The Buddha in Lanna

The Buddha in Lanna

Art, Lineage, Power, and Place in Northern Thailand

Angela S. Chiu

University of Hawai'i Press
Honolulu

Paperback edition 2018

Printed in the United States of America
23 22 21 20 19 18 6 5 4 3 2 1

Library of Congress Cataloging-in-Publication Data

Names: Chiu, Angela S., author.
Title: The Buddha in Lanna : art, lineage, power, and place in northern Thailand / Angela S. Chiu.
Description: Honolulu : University of Hawai'i Press, [2017] | Includes bibliographical references and index.
Identifiers: LCCN 2016044851 | ISBN 9780824858742 (hard cover ; alk. paper)
Subjects: LCSH: Gautama Buddha—Statues—Thailand, Northern. | Buddhist sculpture—Thailand, Northern.
Classification: LCC NB1912.G38 C49 2017 | DDC 730.9593—dc23
LC record available at https://lccn.loc.gov/2016044851

ISBN 978-0-8248-7682-1 (pbk.)

University of Hawai'i Press books are printed on acid-free paper and meet the guidelines for permanence and durability of the Council on Library Resources.

Contents

Acknowledgments

The present volume originated with my graduate studies, completed at the School of Oriental and African Studies, University of London, in 2012. A special expression of deep appreciation is owed foremost to Elizabeth H. Moore, whose illuminating observations and talent for framing inquiry on various levels were hugely valuable to me. She also generously shared her profound knowledge, time, and networks.

I am also immensely thankful to Kate Crosby and Nandana Chutiwongs, who provided insightful suggestions on an early version as well as helped to remedy some of my cavities of ignorance. A major debt of gratitude is also owed to M. L. Pattaratorn Chirapravati, who read drafts and responded quickly, in her wonderfully incisive and forthright manner. I also benefited from the thoughtfulness and sharing of knowledge from Vantana Cornwell, Janit Feangfu, Jotika Khur-Yearn, Stephen Murphy, Navanath Osiri, Matthew Phillips, Pimchanok Pongkasetkan, Peter Skilling, M. L. Surasawasdi Sooksawasdi, Donald Stadtner, François Tainturier, Hiram W. Woodward, Jr., and others. In addition, I much appreciated the insightful comments and suggestions of the two anonymous readers invited by the University of Hawai'i Press. I was also fortunate to receive encouragement from the wise Nattaka Chaisinthop. In Bangkok, the considerate and generous Peter Chiaravanont and Nancy Rojanachotikul devoted extraordinary amounts of time and effort to helping me, arranging some of my stays there and making sure I had plenty to eat.

The research was fueled in part by a grant in 2009 from the Empowering Network for International Thai Studies at the Institute of Thai Studies, Chulalongkorn University, with support from the Thailand Research Fund.

Earlier versions of parts of chapters 4 and 5 were published in Angela S. Chiu, "Drawn to an 'Extremely Loathsome' Place: The Buddha and the Power of the Northern Thai Landscape," in *From Mulberry*

Leaves to Silk Scrolls: New Approaches to the Study of Asian Manuscript Traditions, ed. Justin Thomas McDaniel and Lynn Ransom (Philadelphia: University of Pennsylvania Libraries, 2015), 107–130.

The content of this book has hugely profited from access to the collection of Lanna manuscripts of the École française d'Extrême-Orient at the Princess Maha Chakri Sirindhorn Anthropology Centre in Bangkok, which I visited in 2010 under the auspices of the European Consortium for Asian Field Study. I am extremely grateful to François Lagirarde, who invited me to research the collection. I also benefited from access to the extensive knowledge of all things Lanna of Dr. Lagirarde and of his expert staff, especially Phongsathorn Buakhampan, Rampa Salikarin, and Wisitthisak Sattaphan; it was an honor and a true pleasure to spend time with them.

Warm thanks are also owed to Bernhard Penth, who kindly and quickly gave his permission for the reproduction of illustrations in *Khamcharuek thi Than Phra Phuttha Rup nai Nakhon Chiang Mai* (1976), a book authored by his father, Hans Penth, the pioneering scholar of Lanna. I am also grateful for the kindness of Louis Gabaude, who put me in touch with Bernhard.

I would also like to express my deep appreciation to Pamela Kelley at the University of Hawai'i Press for deftly, patiently, and reassuringly shepherding me through the whole publication process. I am also thankful to Brian Bendlin and Mary Ribesky for the enhancements made to the text by their skillful editing.

Infinite gratitude is owed to my parents, Kao Ding and Shih Yu Chiu, who have provided fundamental and deep support and have been constant role models and inspirations to me.

Abbreviations

Full publication information can be found in the bibliography. For manuscripts from the collection of the École française d'Extrême-Orient (EFEO), the page numbering is not that of the original manuscripts, but that assigned by EFEO, which designates recto and verso sides of a folio as A and B.

CHRONICLE OF THE EMERALD BUDDHA IMAGE

EBCN Camille Notton, trans., *The Chronicle of the Emerald Buddha*, 2nd ed.

EBNJ N. A. Jayawickrama, trans., *The Sheaf of Garlands of the Epochs of the Conqueror, Being a Translation of the Jinakālamālīpakaraṇaṁ of Ratanapañña Thera of Thailand*, 139–145.

EBSM Saeng Manawithun, trans.

EBWN *Tamnan Phra Chan Phra Sing Phra Kaeo*, 14A–16B.

CHRONICLE OF THE SANDALWOOD BUDDHA IMAGE

SWNJ N. A. Jayawickrama, trans., *The Sheaf of Garlands of the Epochs of the Conqueror, Being a Translation of the Jinakālamālīpakaraṇaṁ of Ratanapañña Thera of Thailand*, 174–180.

SWSC Sa-nguan Chotisukharat, *Prachum Tamnan Lanna Thai*, Vol. 2, 68–88.

SWWN *Tamnan Phra Chan Phra Sing Phra Kaeo*, 1A–8A.

Chronicle of the Setangkhamani Buddha Image

CBCN Camille Notton, trans., *P'ră Setaṃgamaṇī.*

Chronicle of the Sihing Buddha Image

SBCN Camille Notton, trans., *P'ra Buddha Sihiṅga.*
SBNJ N. A. Jayawickrama, trans., *The Sheaf of Garlands of the Epochs of the Conqueror, Being a Translation of the Jinakālamālīpakaraṇaṁ of Ratanapañña Thera of Thailand*, 120–126.
SBSM Saeng Manawithun, trans., *Nithan Phra Phuttha Sihing.*
SBWN *Tamnan Phra Chan Phra Sing Phra Kaeo,* 8A–14A.

Chronicle of the Sikhi Buddha Image

SKNJ N. A. Jayawickrama, trans., *The Sheaf of Garlands of the Epochs of the Conqueror, Being a Translation of the Jinakālamālīpakaraṇaṁ of Ratanapañña Thera of Thailand*, 155–158.

Jinakālamālīpakaraṇaṁ

JKM *Jinakālamālīpakaraṇaṁ*
NJSG N. A. Jayawickrama, trans., *The Sheaf of Garlands of the Epochs of the Conqueror, Being a Translation of the Jinakālamālīpakaraṇaṁ of Ratanapañña Thera of Thailand.*

Mūlasāsanā of Wat Pa Daeng

PNPD Prasert na Nagara and Puangkham Tuikhiao, trans., *Tamnan Mulasasana Chiang Mai lae Chiang Tung*, 135–209.
SMPD Sao Sāimöng Mangrāi, *The P̱āḍaeng Chronicle and the Jengtung State Chronicle Translated*, 59–180.
SSPD Sommai Premchit and Donald K. Swearer, "A Translation of Tamnān Mūlasāsanā Wat Pā Daeng: The Chronicle of the Founding of Buddhism of the Wat Pā Daeng Tradition," 73–110.

Mūlasāsanā of Wat Suan Dok

PNWS Prasert na Nagara and Puangkham Tuikhiao, trans., *Tamnan Mulasasana Chiang Mai lae Chiang Tung*, 15–81.

PNYK Prasert na Nagara and Puangkham Tuikhiao, trans., *Tamnan Mulasasana Chiang Mai lae Chiang Tung*, 83–133.

A Note on Transliteration and Terminology

I follow the system of romanization of Thai set out in the "Principles of Phonetic Transcription of Thai Characters to Roman" promulgated by the Royal Institute of Thailand in 1999. However, exceptions are made for names of authors where the author's preferred romanization is known—for example, Piriya Krairiksh instead of Phiriya Krairoek.

Buddhist terms and many other Thai words are transliterations of Pali or Sanskrit words. Because readers of Thai can often recognize the Indic terms behind Thai spellings, while non-Thai readers may not easily comprehend the Thai versions, I have transliterated many Thai terms in Pali or Sanskrit romanization—for example, *bodhisattva* instead of *phothisat*. Otherwise I have left many Thai terms, especially place names, in conventional present-day Thai romanized form—for example, Phitsanulok instead of Viṣṇuloka. It is important to keep in mind that the Thai use and understanding of Indic terms may not be equivalent to their definitions in other Pali or Sanskrit texts, as names and terms have been appropriated into new contexts.

All English translations are my own unless noted otherwise.

The works of art and literature that are the main subject of this book were created and appreciated by people who were Tai, speakers of a family of languages that is part of the Tai-Kadai language group. The Tai include Thai people of Thailand as well as Tai Khuen, Tai Lue, Tai Yuan, and other groups who live mainly in present-day southwestern China, northeastern India, Laos, Myanmar, Thailand, and Vietnam. I use "Thai" to refer to people living within the geographic area of the present-day nation of Thailand, and "Tai" to denote the more widely distributed Tai-speaking people.

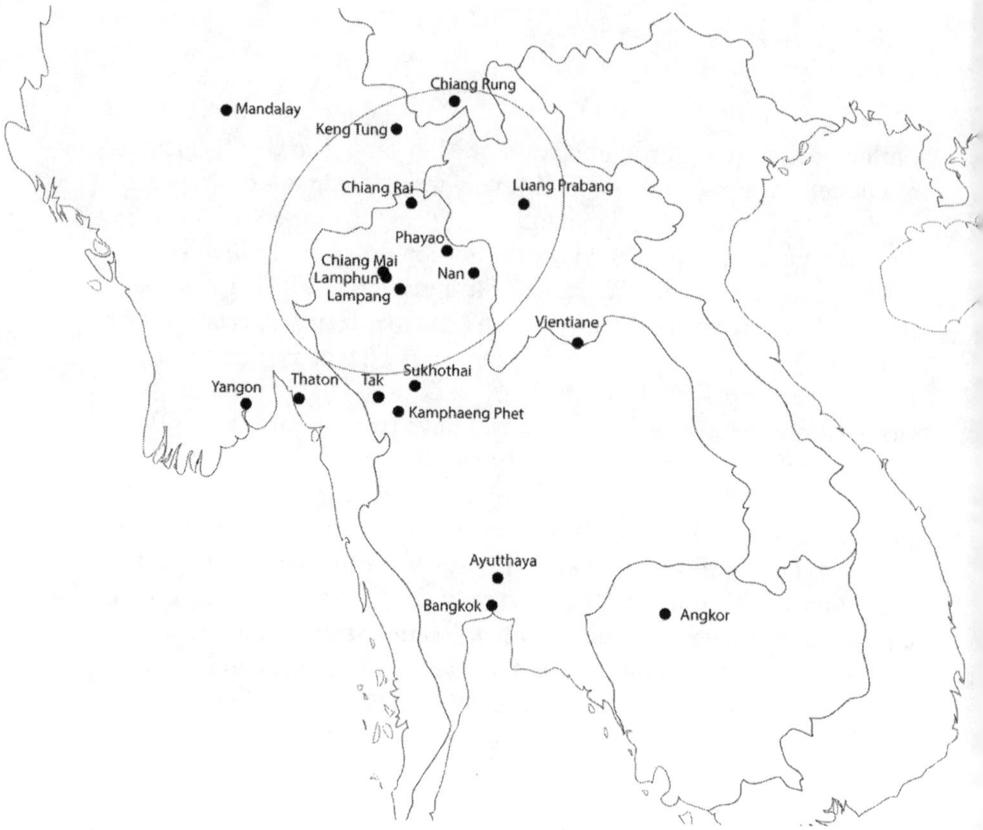

Map: Lanna region

Chapter One

Introduction

Buddha Images of the Tai

For centuries, wherever Tai Buddhists have made their homes, statues of the Blessed One have provided striking testament to the role of Buddhism in the lives of the people. Tai Buddha statues are crafted from a wide variety of materials including bronze, gold, lead, wood, concrete, and even dried flowers and ashes. In Thailand, and across the wider Southeast Asian region inhabited by Tai people who share a linguistic and cultural heritage, each town and province cherishes a special Buddha statue believed to watch over the people and place. Some statues have become famous nationally and internationally, with their photos reproduced on posters, cloth hangings, stickers on car windows, and postage stamps (fig. 1.1). Both within and outside Thailand, the Buddha image has come to symbolize not only Buddhism but Thailand itself. The kingdom's palladium is the Emerald Buddha image, a sixty-six-centimeter-tall statue sculpted from a large nugget of green stone, enthroned in a gold-covered pavilion in its own hall, Wat Phra Kaeo, in the compound of the Grand Palace in Bangkok. Several times a year, the king and his family, together with religious patriarchs and other officials, gather in the hall to conduct ceremonies dedicated to the Emerald Buddha. Attendants regularly refresh the supply of flowers, incense, and candles offered to the image, while every day, devotees and tourists crowd the carpeted span at the foot of the throne to pray, meditate, and gaze up at the statue glowing gently in the dim light of the magnificently decorated hall. Three times a year, the king proceeds to Wat Phra Kaeo to place around the Emerald Buddha's shoulders one of the jewelled gold costumes specially

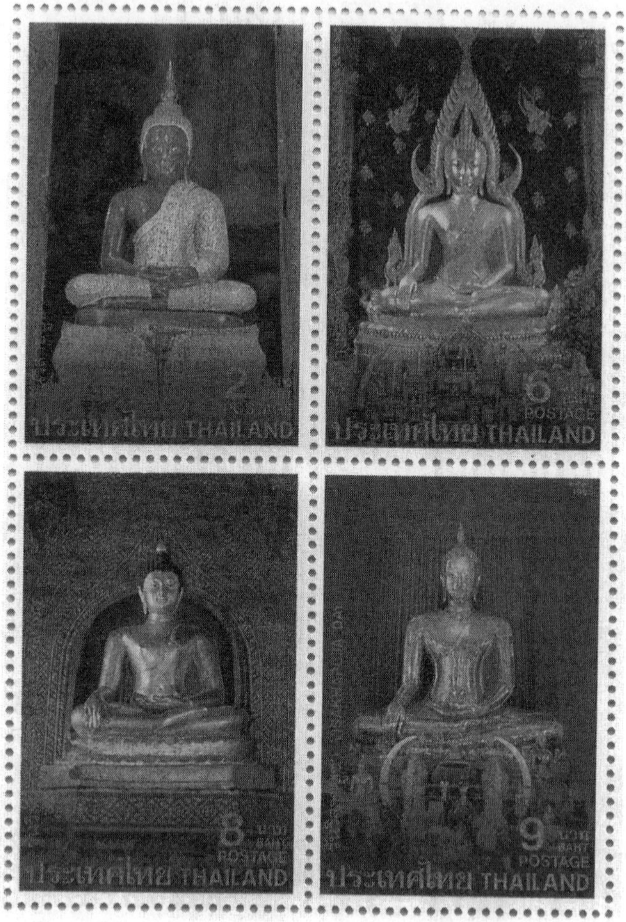

Fig. 1.1. Thai postage stamps, 1995. Clockwise from top right: Chinarat Buddha (Phitsanulok), Mahasuwanna Buddha (Bangkok), Sihing Buddha (Chiang Mai), Emerald Buddha (Bangkok).

made for it to have on during the hot, cold, or rainy seasons. As Princess Maha Chakri Sirindhorn has written, "Wat Phra Kaeo is the repository of the spirit of the entire Thai people."[1]

Why are Buddha images so important in Tai society? Certainly, one must credit the fervency of Tai devotion, in which the tradition of creating portraits of the Buddha has long been one of the most important ways for a devotee to support the religion and to make spiritual merit. This theological rationale in itself, however, does not explain the complex and deep relationships between Buddha images and local societies over many centuries. Nor do the often-repeated definitions of a Buddha statue as a devotional reminder and doctrinal symbol provide a satisfactory explanation. How did a carved green rock become the Emerald Buddha?

This book will suggest that in order to begin to understand Buddha statues, we must understand them as the productions of living societies. The Buddha image is an object arising from the wishes and needs of individuals and produced through a process of craft as well as through social and institutional practices. The Buddha image is an object that not only represents the Buddha himself but also channels the interests of the monks and lay devotees who build, consecrate, and venerate it. It represents a revered being, but one who is not insulated from the world of commodities and politics beyond monastery walls. The image has a "life" in which it continues to be subject to the sometimes divergent interests of lay devotees and monks. The history of the Buddha image is, thus, intertwined with the history of its community.

This understanding of the Buddha statue as a participant in the social world of its worshippers is strikingly depicted in the texts of what are called in Thai *tamnan* (often translated in English as "chronicles"). These texts were composed and disseminated since at least the fifteenth century in Lanna, the region centered in what is now northern Thailand, and which in past times also covered parts of present-day northeastern Myanmar (Burma), southwestern China, and Laos. This book presents the first analysis of descriptions and stories about Buddha statues and relics in Lanna's *tamnan* to illuminate the social and economic roles played by Buddha images for the people of the past who made and venerated them.

The Significances of the Tai Buddha Image

The Buddha images we will consider are anthropomorphic sculptures in the round. Based on current evidence, such representations of the Buddha were apparently first produced in the first to second centuries CE in Gandhara and Mathura in the northern regions of the Asian subcontinent then ruled by the Kuṣāṇa dynasty. There is as yet no consensus among scholars regarding how and why the creation of anthropomorphic Buddha images began. These questions are complicated by the fact that no clear basis exists in Buddhist canonical texts for paying homage to Buddha images. One text that purports to present the Buddha's guidance on sites of commemoration or veneration is the *Kāliṅgabodhijātaka.* According to this text the Buddha declared that there are three kinds of reminder or shrine (Pali: *cetiya*): (1) a shrine for a relic of the body (*sarīrikacetiya*), (2) a shrine for a relic of use (*paribhogacetiya*) and (3) a shrine of commemoration or indication (*uddesikacetiya*). Buddha images are usually thought to belong to this last category.[2] Although the Buddha noted that shrines of commemoration are "lacking in foundation by virtue of their being a matter of mind only," this apparently negative characterization has hardly deterred veneration of Buddha images among the Tai and devotees elsewhere.

In Thailand, *cetiya* (Thai: *chedi*) are categorized as in the scheme delineated in the *Kāliṅgabodhijātaka* with a fourth class also recognized: *dhammacetiya,* a shrine for the words of the Buddha, which are often written or inscribed on such various materials as palm leaves, stones, or plates of silver. The source of authority for the validity of *dhammacetiya* as a shrine has been traced to the Buddha's counsel to his disciples that after his death, or *parinibbāna,* what he had taught them—his *dhamma*—would continue as their teacher.[3]

These four types of *cetiya* in Thailand were described in 1926 in the first modern study of Thai art history to be published in the country, *A History of Buddhist Monuments in Siam* (*Tamnan Phra Phuttha Chedi Sayam;* later retitled *Tamnan Phra Phuttha Chedi*) by Prince Damrong Rajanubhab (1862–1943).[4] Prince Damrong is still highly revered today in Thailand for his leading role in the development of the kingdom, including his pioneering work in establishing Thai history, culture, art, and literature as subjects of academic study. *A History of Buddhist Monuments* is a slim but groundbreaking volume. It begins with a narration of the history of Buddhism and then recounts Buddhist art's beginnings in Gandhara and ancient India and its spread to other areas of Asia. Finally it presents a history of styles and iconographies of Buddhist arts in the area that is today Thailand.

With regard to Buddha images, Damrong expounded a chronological development of styles and iconographies that he depicted as the product of various influences arising from historical phenomena such as the expansion of kingdoms and the spread of religious sects. Damrong addressed the issue of the meaning or significance of Buddha images only briefly, noting that early Buddhist monuments built by King Asoka (in the third century BCE) in ancient India did not include anthropomorphic portraits of the Buddha and seemed to instead only suggest his presence through objects such as his throne, footprints, or sculptures of wheels of the law symbolizing his teaching. Damrong surmised that images of the Buddha were initially made by the people of Greek ancestry living in ancient Gandhara, who already had a tradition of making images as objects of veneration. Perhaps, he proposed, a Gandharan king tasked learned men and craftsmen with developing a form of statue that would be beautiful and give satisfaction to worshippers. The image would have to be recognizable as the Buddha and not as any other deity. As the Buddha had passed away centuries earlier, the image could not resemble him in appearance. Thus the image came to be formed with distinguishing features such as a flame and a bump extending from the top of his head to signify his extraordinary spiritual achievements.[5] The source for this hypothesis on the early development of representations of the Buddha was probably Alfred Foucher, whose work is not acknowledged by Damrong on this particular point but is referenced elsewhere in his book.[6]

Damrong presented Buddhism in Thailand as part of the heritage of global Buddhist theological and historical development. Thai objects were defined as Buddhist *cetiya* consistent with classical Buddhist texts and fitted into the wider history of Buddhism across Asia. At the same time, he presented Thai *cetiya* as art objects that were worthy of aesthetic contemplation and study according to the methods of the Western-originated academic field of art history. His book was not the first treatise of length to do so, but it was the most influential.[7] *A History of Buddhist Monuments* has inspired generations of treatises on Thai art, and the book's structure, topics, and methodology have had a lasting impact on the study of Thai art history. Damrong's system of periodization of art in Thailand, in which the eras of art history are named after different kingdoms or polities, has been modified by subsequent scholars but remains the convention for art history in Thailand. His method of connecting changes in style and iconography with historical phenomena also remains customary today in art historical study in Thailand, and the chief three topics—style, iconography, and dating—that were the focus of Damrong's book continue to be the predominant subjects of Thai art historical study, although this may not have been the intention of the author at the time.

In studies of Tai Buddha images, it has remained conventional for each image to be rendered by the art historian into an example of a type of style and iconography so that it may be inserted into a chronology of objects. "Style" refers to the manner in which the form of the statue has been rendered to create visual effects; "iconography" includes the bodily traits, postures, and gestures of the statue as well as the adornments and items borne by or surrounding it, which in combination serve to distinguish the particular personage or event the statue is intended to evoke. Most art historical inquiries aim to establish chronology according to stylistic and iconographical features, with only brief consideration devoted to other meanings of the objects.[8] Typically art historians have emphasized the Tai Buddha image as an icon that makes present the absent Buddha, as a symbol of his teachings, and as a materialization of positive karma, pointing to the devotees' desire to make merit as the main motivation for producing images. Deeper investigation of the abstract, nonvisual, or even other material aspects of Buddha images are still minority studies, produced by art historians such as Alexander B. Griswold, M. L. Pattaratorn Chirapravati, Phiset Chiechanphong, and Piriya Krairiksh, all of whose works will be discussed in this book. There is certainly nothing inherently problematic with the connoisseurial focus on style, iconography, and dating; the consideration of these characteristics of the statues is a fundamental and extremely valuable aspect of art historical inquiry. Nevertheless, the art historical survey's parade of photos of statues has had the unfortunate side effect of literally flattening the Buddha statue, in both its physical and conceptual senses. Basic questions about Tai Buddha images deserve more intensive investigation. For example, what did the physical characteristics of the images such as the style, iconography, and material mean to the people who created and venerated them? If the Buddha image was built primarily to make merit, what motivated people to make Buddha images as opposed to other kinds of *cetiya?* If style was a matter of "influences" perpetuated by copying, which models or features were chosen to be copied, and why? The risk that art historians of Thailand take in setting aside such questions is that we lose sight of what the art objects actually meant to the people who created, used, and viewed them. The people of the past, by making and caring for these images, were indeed the very generators of art history.

Historical evidence for how Tai Buddha images may have been used by devotees has been more elaborately considered by researchers of social, historical, and religious studies in Thailand. Their studies have drawn attention to the fact that Buddha images, relics, and other *cetiya* feature prominently in early northern Thai *tamnan.* Such texts have been little used by art historians, even though certain manuscripts center on Buddha images; a history of the Emerald Buddha image, for instance, was probably composed in the fifteenth century or earlier. Historians and anthropologists, on the other hand, have in their reading of *tamnan* perceived Buddha images as devices used by people of the past to promote political and sectarian interests. The early written accounts about Buddha images suggest that they played a significant role in introducing and cultivating devotion to Buddhism in Tai territories. Rulers promoted the spread of Buddhism through the distribution of statues and relics across Lanna to provide means of spiritual advancement for their people as well as to assert political dominion and consolidation. The historian Dhida Saraya has suggested that the extensive patronage of the cult of Buddha relics and images was a strategy initiated by the kings of Lanna in the 1400s to establish their paramountcy over the cults of local guardian deities in the various parts of Lanna. For example, in the fifteenth century King Tilok installed the Emerald and Sihing Buddha images in special monasteries in Chiang Mai, the center of Lanna. The worship of special images was instituted as the prerogative of the king.[9] Furthermore, certain Buddha images were presented as "authentic" portraits of the Buddha and therefore magically powerful; a king in possession of such a statue could claim rights to supremacy over other regional kings.[10] In such understandings highlighted by historians and anthropologists, the images are not only productions of merit but also express a significance beyond narrow theological concerns because they are integrated into the systems and strategies of the social and political worlds of people of the past. On the other hand, these interpretations tend to present images—as well as the revered remains of the Buddha, such as strands of his hair and particles of his ashes—in terms of their quality as abstract symbols, allowing emphasis to be placed on statues' and relics' similarities in spite of their differences as physical objects.

In a sense, contemporary researchers have fragmented the Tai Buddha image, with historians and anthropologists focusing on the social functions and other conceptual significances of the image while art historians have hewed to its physical form. Surely all would agree that the multiplicity and potency of the significances of the image are inseparable from its form as a material production. In this respect the insights of Robert Lingat and Stanley Tambiah are instructive. Lingat has suggested that the Emerald Buddha image may have been carved long ago from a green stone that people worshipped as a form of a guardian spirit. The transformation of the stone into a Buddha image, if this in fact occurred, suggests how Buddhists subsumed veneration of local spirits to Buddhism in Tai territories.[11] This hypothesis highlights that the particular form of the Buddha image as an object resulting from a process of craft had specific consequences for the nature of its role in society. Likewise, Tambiah has examined the way famous Lanna statues were copied by ambitious kings who sought political legitimacy through the possession of powerful objects;[12] the ability to copy sacred artworks at will had political implications. Lingat and Tambiah indicate that the popularity or value of the Buddha image in Tai areas was due not only to the image's symbolism or its function as a manifestation of the Buddha but also to its material features and the process of its production. Moreover, these latter aspects distinguish the image from a bodily relic of the Buddha and suggest an important way people in the past differentiated these objects. Tambiah and Lingat thus reconstitute the Tai Buddha image as a single entity by recognizing that it is formulated of material and conceptual inputs by its devotees.

Elaborating this point, I suggest that to understand the image, we need to restore the role of past Tai people as not only elements of context or background but as the agents or drivers of Buddhist art production. A more sustained and detailed study of the nature and practices of patronage is needed. The Buddha image in Tai history could then be understood as both a product of craft and as a creation arising within individual, cultural, and institutional contexts of social interaction. This reorientation towards viewing the image as a social object provides an opening to expand the interpretive range of Tai art history beyond iconography; it also sets up an alternative vantage point from which we may examine the assumptions of past studies about the creation of Buddha images. Furthermore, we need to consider the cult of bodily relics of the Buddha in comparative perspective in order to clarify the distinctive roles of the image in Tai devotion. The study of narratives and descriptions of relics also permits a new assessment of the relationship between images and relics.

With this approach in mind, we turn to the writings about Buddha images by the devotees who made and worshipped them in the rich archive of the *tamnan* of northern Thailand.

The Study of Local *Tamnan*

Together with inscriptions, the *tamnan* produced in the Lanna region have been key sources for the construction of the chronology of Tai history. These writings consist of histories and stories with a Buddhist flavor about places, Buddha images, relics, and lineages of monks and rulers. Likely derived from oral accounts and meant to be preached, the *tamnan* were written mostly by monks and perhaps some monastically educated laymen. The writings contain some elements inspired by the monastic chronicles of the island of Lanka (present-day Sri Lanka), such as the *Mahāvaṃsa,* written sometime between the late fifth and early sixth centuries. The *tamnan* also share some elements with the literature of Burmese/Mon cultures with whom the Lanna Tai have had a history of exchange. Evidence to account for the beginning of the tradition of writing *tamnan* has been lost to time, but because of commonalities with Lankan manuscripts there may have been a correlation with the rise of Lankan-associated monastic lineages in Lanna during the fifteenth century.

Before modern mechanical printing became popular in the early twentieth century, the text of *tamnan* were commonly inscribed on dried palm leaves cut into narrow rectangular pages about four to five centimeters tall and fifty to sixty centimeters wide. A sharp stylus was used by a scribe to etch the letters on the leaf, and then soot was rubbed over the surface to fill the incisions. The leaves were then bundled and tied together. The vast majority of *tamnan* are written in vernacular languages (often Tai Yuan or *Kham Mueang,* as well as other Tai languages, particularly Khoen, Lao, Lue, and Shan) interspersed with Pali, the Indic Buddhist literary language. A smaller number of texts are composed only in Pali. The script most often used is Lanna Tham (also called in Thai, Tua Tham, or Dhamma letters), but the scripts Fak Kham and Thai Nithet (or Khom Mueang) are also employed.[13] The leaves are unillustrated.

The number of different stories or accounts of *tamnan* is estimated to be in the low two hundreds.[14] Today one can find hundreds of thousands of palm leaf manuscripts, including *tamnan* and other kinds of literature, stacked in northern Thailand's monastery libraries; many other manuscripts have been lost to age, fire, and insects.[15] Monasteries with well-known relics or images now publish their chronicles in Thai and sometimes English in the form of booklets for sale to the public. The long history of production of chronicles attests to the popularity of the stories; it also reflects the fact that *tamnan* have been common items given by monastic and lay sponsors to monasteries to make merit.

An important characteristic of *tamnan* is their portability. For hundreds of years, they were carried by monks from monastery to monastery across an extended area. Many of Lanna's cultural features, including literature in the Tham script, were spread across the area, a movement that seems to have increased during the fifteenth and early sixteenth centuries, when Lanna reached its so-called golden age and became a regional power. In the area that comprises today's northern Thailand, northwestern Laos, northeastern Myanmar, and southwest China, Hans Penth has identified a "Culture of the Region of the Dhamma Letters." In this region, many shared aspects of culture are still visible today.[16] The spread of features of literary culture was developed through a network of monasteries, in which teachers, students, and texts circulated to create, as Justin McDaniel has described, " 'vernacular landscapes' made of rhetorical styles, local legends, and scribal lives."[17]

Because of the vulnerability of the materials to physical damage, most of the extant manuscripts found today in Lanna's monastic libraries are those inscribed in the nineteenth and twentieth centuries.[18] However, the texts of these documents may have been originally composed centuries earlier. Due to a tradition of respect for original texts that drives copying, "today's historian can with a good deal of confidence work with the material that has been handed down."[19]

Interpreting *tamnan* has posed a challenge for present-day scholars. Dating the works is usually difficult: the authors of *tamnan* often did not record their names, nor the dates or places of composition; and the style of writing has not made the content of *tamnan* easy to assess for the contemporary historian, as in these texts "[h]istorical memory, the supernormal, the divine, and the miraculous are inextricably entangled."[20]

Because of the mythical content of the chronicles, among other issues, the ways in which they have been interpreted so far have been limited and they are still understudied as a historical resource. As Peter Skilling notes, "It is clear that we know far too little of the pre-modern literature of the region. Yet it is this literature that is the key to the understanding of the ethics, ideals, ideology, and imagination of the pre-modern period."[21] Scholarly biases have also played a role in this lack of attention. Regarding Theravada, the main form of Buddhism practiced in Lanka and mainland Southeast Asia, Kate Crosby notes that the view of Theravada as "early, rational-scientific and anti-ritual is so strong that it prevents evidence to the contrary from being revealed or taken on board. Theravada as a historical and developed religion is hardly represented at all."[22] A kind of linguistic chauvinism in which scholars of Buddhism have favored Pali, the liturgical language, goes hand in hand with this influence. As McDaniel has observed, although Pali is revered in Lanna, it is usually reserved for recitation, while vernacular language is used for composition and discussion: "Unfortunately, most Buddhist Studies scholars have not engaged in that local discussion. There are whole genres of vernacular Buddhist literature ignored by the field."[23]

Extracting factual information from the mass of myths in the chronicles has been a productive line of inquiry for a number of researchers. An early example of this orientation is George Cœdès's use of *tamnan* to construct chronologies of events and reigns in Lanna.[24] Art historians have made so far very limited use of *tamnan,* and their approaches have tended to be in this mode of separating fact from myth;[25] this style of approach may be accompanied by a certain predisposition. As Udom Rungrueangsi remarks, the magical happenings in the texts "reduce the historical value of the *tamnan,*" but "if an appropriate analysis is made, the scholar would be able to see that the erudite composers of *tamnan* hid some traces of the past and historical truth within the texts."[26]

On the other hand, might we view the texts' interweaving of fact and legend as intentional and meaningful? Taking up such a perspective, we may then perceive how *tamnan* reveal another dimension, as assertions of a particular construction of knowledge within a Buddhist framework.[27] For instance, one genre of chronicle describes visits by the Buddha to Lanna. Such stories were apocryphal, but Donald K. Swearer has suggested that they had an important function: "The Blessed One's journey throughout northern Thailand is a cosmogonic event that creates an ordered, meaningful world."[28] Swearer's insightful writings on the subject draw attention to Buddhist and universal motifs in the *tamnan* to situate Lanna within the larger sphere of Buddhist history and thought in Asia.[29]

The use of structures and motifs that integrate local values with classic Buddhist values reflects the influence on Lanna authors of Lanka's Pali *vaṃsas* such as the *Mahāvaṃsa,* which presented Lankan dynastic history in the context of the progression of Buddhism. As with the *tamnan,* the *Mahāvaṃsa* has been studied as an empirical account of Lankan history. However, the scholarly reading of the Lankan *vaṃsas* as sources of empirical historical fact is a relatively recent concept originated by nineteenth-century British colonial officials "seeking to appropriate Ceylon by appropriating its past." As Jonathan S. Walters has pointed out, the texts should instead be understood as "partisan rearticulations of the past" that reflect "people in Sri Lanka as making their polity and way of life rather than as passive guardians of a pure, early Buddhism."[30]

A similar dialogic understanding was in fact brought to bear in the consideration of *tamnan* by Dhida Saraya, who has suggested that the proliferation of the chronicles in the fifteenth and sixteenth centuries was linked to the expansion of the authority of the Mangrai dynasty of Lanna in the region. The histories narrated in *tamnan,* she explained, were written in order to integrate the oral myths of each locality with the history of the lineage of the ruling dynasty. The objective of this integration was to promote a sense of unity among the various polities being absorbed into Lanna.[31] Thus, while the myth content of *tamnan* has been viewed by some scholars as detracting from the scholarly value of the texts, it was precisely these myths that increased the credibility of the chronicles in the eyes of people of the past.

In a similar vein, David K. Wyatt has posited that *tamnan* should be understood as expressions of "cultural and intellectual history." For example, he demonstrates how comparison can be made of chronicles' ways of explaining similar events at different dates in order to understand changes in biases over time. In this approach the texts are understood as modes of thought or exposition that reflect "what was going on inside people's heads." Wyatt suggests that this "internalist" approach would avoid the possible pitfalls of categorizing phenomena of the past according to present-day conceptions of what may be deemed "political" or "economic" by instead focusing on the past "*as it really was* to those who lived *in* that past."[32] Recently, François Lagirarde's analysis of nineteenth-century prophetic *tamnan* has followed this train of thought, observing that the chronicles "permit us to approach a historical and moral conscience at the human, nearly individual, scale, very rarely accessible in the culture of the Thai peoples."[33]

Following Dhida, Lagirarde, and Wyatt in their orientation towards the *tamnan* as reflecting the interests and concerns of their writers and audiences, this book will approach the *tamnan* with a new method: gathering examples of how a single subject (Buddha images) are discussed across a range of *tamnan* and focusing attention on modes of description, narrative, structure, motifs, and themes of the texts to illuminate patterns of thought, methods of argument, objectives, and values. The chronicles frequently recount devotees interacting with and through Buddha images; these images were presented not as static objects but as lively participants in the social worlds of their authors and audiences. Issues of Buddhist doctrine, economy, politics, and gender are evidenced in *tamnan* that cast a new light on the role of Buddha images in their societies, particularly in mediating monastic-lay relations.

The Social World of the Buddha Image

There are numerous examples across Asia of stories that recount particular Buddhist statues' origins, miraculous powers, and adventures. The texts situate the images in the histories, societies, and landscapes of their devotees; Buddhist liturgy and art, in other words, are interdependent.[34] Of Japanese Buddhist stories, Robert H. Sharf has noted that these accounts "would have been more significant in vivifying the image for its Japanese devotees than the consecration ritual, objects inside the statue, or scholastic theories of multiple Buddha bodies."[35] Such a characterization would also be applicable to Lanna accounts about images. Buddha images feature prominently in many *tamnan,* to the point that some chronicles could be said to be "biographies" narrating the origin and subsequent "lives" of specific statues. As we shall see, Lanna Buddha images were depicted as the focal points of panregional politicoreligious lineages and rivalries—indeed, as the very catalysts of history itself. In the *tamnan,* Buddha images also physically and conceptually unified the Buddha with local places, thereby integrating the Buddha into Lanna conceptions of the divine character and social significance of the northern Thai landscape.

To illuminate the role of the Buddha image in Lanna society, I will follow the approach to the social world of artworks developed by the anthropologist Alfred Gell in his posthumously published book *Art and Agency* (1998). Gell sought to approach art in a way that was truly anthropological—that is, he aimed to create a theory of art that would fit anthropology's goal to "make sense of behavior in the context of social relations." He rejected theories of aesthetics, which in his view could not account for art as an object that was produced, circulated, and received in social contexts. He also criticized explanations driven by linguistic theory, rejecting cultural conventions as an explanation for how art is received.[36]

Instead Gell took note of the importance of the social relationships created through the making, use, and viewing of art objects. Art, he observed, is more than a system of aesthetics or symbols. Art objects are means by which people communicate and influence each other; such objects are not passive participants in social contexts but truly express agency: "Agency is attributable to those persons (and things, see below) who/which are seen as initiating causal sequences of a particular type, that is, events caused by acts of mind or will or intention, rather than the mere concatenation of physical events. An agent is one who 'causes events to happen' in their vicinity. As a result of this exercise of agency, certain events transpire (not necessarily the specific events that were 'intended' by the agent)."[37] Furthermore, "To be an 'agent' one must act with respect to the 'patient'; the patient is the object which is causally affected by the agent's action. For the purposes of the theory being developed here, it will be assumed that in any given transaction in which agency is manifested, there is a 'patient' who or which is *another 'potential' agent,* capable of acting as an agent or being the locus of agency."[38]

The social nexus of an art object consists of the actions and intentions of agents and patients who interact in the vicinity of the object, and the art object itself is able to take on agent and patient roles within these interactions.

Gell's theory can help us to cast a new light on the process of how a Tai Buddha statue is made. In the first stage, a patron is inspired to create a statue on a certain occasion, such as the celebration of a birthday or the fulfillment of a vow. A craftsman is then hired to make the image. Certain rituals involving the participation of a monk may be performed during the work. When the image is finished, the monks lead an assembly consisting of the sponsor and other members of the local community in undertaking a consecration ceremony for the image. Thus a chain of agency is created: the patron as agent acts on the artist, who picks up his tools in order to meet the patron's wish. The artist also attempts to channel the agency of the Buddha in forming the image in his likeness. The Buddha's agency is channelled again via monks during rites to consecrate—or ritually make worthy of devotion—the statue. Because the ceremony is also executed by the sponsor and the temple's lay congregation, their agency also acts upon the image as patient. After its consecration and establishment in a hall, the image brings merit to the initial patron and enables him to achieve his goal. The image may continue to act as an agent by drawing further devotees to venerate it. These new devotees may be moved to donate flowers, to speak to the image, to become more faithful, or even to start a war to seize possession of it. As these devotees are drawn to the statue, they may inspire other patients to follow them. Thus the chain of agency is continued. The creation and worship of a Tai Buddha image exemplify Gell's proposal that art is a "system of action, intended to change the world rather than encode symbolic propositions about it."[39]

I have here related only in brief the central hypothesis about the social nexus of works of art in *Art and Agency*, simplifying Gell's elaboration of the theory in his book. For example, Gell's study includes an extended discussion about how certain artworks made through apparently virtuosic skill exercise agency by "captivating" their viewers. I do not elaborate on this part of Gell's theory here as it does not pertain to the way Buddha images are described in *tamnan*. Gell also expounds on what he sees as the failures of aesthetic and semiotic theories for understanding art objects, a repudiation that has been criticized as too extreme by the anthropologist Robert Layton and others who have pointed out the relevance for these theories in certain cultural contexts.[40] There are also examples of the operation of agency that expand or add complexity to the theory as described in *Art and Agency*.[41] In my view, much of these criticisms of Gell's work have credibility. On the other hand, one does not need to take the presentation in *Art and Agency* as being comprehensive (which Gell himself may not have intended). Indeed, despite criticism, Gell's work has since its publication stimulated researchers to scrutinize the social contexts that surround art objects. The analysis that follows will be guided in part by Gell's fundamental principle—which has received widespread acceptance among scholars, including his critics—that artworks may be productively studied as objects enmeshed in social relations. Aesthetic, semiotic, and other approaches that analyze the visuality of artworks are not utilized in the present volume because the *tamnan* tend to hardly describe the visual features of the images—an intriguing absence that we will also examine.

An approach to artworks that has affinities with Gell's is Richard H. Davis' presentation of the history of Indian religious statues as a succession of "communities of response"—individuals and groups who drew on their own worlds of belief, assumptions, needs, and hopes to define and use Indian statues over time. These communities include, for example, the rulers who created the images centuries ago, the conquerors of later generations who seized the images as booty, and the worshippers who visit the shrines today. In recent times, scholars and curators who have constructed their own meanings and visions of Indian statues also constitute a community of response whose agenda must be critically evaluated.[42] Davis' approach has been recently deployed to highlight the history of social contexts of Japanese Buddhist images.[43] For Davis the response to an image is not founded primarily on universal aesthetic notions, general human psychology, or the neurology of vision but on the cultural understandings of viewers. Like Gell he sees the identities of images as subject to constant revision through the agency expressed in different contexts over time. Yet Gell also focused attention on the directions of different agencies and exchanges between them, indicating the way art objects instigate action, create new communities, mediate relations between people, or create new contexts for interaction among people. Art objects may not only evidence cultural understandings but may also contribute to the development of new directions in society and history. They are person-like and can assume special societal roles. The northern Thai *tamnan* recount the initial production of particular Buddha statues and describe their whereabouts and their audiences of worshippers over the course of hundreds, even thousands, of years. In this way these texts are assertions of a specific monastic claim to how a Buddha statue should be understood and to a particular vision of history. However, by paying close attention to the topics and ideas raised in *tamnan* and to the structures, motifs, and themes of the texts, we can discern the interaction of monks and lay devotees in the creation and deployment of the images. The Buddha image is a channel for the assertion of different agencies and can act as a point of mediation between agencies. As we shall see, in sixteenth-century Lanna, monastic orders carried out a struggle for power invoking Buddha images in order to criticize each another and to pull the lay worshippers of images into the dispute. The monastic authors of *tamnan* seem to have well understood the possibilities and challenges involved in any attempt to direct the social agency of images.

Significantly, Gell's work also focuses attention on how the precise form of the artwork is related to the interplay of agencies. In the case of Buddha statues, we must particularly account for the agency of their materials. The precious metals and gems that were shaped into Buddhist images were consecrated through specific rituals to "singularize" them as sacred objects and shield them from the market forces of "commoditization," to use Igor Kopytoff's terms.[44] There is nonetheless "a contestation of the Buddha with the material body of the

Buddha image"; for despite sacralization, the materials of Buddha statues render them ever subject to the forces of the wider economy of commodities outside the temple.[45] Moreover, Buddha images were often understood by monastics as having an economic function. Gregory Schopen has shown for ancient India that texts on monastic regulation and archaeological data from as early as the first centuries provide evidence of the significance of financial and, for want of a better word, related *legal* aspects of monastic management of the cults of Buddha images and relics.[46] As we shall see, the attitudes towards and practices relating to Lanna Buddha images expressed in *tamnan* provide insight into how forces of commoditization were not necessarily in opposition to those of singularization but could contribute to the fame and power of specific Buddha statues. Moreover, the limited set of iconography of statues facilitated the practice of copying and so must also be considered as a factor in the commoditization of the Tai Buddha image.

In this study, we will consider versions of *tamnan* in Thai, English, and French. These will include *tamnan* from the collection of the École française d'Extrême-Orient (EFEO) at the Princess Maha Chakri Sirindhorn Anthropology Centre in Bangkok, a collection that has, happily, recently been made publicly available online.[47] I have consulted the EFEO's transpositions and translations of the texts from their original language (mostly Yuan) to modern central Thai. Translations to English are mine unless noted otherwise. This study includes twenty-four chronicles; for fourteen of these, two to four versions of the same chronicle were read to look for consistencies and divergences in the texts. I focus on the narrative portion of the texts, omitting introductions that typically entail standard expressions of praise for the Buddha. To provide a comparison to *tamnan,* I additionally consider Hans Penth's 1976 catalogue *Khamcharuek thi Than Phra Phuttha Rup nai Nakhon Chiang Mai* (*Inscriptions on the Bases of Buddha Images in Chiang Mai*). I will also compare stories of Buddha images and relics of the Lankan and Burmese/Mon who shared many aspects of Buddhist tradition with the Tai.

As noted earlier, one challenge to studying *tamnan* is their lack of confirmed dating. In this book, dating suggested for each *tamnan* by different researchers is noted. I also provide my own observations about clues in the texts that might reflect dates of composition. I put forward some suggestions about how the composition of some texts might have been related to dated historical phenomena such as reigns and wars, but identifying such relationships is not the primary objective of this study. On the other hand, there is a notable consistency in the modes of discussion about Buddha images across the texts regardless the dating. The fact that the stories were copied and recopied for centuries indicates that they had features that were positively received by devotees of various periods.

Chapter Two

BUDDHA IMAGES AND DEVOTEES

Lineages of People and Places

The fifteenth to early sixteenth centuries, extending from the reign of Phraya Sam Fang Kaen (1402–1441) to that of Phraya Kaeo (1495–1525), has been remembered as the golden age of the kingdom of Lanna, which had its capital at Chiang Mai.[1] This was a period of territorial expansion for Lanna, which put it into competition with a powerful rival to the south, the kingdom of Ayutthaya, forerunner of the kingdom of Siam centered in Bangkok. The growth and development of Lanna and Ayutthaya involved a strengthening of political and military systems, as well as cultural development—particularly the spread of Buddhism and the growing institutionalization of the monarchy as chief supporter and propagator of the religion. Royal donations to support communities devoted to Buddhist thought and practice (Pali: *sāsana*) in the form of land, buildings, labor, money, and other assets reached an unprecedented scale in the Tai kingdoms at this time. Buddhist statuary images proliferated as never before. Indeed, the Emerald Buddha probably became famous during this period in Lanna. Yet in conventional art histories, the meaning of the Tai Buddha image has been little explored; it has been defined as an icon, a materialization of merit, or a symbol of the politically powerful. In this chapter, we will look at the evidence in northern Thai chronicles, *tamnan,* that indicate that images were valued not only for their symbolic value but because they embodied local conceptions of lineage and place.

I will first introduce the Buddha image *tamnan* and its structure and themes. Then I will consider, via Alfred Gell's approach to agency (see chapter 1), how the statues' effective embodiment of local interests enabled them to play an important role in the society of sixteenth-century Lanna.

Five well-known Lanna Buddha images will be considered: the Emerald, Sihing, Sikhi, Sandalwood, and Setangkhamani Buddhas. The histories of these images are the main subject of specific *tamnan,* and the first four also feature in the *Jinakālamālīpakaraṇaṁ* (*JKM*), the *tamnan* of Buddhist history said to have been written by the monk Ratanapañña Thera of Wat Pa Daeng, near Chiang Mai, between 1516 and 1527. The chronicles about the statues are narratives relating the movement of the images across Asia over time. Thus, I refer to this group of statues as travelling images.

The Travelling Images of Lanna

The Sihing Buddha: From Sri Lanka to Southeast Asia

The bronze Sihing (Thai: Phra Phuttha Sihing, Phra Sing; Pali: Buddha Sihiṅga, Sīhaḷapaṭimā) is today one of the most famous Buddha images in Thailand.[2] It resides in Chiang Mai in a modest-size but elaborately decorated hall on the grounds of the monastery named for it, Wat Phra Sing Woramahawihan (fig. 2.1), where its gilded surface glows warmly against the crimson and gold of the murals that cover the walls. In local belief, this statue has resided in Chiang Mai as a protective presence since the sixteenth century. Elsewhere in Thailand, there are several statues that are also called the Sihing Buddha, such as the principal image in the Phutthaisawan Chapel at the National Museum in Bangkok. The chronicle of the Sihing relates that it was cast on the island of Lanka, now the nation of Sri Lanka. The name Sihing may be related to *siṃha* or *sīha,* the Sanskrit and Pali words, respectively, for lion, a symbol of the Sinhalese people of Lanka as well as of the Buddha Gotama. The statue's robust chest is said to imitate that of a proud lion. References to the Sihing can be found in manuscripts from around the region, including Laos, the Tai (Shan) areas in Myanmar, and southern Thailand.[3] The *tamnan* was written in Pali by a monk, Bodhiraṃsi (Thai: Phra Phothirangsi), probably in the first half of the fifteenth century.[4]

The Emerald Buddha: Palladium of the Kingdom of Thailand

According to the *tamnan* of the Emerald Buddha (Thai: Phra Kaeo Morakot, Phra Ratanapatima; Pali: Ratanapaṭimā, Ratanabimba;

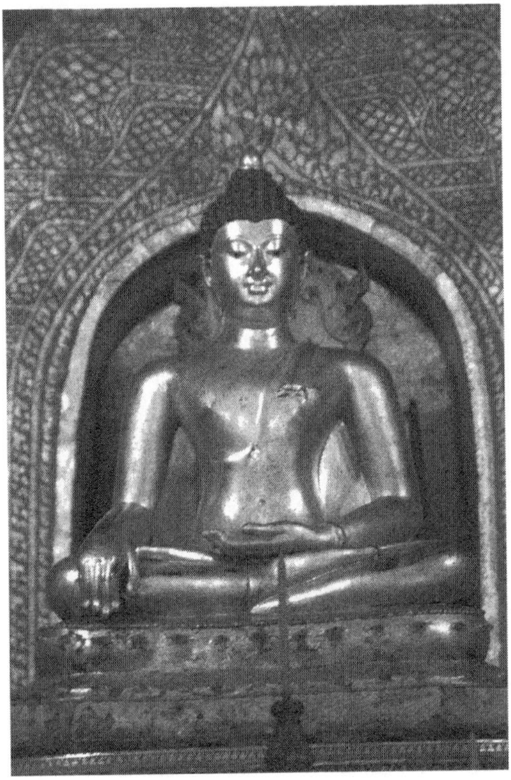

Fig. 2.1. Sihing Buddha image, Wat Phra Sing, Chiang Mai.

fig. 2.2),[5] the statue was discovered accidentally in the fifteenth century in the northern Thai city of Chiang Rai. One day a lay devotee was washing a stucco Buddha image at the monastery and noticed that where bits of the stucco had chipped off, he could see a green stone beneath. The monks had the rest of the stucco chiseled away and were elated to uncover the Emerald Buddha, which had probably been covered during a time of war. According to its chronicle, the image has an illustrious history. It was created in ancient India at the instigation of Nāgasena, the highly accomplished Buddhist monk and scholar who famously answered over two hundred knotty questions of doctrine and practice posed by a skeptical king, Milinda (possibly the Indo-Greek king of Bactria also known as Menandros, around the second century BCE).[6] Their marathon dialogue is recounted in the classical Buddhist text, the *Milindapañha* (*Questions of Milinda*). According to the *tamnan*, Nāgasena later expressed a wish to create a Buddha image to benefit

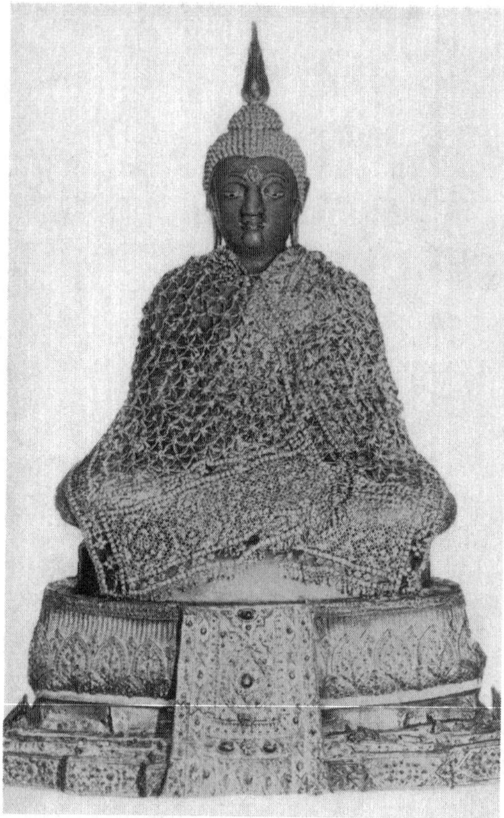

Fig. 2.2. Emerald Buddha image, Wat Phra Sri Ratanasadaram, Bangkok.

the world; this spurred the gods to obtain a divine gem and sculpt it into a beautiful statue. The image was then enshrined in India as a long-standing object of enthusiastic devotion, but eventually was transported away. Over the course of many centuries it was carried from India to Lanka, then to Angkor in contemporary Cambodia, and from there to various cities in Tai territories. The text of the Emerald Buddha chronicle states that it was written by a monk called Brahmarājapaññā (Thai: Phra Phromarachapanya), who at age twenty-three had been ordained for two years and was living at the monastery Wat Doi Mahathammaracha. It is estimated that he set the chronicle down in writing in the mid- to late fifteenth century.[7] Brahmarājapaññā wrote that he based his composition (in the Pali language) on an existing account in the local language, so the story of the Emerald Buddha was known from some earlier time, from oral and probably also written accounts.[8]

The Sikhi (Flaming) Buddhas: From Black Rock to Sacred Icon

The Sikhi images (Thai: Phra Sikhi Phutthapatima; Pali: Buddhapaṭimā Sikhī) were originally produced in a set of five.[9] As far as I have been able to ascertain, none of the images is known to exist anymore.[10] Their chronicle recounts that during his lifetime the Buddha travelled to mainland Southeast Asia, using his extraordinary powers to fly from ancient India, accompanied by five hundred disciples. He rested upon a black rock and then preached a sermon to people living nearby. The rock was later sculpted by a ruler of the Rāmañña country (probably referring to today's Lower Myanmar) into five Buddha statues, which were sent out to various cities in Burmese, Cambodian, and Tai lands. Because the Sikhi images are discussed in the *JKM,* their history was apparently known by the early sixteenth century.

The Sandalwood Buddha: The First Image of the Buddha

This image (Thai: Phra Phuttharup Kaenchan; Pali: Candanapaṭimā, Kosalabimba) may not exist anymore in Thailand,[11] but it is distinctive among this group of images because it is referred to in Buddhist lore across Asia. For instance, in the account written in the year 400 of his travels in ancient India, the Chinese monk Faxian states that the sandalwood statue was the first image ever created of the Buddha Gotama. He recounted that at the time the Buddha was living in Kosala, he made a trip to heaven to preach to his mother, then residing there with the gods. Back in Kosala, King Pasenadi was so pained by the Buddha's absence that he had a statue of him carved.[12] In Japan, a story dating to at least the late twelfth century extends this account to say that the sandalwood image was conveyed to China, and then was later carried away to Japan by a Japanese monk; today it is known as the Shoji Shaka or Ikimi Shaka and is enshrined at the Seiryōji Temple in Kyoto.[13] The Lanna chronicle, on the other hand, asserts that the image was transported from Kosala to the northern Thai region, where it circulated for centuries. Some believe that it is now enshrined in a *stūpa,* a reliquary monument, at Wat Suan Dok (Wat Buppharam) in Chiang Mai.[14] As the chronicle is summarized in the *JKM,* the story was likely in circulation in Lanna by the early sixteenth century.

The White Crystal (Setangkhamani) Buddha: A Buddha Image amidst a North-South Rivalry

Alongside the Sihing in Chiang Mai, the Setangkhamani or White Crystal Buddha (Thai: Phra Setangkhamani, Phra Kaeo Khao; Pali: Setaṃgamaṇī) is today considered to be one of the most important images in northern Thailand (fig. 2.3).[15] It is sculpted from clear stone and stands just thirty-four centimeters in height. It is housed at Wat Chiang Man, one of Chiang Mai's most venerable monasteries. The *tamnan* recounts that the statue was created long ago at the request of the king of Lavo (today Lopburi in central Thailand); a god who had been wearing a white crystal on his head donated it to be sculpted into an image. The statue was later passed to the king's daughter, Cāmadevī (Thai: Chamathewi), and taken by her to Haripuñjaya (Thai: Hariphunchai; now the northern Thai city of Lamphun), where she became queen and established an eminent dynasty. The statue was later transported to Chiang Mai, from where it was stolen by a prince of Ayutthaya but eventually recovered by the king of Chiang Mai. The

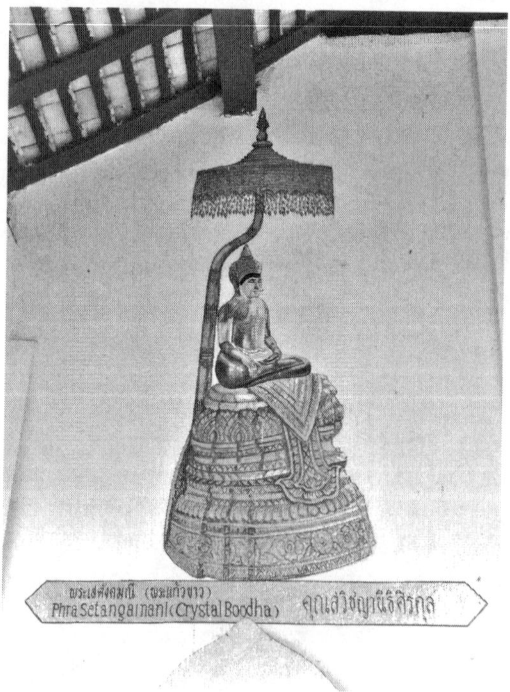

Fig. 2.3. Mural of Setangkhamani Buddha image, Wat Chiang Man, Chiang Mai.

name of the author of the chronicle is unknown. The story does not appear in the *JKM,* but all known versions of the text are missing events of the years 1455–1476. The Setangkhamani story focuses in detail on Chiang Mai's rivalry with Ayutthaya in the late fifteenth century and ends in the reign of King Kaeo of Chiang Mai (1495–1525), suggesting a possible time of original composition in the sixteenth century.[16]

The *tamnan* for all of these Lanna Buddha images share a similar narrative structure. They begin hundreds or thousands of years in the past with a description of how a particular image was produced and consecrated, and then provide a chronology of who possessed the statue at what times, and where, up until the time of the writing of the chronicle.

The *Chronicle of the Sihing Buddha Image*

As an example, let us consider the following summary of the chronicle of the Sihing Buddha image.[17]

Bodhiraṃsi, the author of the *Chronicle of the Sihing Buddha Image* [*Tamnan Phra Buddha Sihiṅga*], prefaces the story with traditional brief expressions of homage to the Buddha, the *saṅgha* (the community of monks), and the *dhamma* (the Buddha's teachings) before opening the narrative on the island of Lanka. There, seven hundred years after the Buddha's death (or *parinibbāna*) (parinirvana), three kings were ruling, and Buddhism (the *sāsana*) was flourishing there thanks to the efforts of twenty enlightened individuals, *arahants.* One day the kings asked the *arahants* if they had ever seen the Buddha when he was still living. They admitted that they had not, but suggested that there should be someone who had, perhaps a god. The conversation was overheard by a long-lived *nāga,* or snake god, who appeared before the assembly and declared that he had seen the Buddha. The *nāga* offered to magically transform himself into an image of the Buddha. He warned the people, "When you see the form like the form of the Buddha, I ask the lords not to pay homage to me at all, an impure image which should not be reverenced," as in essence the image would not be the Buddha but only the snake god.[18]

Through the accumulated power of the good deeds the *nāga* had performed in previous lives, he transformed his body into the form of the Buddha. The beautiful, elaborate vision presented the Buddha seated cross-legged in meditation upon a throne of seven jewels within the Jetavana Monastery in Sāvatthī, in ancient India. His body, complete with thirty-two distinguishing characteristics of the Great Man (Pali: *mahāpurusa*) and eighty major and minor aspects, broadcast a *rasmi* (radiance) of six colors. Around the Buddha were arrayed his eighty great disciples. When the kings and the people of Lanka saw the vision, they were overwhelmed with faith and, apparently forgetting the snake god's warning, they venerated the image with shouts of joy, prostrations, the waving of cloths, and offerings of jewelry, gold, and silver.[19] The *nāga* maintained the vision for seven days, and then he returned to the land of the *nāgas*.[20]

The three kings decided to make a copy of the Buddha image in metal. They summoned craftsmen to cast the statue. First, the craftsmen sculpted a model in beeswax based on the witnesses' memory of the *nāga*'s image. Groups of different kinds of deities, such as *asuras, garuḍas, gandhabbas, devas,* and *yakṣas,* came to contribute bits of metal such as gold, silver, and brass. The metal was placed in a crucible that was heated, and when the metal was fluid, a large pair of tongs was used to grip the crucible and pour it into a mold. While observing the process, one of the kings noticed that a craftsman was ignoring royal orders and struck that craftsman on the finger. Later, when the casting was completed, it was discovered that one of the fingers of the statue had a defect. Upon seeing what had happened, the *arahants* made a prophecy. They declared that in the future the Buddha image would go to Jambudvīpa: "There will be a king in that country with faith who will support this Buddha image. He will cut the Buddha image's finger and make a new one, rendering it perfect. When our Buddha *sāsana* reaches two thousand years of age, a righteous king (*dhammikarāja*) on this Sīhala island will bring the Buddha image back here again." Hearing the prophecy, the kings and people of Lanka shouted with happiness. They polished the image and placed it upon an excellent throne in a newly built pavilion. For seven days and seven nights, the people, and huge numbers of gods, celebrated and offered fragrant garlands and beautiful and fine banners to the image. On the eighth day, the image was placed in a pavilion shared with the Tooth Relic of the Buddha.[21]

From then the Sihing image was worshipped by men and deities for many centuries. Fifteen hundred years after the Buddha's *parinibbāna,* there was a righteous king called Phra Ruang ruling in the city of

Sukhothai, in the central part of present-day Thailand. Ruang, endowed with great wisdom and courage, had immense power and wealth, ministers from prominent families, and a large force of soldiers at his command. He possessed a kingdom of vast territory, and his people enjoyed happiness and riches. Ruang journeyed south to Nakhon Sri Thammarat, on the coast of contemporary Thailand, where he was informed by the king of that city that on Lanka Island "there is a Buddha image with great power. Indra, Brahma, *devātas, asuras,* and men, with *arahants* as their leaders, together built it within one day. It is established on that island and is worshipped every morning, day and night, constantly. There are four gods—namely, Sumanadeva, Kāmadeva, Rāmadeva, and Lakṣaṇadeva, those with power—taking care of that Buddha image all the time." Upon hearing this, Ruang became determined to possess the image and so had the king of Nakhon Sri Thammarat send an emissary to Lanka to ask for it. The emissary described Ruang's power, might, and cleverness to the king of Lanka. The king agreed to Ruang's request to turn over the Sihing, regarding it as fulfillment of the prophecy that the image would go to Jambudvīpa.[22]

The Lankan king worshipped the Sihing image for the last time, and then arranged a boat filled with lavish amounts of special offerings, in the middle of which a beautifully decorated throne was installed as the statue's seat. The king requested that the image perform some final miracle (probably of levitating in the air), and then the boat sailed off. In the middle of the ocean, however, the boat struck a rock and was demolished. All of the people on board fell in the water and were eaten by turtles and fish. The Sihing also tumbled into the sea but did not sink. It floated along, beautiful in its splendor, turning to face the direction of Nakhon Sri Thammarat.[23]

At that time, the gods of the sea and sky were occupied in an assembly of deities and thus did not immediately go to the aid of the Sihing. As the statue glided closer to Nakhon Sri Thammarat, the gods were returning from their assembly, and saw the Sihing in the ocean. In the night they entered the dreams of the king of Nakhon Sri Thammarat and informed him that he should send a boat to welcome the Sihing. Upon waking, the king summoned boatmen to arrange a flotilla of eight boats, which he loaded with offerings. The boatmen found the Sihing and conveyed it to the pier. The king led the whole population of the city in venerating the image with special offerings of fragrant items such as flowers and sandalwood, as well as fans, banners, umbrellas, and music played on many kinds of instruments. The king declared that Buddhism, the *sāsana,* would flourish for five thousand years with Ruang at the forefront. The king and people paid homage to the Sihing image for seven days and seven nights with various offerings, while the gods in heaven, led by Indra and Brahma, scattered offerings that fell like rain from the sky. The king asked the Sihing to "please help and have compassion for the servant of the Lord Buddha who requests you to perform miracles in the middle of the populace to increase happiness and benefit the people." The image floated into the sky, emitting a radiance of six colors in all directions, causing the people to raise their hands in reverence, wave cloths, and shout in homage.[24]

The king of Nakhon Sri Thammarat sent word to King Ruang of the arrival of the Sihing. Hearing the news, Ruang's heart filled with happiness and he proceeded to Nakhon Sri Thammarat. He invited the statue to return with him to Sukhothai. He then entreated the image to perch on his head, and the Sihing miraculously flew and rested upon the king's head, causing the people to cry out with joy. The Sihing was then transported to Sukhothai on an excellently decorated palanquin, accompanied by offerings too numerous to count and surrounded by a vast entourage of nobles, charioteers, horse cavalry, elephant cavalry, and infantry. In Sukhothai, Ruang built a hall for the Sihing and worshipped it continuously.[25]

After Ruang died, his successors likewise venerated the Sihing. During the reign of King Luethai, another king, Rāmādhipati (Thai: Ramathibodi) of Ayutthaya, conquered Sukhothai. Rāmādhipati deposed Luethai but permitted him to go to rule in Songkhwae (present-day Phitsanulok), and Luethai brought the Sihing image with him there. After Luethai's death, the Sihing image was sent to Ayutthaya,[26] transported on a large boat laden with offerings. People unfamiliar with the Sihing noticed this and understood that the statue was different from others but did not know why.[27]

At that time, a king named Ñāṇatissa (Thai: Yanadit) was ruling in Kamphaeng Phet, today in Thailand. A man of knowledge and perception who followed the *dhamma,* Ñāṇatissa heard of the prestige and power of the Sihing and determined to obtain it. He dispatched his mother, Mae Luang, to Ayutthaya; endowed with great beauty, she was "clever in womanly deceptions and able to coax and ensnare the hearts of men." Her beauty caught King Rāmādhipati's eye, and they began living together. Mae Luang, aware that the king had fallen in love with her, waited until he was feeling cheerful and requested that the king give her a bronze Buddha image to send to Kamphaeng Phet. The king, whose love for her at that time was only growing greater, agreed. Mae Luang then picked up offerings including candles, incense, and garlands and proceeded to the hall of Buddha images. There were many images there, and she did not know which image was the Sihing, so she bribed the curator with gold to identify it. She performed a worship for the statue and then had it put on a boat to go by river to her son, Ñāṇatissa. Receiving the image, Ñāṇatissa exclaimed, "My hope has borne fruit! My thought has borne fruit!" He planned to venerate the image constantly.[28]

Meanwhile, in Ayutthaya, the disappearance of the Sihing from the hall of images was noticed three days after the fact. Rāmādhipati furiously scolded Mae Luang, but she replied, "I followed the course of the king's approval and invited one Buddha image [to Kamphaeng Phet] in order to worship it for merit. I did not know that that image was the Sihing Buddha. If the Sihing Buddha is the one I invited, I will have a new copy cast in bronze and will return the excellent Sihing Buddha here." Listening to her sweet words, the king was calmed, and Mae Luang again became the beloved of the king.[29]

Word of the powerful Sihing image spread to people and their leaders. At the time, the king of Chiang Rai, a city in the far north of today's Thailand, was Mahābrahma (Thai: Mahaphrom). This king was skilled in various crafts such as writing, carpentry, and sculpture. His older brother was King Kli (Thai: Kuena; r. 1355–1385), the ruler of Chiang Mai.[30]

One day a monk from Kamphaeng Phet brought to Chiang Rai a beeswax sculpture he had made of the Sihing. He showed it to Mahābrahma and regaled the king with the Sihing's virtues. Mahābrahma determined to possess the statue and assembled many tens of thousands of brave soldiers to march on Kamphaeng Phet. The procession of the huge force crushed trees and grass, and "the sound of the elephants, horses, chariots, and troops marching made the sky seem too small and the ground as if it would collapse." At Kamphaeng Phet, Mahābrahma threatened war against King Ñāṇatissa. Ñāṇatissa did not want to fight and replied, "It is believed that Brahma [the Indic god of creation] is the father of all beings in the world. In that case, I am the son of the king, and the king is my father. It is said that he who is the father of all beings in the world usually renders aid to his sons. I request you to spare my sons, wives, territory, and myself. Outside of those, I bow my head and request you not to bring destruction on me." Ñāṇatissa further agreed to Mahābrahma's request for the Sihing but knew that Rāmādhipati of Ayutthaya would crush him if he knew that he had given away the statue. Therefore, during the night he had the Sihing placed on a boat and spirited to Tak, where Mahābrahma received it. Mahābrahma mounted the statue on a golden litter, which was borne to Chiang Mai, where he told his older brother King Kli that he would give the Sihing to him after he made a copy of it in Chiang Rai. Mahābrahma then transported the Sihing to Chiang Rai, venerating it all along the route, even inviting it to be honored on a throne on an island in the middle of the Mekong River. After they reached Chiang Rai, Mahābrahma had the image's defective finger repaired. He also had a copy of the Sihing cast in gold. Mahābrahma worshipped the two Buddha images ceaselessly; he exclaimed, "The Buddha image named Sihing has come to find us. The kings in Jambudvīpa do not have merit equal to ours!"[31]

Meanwhile, in Chiang Mai, Mahābrahma's brother King Kli, although replete with prestige, happiness, and royal accoutrements, became worried about his next life and thus performed several meritorious acts, including building *stūpas* containing Buddha relics and *vihāras* (monastic halls) for Buddha images. When Kli died he was succeeded by his son, Sirirājaputta (Thai: Sirirachabut or Saen Mueang Ma; r. 1385–1401), a man of compassion and gentle speech who was beloved by the people of Chiang Mai. King Mahābrahma, who was Sirirājaputta's uncle, conscripted an army and tried to seize Chiang Mai. He failed; Sirirājaputta captured him on the battlefield "like a lion catching an elephant." King Sirirājaputta had the Sihing and the golden Buddha image, plus the gold, silver, and other possessions of Mahābrahma brought from Chiang Rai to Chiang Mai. He venerated the Sihing with an extremely large collection of offerings.[32]

When Sirirājaputta was near the end of his life, he handed over the kingdom to his son, Vijayatissa (Thai: Wichaidit or Sam Fang Kaen; r. 1402–1441), who likewise had high merit, was beloved by the people, and worshipped the Sihing image constantly.[33]

The chronicle ends with a reiteration of the prophecy of the Sihing image's return to the island of Lanka at the two thousandth anniversary of the Buddha's *nibbāna* (nirvana) and an expression noting the prestige of the Sihing image and its great veneration in Chiang Mai.[34]

This summary conveys the flavor of the Lanna chronicles, in which Buddhist themes are combined with local history, legend, and magical happenings. The text is largely narrative, with relatively little description. Humor is not lacking, however. We can imagine how stories such as this would have engaged Buddhist devotees who sat in temple halls listening to them preached by monks.

Biographies of Buddha Images

Because the Sihing and the other travelling images at present appear stylistically to date no earlier than the fourteenth century, many scholars doubt that the statues were created thousands of years in the past, as some chronicles say. *Tamnan* like these are tantalizing as potential sources of information about royal lineages, ancient city names, and events such as wars between states that are not found in other sources. At the same time, modern scholars approach the chronicles with skepticism because they evoke legend and miracle. Nonetheless, it is worthwhile reading these documents not only for what they say but for how they say it. Studying the structure and themes of these *tamnan* will help us to illuminate how people of Lanna's golden age regarded Buddha images.

The Lanna focus on the original production of a statue and the detailed recounting of its history over hundreds of years suggest an understanding of a Buddha statue as capable of having its own biography. Based upon accounts described in existing scholarship, commonalities of motif and theme may be perceived between the Lanna stories and examples from China and Japan, such as the preference for detailed discussion of the origins of an image, attention to its miraculous powers, and the sense of the image as having its own life or at least an autonomous sense of where it should go on its travels.[35] Yet the Lanna style of the extended biography of the travelling statue seems to be without equivalent elsewhere. The varying themes and emphases of the various Asian narratives reflect the different contexts of their composition. A comparison with Buddhist stories from across Asia is well beyond the scope of this book, but a set of Burmese stories of images will be considered in chapter 4.

The stories of the Sihing and other travelling images are largely narratives of how the statues journeyed between esteemed patrons—

mostly kings who were glorified as pious and mighty—in various locations across Asia. The relationship drawn between an image's residence and a host's merit echoes circumstances from the Buddha's life story. The Buddha wandered for twenty years and then for a twenty-five-year period lived in just two places, Jeta's Grove (Jetavana) and the Eastern Monastery (Pubbārāma); as Ratanapañña Thera, the author of the *JKM* remarked, the choice of residence was due to the immense virtue of the two patrons' families.[36] The Lanna images likewise gravitated away and towards potential patrons according to those patrons' merit. Thus, for example, in the chronicle of the Sihing Buddha, King Rāmādhipati of Ayutthaya lost the Sihing when he was seduced by Mae Luang of Kamphaeng Phet and carelessly permitted her to take the statue away.[37] In the Emerald Buddha chronicle, it is recounted that the king of Angkor lost the statue after he ordered an unduly harsh punishment, execution, for the son of an official who killed his son's pet greenflies.[38] One measure of a patron's merit often noted in the chronicles is military prowess; in the Sihing Buddha story, Ruang obtained the Sihing Buddha image from the king of Lanka after the latter was implicitly threatened with war, being informed by the Tai emissary of the warrior king Ruang's power, strength, and spirit.[39] The story of the Sikhi images recounts that King Anawrahta (called Aniruddha in the chronicle; r. ca. 1044–1077) of Bagan invaded the Rāmañña country and defeated its king in order to take a Sikhi image.[40] The chronicles often highlight a ruler's military ability, merit, and fitness to possess a certain Buddha image. Indeed, going to war to seize a particular statue was evidence of a king's confidence in his own excellence.

Focusing on patrons and how they supported Buddha images and were strengthened by them, the chronicles essentially concern the sphere of social interactions generated by Buddha images. Each text recounts a chain of agency. In the story of the Sihing, the kings of Lanka are agents who caused the snake god to transform himself into a vision of the Buddha; this vision in turn made the kings its patients when it inspired them to hire craftsmen to make a Buddha statue. The casting also attracted the agency of the gods, who donated metals for the casting, and later, together with the king, monks, and people of Lanka, consecrated the statue. The image became a patient receiving veneration from its original patrons and subsequent ones, but then also became an agent in that it enabled devotees across Asia to make merit, helped them achieve their wishes, and inspired other patrons to obtain the image. Because the Lankan kings decided to make an image, their agency effectively continued to act on worshippers well after their deaths.

The sequence of worshippers of travelling images includes famous figures of the past. The Sihing Buddha story features Ruang, which may in this case refer to the thirteenth-century king Ramkhamhaeng, considered a great hero of Thai history. In the Emerald Buddha *tamnan*, illustrious persons from different points in history become connected to the statue. The originator of the Emerald Buddha is the wise and clever Nāgasena, who dispelled King Milinda's doubts. King Anawrahta, one of the most powerful monarchs of the early Upper Burmese kingdom of Bagan, caused the Emerald Buddha to depart Lanka for the Southeast Asian mainland. Anawrahta also plays a role in the history of the Sikhi images, as does Cāmadevī, said to be the first queen of Haripuñjaya (Thai: Hariphunchai), an early kingdom in northern Thailand.

The statues' networks of relationships link eminent past figures to fourteenth- and fifteenth-century Lanna sovereigns. The recounting of each image's story takes the form of a lineage. The image biography envisions history as a lineage of meritorious persons (table 2.1). It is notably almost entirely a line of men, predominantly kings; in chapter 4 we will consider the scarcity of women in such lineages.

The travelling image chronicle presents an alternative version of the history of Lanna to that expounded in the *JKM*, an important source for much information about what is known of Lanna's early rulers and their activities, and particularly their patronage of Buddhism. The text of the *JKM* commences in the distant past, with the recounting of rebirths of the Buddha Gotama hundreds of thousands of lives ago. It then enumerates the lineage of twenty-seven Buddhas born previously in the world over eons and summarizes the career of Gotama, and then describes early Buddhism in India and Lanka before moving on to mainland Southeast Asia with a short history of Haripuñjaya in the late seventh to late thirteenth centuries. The rest of the text lists Lanna kings beginning with King Mangrai (r. 1261–1311), the founder of the dynasty, and their activities from the late thirteenth to the early sixteenth centuries.[41]

The *JKM* presents local history in the form of a chronology of Haripuñjaya and Lanna sovereigns. It also incorporates within its text

Table 2.1. Patrons of travelling images. Based on CBCN, EBSM, SBSM, SKNJ, and SWNJ.

Emerald	Sihing	Setangkhamani	Sikhi	Sandalwood
Monk Nāgasena	Kings of Lanka	King Rāmarāja of Lopburi	King of Rāmañña	King Pasenadi of Kosala
King Anawrahta of Bagan	King Ruang of Sukhothai	Queen Cāmadevī of Haripuñjaya	King Anawrahta of Bagan	King of Suvaṇṇabhūmi
King of Angkor	King Phokhunban of Sukhothai	King Mangrai of Chiang Mai	King of Angkor	King Ādicca of Suvaṇṇabhūmi
King Āditta of Ayutthaya	King Lithai of Sukhothai	King Khram of Chiang Mai	Queen Cāmadevī of Haripuñjaya	King Suvaṇṇasāma of Tak
King of Kamphaeng Phet	King Namthuam of Sukhothai	King Sam Fang Kaen of Chiang Mai	King Sudhamma of Tak	King Muddikanetra of Sob Soi
King Mahābrahma of Chiang Rai	King Luethai of Sukhothai	Prince Suriya of Ayutthaya	King of Ayutthaya	A hunter of Bang Phlu
Minister Sandha of Lampang	King Rāmādhipati of Ayutthaya	King Muang Yot of Chiang Mai		Monk Abhaya of Balima
Minister Uttarasunoma of Lampang	King Ñāṇatissa of Kamphaeng Phet	King Kaeo of Chiang Mai		Moḷī, a layman of Phayao
Minister Sumana of Lampang	King Mahābrahma of Chiang Rai			Phya Yuddhasaṇṭhira of Phayao
	King Sirirājaputta of Chiang Mai			Monk Dhammasenāpati of Asoka Monastery
	King Vijayatissa of Chiang Mai			Great Minister Pādepa of Phayao
				King Kaeo of Chiang Mai

short versions of four travelling image histories. The accounts of the Emerald, Sandalwood, Sihing, and Sikhi Buddhas are inserted into the narrative of kings at the specific point when a king captures the image in a war (Sikhi) or installs the image in a new shrine (Emerald, Sandalwood, and Sihing). Each account of a statue, in other words, is a digression from the chronicle's chief chronological sequence.

The *JKM* shifts between two narrative viewpoints, one focused around the succession of monarchs of the Mangrai dynasty, the other around a particular statue. The role of the monarchy and the role of the Buddha in northern Thai society thus follow distinctive historical paths across time and space, with both ultimately converging in Lanna and intertwined in the Buddha image.

The travelling image chronicles underscore that the statues were created through the initiative of specific patrons. In at least one version of the Emerald Buddha chronicle, the importance of Nāgasena as the initial patron of the statue is emphasized by the fact that the first quarter of the text is devoted to an extended account of the monk's biography, including his past lives. Great attention is paid to describing his education and listing the spiritual feats he attained through the course of his rebirths. Nāgasena mastered the massive corpus of the Vedas by the age of seven. He memorized every word of the Buddhist canon in the space of three months, and it took him only three more months to memorize the words' meanings. By the time of his famous encounter with Milinda, "the earth shook, the sea was in turmoil, and the mountains shook with the power of Nāgasena Thera."[42] Thus the monk was able to deftly respond to Milinda's questions. Yet the culmination of his achievements is presented not as his triumph in this momentous debate, which is in fact only very perfunctorily noted, but the creation of the Emerald Buddha. The author of the chronicle summarizes his life thus: "Nāgasena Thera, a person of great prestige, appeared to the whole world like the moon in the sky. He had destroyed darkness—that is, delusion—through illumination, the powerful insight of the *thera* [monk]. He had them carve the Buddha image, which appeared in the era of the *sāsana,* and worshipped it his whole life until his attachments—that is, desires, all bindings—ceased. He entered *parinibbāna* [death] and through the *nibbāna* [nirvana] of the *dhātu* [components of being], had no attachments remaining at all."[43] The Buddha image is here described as the result of Nāgasena's achievements as well as a catalyst for his further achievements: the monk's agency brought about the creation of the wonderful Emerald Buddha;

then, owing to the statue's empowerment of his further development, he was able to reach *nibbāna*. After describing Nāgasena, the *tamnan* narrates the lineage of further sponsors; the themes of the image's attracting sponsors of high merit and the benefits of venerating the image are extended through the rest of the text.

At the same time that the chronicles elevate the patron who originated the idea to make a Buddha image, the texts also present the creation of statues as projects involving collective efforts. For instance, the Setangkhamani image came into being when King Rāma of Lopburi desired to make an image out of crystal. Kumārakassapa, the head of the *saṅgha* (the Buddhist monkhood), got involved, and a god contributed the crystal. The king had his officials and people erect a jewelled pavilion and arrange a festival with music and dance. The stone was sculpted into a Buddha image by the gods Vishnu and Vissakamma with the help of humans. When the image was finished, it was the gods who washed it. Then Indra presented five relics of the Buddha, which miraculously implanted themselves into the image following an invocation intoned by *arahants*.[44] The process of production of each statue and the different parties who contributed to its making are significant aspects of the travelling image chronicles, emphasizing the importance of patronage and the collaborative effort needed by craftsmen, monks, and lay devotees in order to create a Buddha image. The image embodies a collectivization of agencies.

In the *tamnan,* the Buddha statue is depicted as constantly subject to the agency of those who make and honor it, who not only influence its location and movement but through their piety summon the expression of its special powers. The author of the Sihing Buddha chronicle attributed the image's supernatural power to not only its association with the Buddha but to the agency of its patrons as well. While the image was being transported by boat across the sea from Lanka to Nakhon Sri Thammarat, the boat was destroyed in a storm. The Sihing Buddha tumbled into the ocean but did not sink and floated along the surface of the waves. The chronicle's author himself asked, how could the heavy object have such buoyancy? Following an extended discussion, he concluded that this miracle was due neither to the power of the image alone nor to the power of helpful gods: "the Buddha image Sihing has no life but has power through the strength of the resolution [Thai: *athitthan;* Sanskrit: *adhiṣṭhāna*] of the *arahants,* the strength of the resolution of the Lankan king, and the strength of the *sāsana* of the Fully Enlightened One. It is not the image itself alone."[45] In other words, the virtuous thoughts and practices of lay and monastic supporters helped propel the image.

Images could embody the agency of the people who produced them in a literal sense. When the Sihing Buddha was in the process of being cast, one of the Lankan kings struck and injured a craftsman's finger, and when the casting was finished, the Sihing itself was found to have one defective finger.[46] Likewise, the Sihing is depicted as performing miracles not at its own initiative but in response to specific worthy patrons. As noted above, the chronicle author said that the miraculous power of the Sihing arose in part from the resolution of a Lankan king, which was expressed by the king when he was about to invite the image to board the ship to go from Lanka to the mainland to help King Ruang of Sukhothai. He also asked the image to perform miracles for the people there.[47] Later, after the Sihing arrived in Nakhon Sri Thammarat, the king of that city requested that it perform miracles to benefit the people; the Sihing then floated up into the sky, emitting a multicolored radiance. Ruang, who had come to invite the Sihing to return with him to Sukhothai, asked the image to come down and perch on his head, and it did so.[48]

The attribution of the Sihing's miracle performance to virtuous patrons echoes an explanation given for miracle performance given by Nāgasena. According to the *Milindapañha,* King Milinda asked Nāgasena how it was possible that miracles could appear at the reliquary mounds (Pali: *cetiya*) of deceased *arahants,* given that these enlightened beings had already died and passed into *nibbāna.* Nāgasena replied that there were three possible causes for such miracles. One was that the *arahant,* out of pity for gods and humans, had made a resolution during his lifetime that miracles should happen at his *cetiya* after his passing. The second was that a similar resolution for miracle performance was made by a god visiting the *cetiya.* The third cause was that "some woman or some man of believing heart, able, intelligent, wise, endowed with insight" brought offerings to the *cetiya* and resolved that a miracle should occur there.[49] This may represent a precedent for the concept of the Sihing Buddha image performing miracles because of the virtue of lay patrons and not only due to the powers of the Buddha, monks, or deities.

The pairing of patrons and images in the travelling image chronicles was not just a symbolic pairing but indeed the fuel that gave each image its special power. The travelling images were distinguished from other Buddha statues by their lineages of illustrious makers and worshippers. This understanding of a Buddha image as not being merely symbolic but as having an active orientation and its own biography is perhaps the underlying rationale for devotees' wish to produce images for different occasions: to commemorate vows, to celebrate birthdays, to present a final testament. A patron sponsors an image because he wants the image to do something in the future, to be an agent acting upon others.

Those who heard the chronicles preached were invited to join these glorious lineages, to associate themselves with the heroes of the past and position themselves and their heirs as leading supporters of Buddhism. The statues were deployed to become the central organizing pivots of history—indeed, the very generators of Buddhist history.

Buddha Images and the Spread of Buddhism

The lineage of patrons in the chronicles is connected to a lineage of places, the residences of each travelling image. For example, the five Sikhi images were sculpted near Ayutthaya and distributed to Angkor in present-day Cambodia, Lopburi in central Thailand, and the Rāmañña country and Thaton of present-day Lower Myanmar; later, they were sent on to Lampang, Lamphun, Lopburi, and Tak in Tai territories and to Bagan in Burmese lands. The Sandalwood Buddha emerged from India and went to the northern Thai polities of Chiang Mai, Phayao, and Tak and to other villages in Lanna. The Sihing Buddha linked Lanka with the Tai cities of Ayutthaya, Chiang Mai, Chiang Rai, Kamphaeng Phet, Nakhon Sri Thammarat, Phitsanulok, and Sukhothai.

It has been proposed that the travelling images were symbols that marked the spread of Buddhism or perhaps the transmission of particular Buddhist orders. For instance, Phiset Chiechanphong has suggested that the travels of the Emerald Buddha image were meant to symbolize the expansion of Theravāda Buddhism, while those of the Sihing Buddha image, which was made in Lanka, were intended to represent the spread of the Lanka-linked Wat Pa Daeng, the Monastery of the Redwood Grove, a forest-dwelling order (Pali: *araññavāsī*).[50]

This concept of an image standing for the territorial expansion of Buddhism is found in other Asian traditions. One of the most valuable records available today of Buddhism in ancient India is the travel account written by the Chinese monk Xuanzang, who made a pilgrimage to numerous Buddhist sites there during the seventh century. Xuanzang reported that in a monastery in the valley of Ta-li-lo (Daril or Darail), there was a wooden statue, a hundred feet tall, of the Bodhisattva Maitreya. The statue was sculpted by a craftsman who was dispatched, through the spiritual power of the Arhat Madhyântika, to Tuṣita heaven to observe the Bodhisattva in person. Xuanzang noted, "From the time of the execution of this image the streams of the law (religious teaching) began to flow eastward."[51] Thus the expansion of Buddhism was attributed to the creation of the image. This function of an image may perhaps also be seen in the way the Sihing and Emerald Buddhas were depicted travelling to some important locations in the history of Tai Buddhism. Moreover, it seems probable that the authors of both statues' chronicles were members of the Wat Pa Daeng order. Perhaps the confidence of the author of the Sihing chronicle in the important role of his order can be seen in the way he remarks that happiness and an increase in faith resulted wherever the Sihing Buddha is said to have gone: the statue "was like a lamp illuminating the *sāsana,* making it bright and prosperous."[52] On the other hand, the symbolism seems to apply only in a generalized sense; for instance, there is no involvement in the Emerald and Sihing chronicles of influential sources of Buddhist transmission in mainland Southeast Asia such as Martaban (Mottama in present-day Myanmar) or Haripuñjaya (Lamphun) and Lopburi (in present-day Thailand).

For their worshippers, the statues were more than symbols; their condition as the crafted productions of devotees and their physical position in their communities enabled the statues to be integrated into local communities through the embodiment of local conceptions of place and lineage to a depth beyond the merely symbolic. As we shall see in chapter 4, some stories of Buddha statues were deliberately composed to emphasize the connection between a statue and its place of enshrinement.

Precedent and Tradition in Buddhist Literature

Some evidence suggests that before the mid-fifteenth century, manuscripts were not written in significant quantity in Lanna, and that there seems to have been a new impetus or trend in literature, with an increase in the number of texts produced and the composition of influential texts during this so-called golden age.[53] At present there is no consensus on what caused the growth in importance of literature.

Lanna's authors appear to have taken inspiration from chronicles from Lanka—especially those involving stories of bodily relics of the Buddha. The dissemination of Lankan texts may have originated in the fourteenth to sixteenth centuries when Tai monks journeyed to Lanka to study at the island's monasteries, where many were reordained in Lankan orders that they then propagated in Tai territories after they returned home. Lankan literature was the subject of a flourishing tradition, having enjoyed a renaissance that began in the mid-twelfth century and lasted for at least two hundred years.[54] Copies of Lankan texts, as well as newly written texts claiming a Lankan heritage, may still be found today in Lanna's monastic libraries. Summaries of the histories of the Tooth Relic (Lanka's most famous relic) and of other Lankan relics appear in the *JKM*.[55]

The Tooth Relic is enshrined today in Kandy, Sri Lanka, and is the subject of the *Dāṭhāvaṃsa*, a manuscript traditionally said to have been written in the fourth century in a Sinhalese language and translated into Pali in the thirteenth century by Dhammakitti Thera.[56] The *Dāṭhāvaṃsa* narrates the Tooth Relic's journey from the Buddha's funeral in what is now northern India to the Lankan royal court.[57] It begins with a monk named Khema plucking the tooth from the funeral pyre and presenting it to the king of Dantapura. The king and his successors greatly venerated the sacred Tooth Relic, though it also attracted skeptics. In one episode, described at length, a heretic king tried to destroy the Tooth Relic in various ways but ended up being converted to Buddhism because of the hardy tooth's performance of amazing miracles. Later another king started a war against Dantapura to obtain the Tooth Relic, but the Dantapura royal family managed to smuggle it out of the city and away to Lanka. Along the way the relic's journey was temporarily obstructed on two occasions by snake gods who desired it as an object of worship for themselves. Both times an *arahant* appeared and compelled the snake gods to release the Tooth Relic and allow its journey to continue. Ultimately it reached Lanka, where it became established as an object of homage for kings and people.

Like the travelling image chronicles, the *Dāṭhāvaṃsa* lists the royal patrons of its object of veneration. A royal couple, the prince and princess of Dantapura, were the ones who accompanied the Tooth Relic from Dantapura to Lanka. Their journey occupies much of the text of the chronicle. However, the two royals are depicted as rather uncertain and vulnerable; the snake gods easily snatched the relic from them, only surrendering it when an *arahant* overwhelmed the snake gods with the magical powers he had obtained through his study of higher Buddhist knowledge. The Tooth Relic chronicle emphasizes the supernatural abilities of the Buddha, as manifested by both his tooth and the *arahant,* and relates how these abilities propelled the relic's journey from India to Lanka: the Buddha's magical powers converted the heretics, triumphed over the snake gods, and stimulated the religion to flourish in Lanka. An important purpose of such accounts of Lankan relics was apparently to establish the relic as authentic to the Buddha and thereby legitimize Lankan religious and political authority.[58] The long string of miracle performances presented in the Tooth Relic chronicle contrasts with the travelling image stories' focus on the lineage and activities of patrons; the differences in emphases reflect the differing local political and social environments of Lanka and Lanna.

Nonetheless, both Lankan and Lanna chronicle authors may have been spurred to take up writing implements in response to an old prophecy that warned that Buddhism would progressively decline over the course of five thousand years after the Buddha Gotama's *parinibbāna,* so the world would then be deprived of Buddhism until the emergence of the next Buddha, Maitreya (Pali: Metteyya). This prophecy has been expounded in Lankan texts such as the *Manorathapūraṇī* by the fifth-century Lankan commentator Buddhaghosa,[59] as well as the *Anāgatavaṃsa,* a text attributed to the Buddha Gotama that was composed sometime before the early fourteenth century.[60] Rescensions of the *Anāgatavaṃsa* have been found in northern Thailand.

A version of the gloomy prophecy, discovered on a Thai stone inscription attributed to King Mahādhammarāja I of Sukhothai and dated 1345,[61] can be summarized as follows.

The inscription begins with the dismal disclosure that since the time of the Buddha's enlightenment, human lifespan has been gradually becoming shorter and shorter. At the same time, the religion has been deteriorating and will continue to do so. Ninety-nine years from the time of the inscription, the *Three Piṭakas,* the canon of Buddhist texts, will disappear as knowledge of them dwindles among the people. A thousand years later, monks will stop observing monastic rules. A thousand years after that, monks will no longer don robes but only tuck a bit of yellow cloth behind their ears as a marker of the Buddha's religion. A thousand years after that, there will be no yellow cloth and no monks by whom the *sāsana* can be identified. Meanwhile, the relics of the Buddha Gotama will still be present, but on the last day of the *sāsana* at the end of the five thousand years, all of the relics enshrined on earth and in heaven will soar up and together enter the Ratanamālikamahāstūpa (the Mahāthupa, a reliquary monument in Anurādhapura, Lanka). Then they will fly to the Mahābodhi tree beneath which the Buddha had attained enlightenment. There the relics will be consumed by a huge fire, and the Buddha *sāsana* will end. Humans will then be ignorant of the meaning of meritorious action and will continually commit sins and be doomed to hell. The inscription makes an exhortation to people of the present:

> From now on, all good people should make haste to perform meritorious actions in (accordance with) the Buddha's religion while it still survives. The present generation has the immense advantage of being born in time (to know) the Lord's religion; so everyone should be assiduous in doing homage to *stūpas, cetiyas,* and *śrīmahābodhi* trees, which is the same as (doing homage to) our Lord in person. If anyone (when doing homage to them) makes a wish with perfect faith, it will come true, even if he makes the wish that he will be reborn in heaven, (that he will stay there) until Śri Āriyamaitri (Maitreya) comes down (to earth) to become a Buddha, and that he will be reborn on this earth at the same time.

The two thousandth anniversary of the Buddha's religion occurred around 1456–1457. Consistent with the inscription's call to action, devotees may have responded to the millennial anniversary of the *sāsana* by performing various actions to try to support its welfare. The composition of the chronicle of the Emerald Buddha and the making of the statue may have been among the activities; in the chronicle of the Emerald Buddha, Nāgasena was said to have conceived the thought to make the statue because he was looking for a means to make the *dhamma* of the Buddha "prosperous and secure in the future."[62] According to the *JKM,* the Emerald Buddha appeared in Chiang Mai during the reign of King Tilok (also called Tilaka or Bilaka; 1441–1487), who was ruling at the time of the two thousandth anniversary.[63] Two other projects by Tilok may also have been great acts of merit related to this anniversary, though no records have yet been found to attest to the fact: the construction at Chiang Mai of the Mahābodhārāma (now popularly known as Wat Chet Yot), as a copy of the Mahābodhi Temple of Bodh Gaya in India, where the Buddha achieved enlightenment, and the convening at the Mahābodhārāma of the Eighth Buddhist Council (Pali: Saṅgāyana) in 1477.[64] Moreover, the writing of the *JKM* and other texts may also have been projects inspired by the need to support the *sāsana* at the two-thousandth anniversary.[65]

The trope of material representations of the Buddha—images, *stūpas,* or relics—being considered to reflect this sense of Buddhist temporality is found in manuscripts from across Asia.[66] One example is the Buddha's alms bowl. According to tradition, the Buddha, after his enlightenment, was offered four alms bowls, one from each of the Four Heavenly Kings; he fused them together into one bowl, which he then used throughout his life. After his death, the bowl miraculously transported itself to different places across Asia, stimulating people's conversion to Buddhism. Chinese tradition claims that the bowl will eventually withdraw from the human world, and this disappearance will signal the decline of the *sāsana*. The bowl will go to wait in the kingdom of *nāgas* until the next Buddha (Maitreya) becomes an enlightened being on earth, at which time the Four Heavenly Kings will again offer bowls. Then the combined bowls will be used by Maitreya. Throughout time the same bowl is in fact used by all of the Buddhas.[67] The bowl in this account is depicted as framing the timescale of each Buddhist era and providing continuity across eras.

In other examples, the ongoing state of decay of the *sāsana* in the current Buddhist era has been said to be reflected in the declining physical condition of specific Buddhist material objects. For instance, Xuanzang reported that he beheld two statues of the Bodhisattva Avālokiteśvara near the seat of the Buddha's enlightenment at Bodh Gaya. One statue of the Bodhisattva was positioned to the north of the seat, and the second to the south of it. Xuanzang recounted, "The old people say that 'as soon as the figures of this Bôdhisattva sink in the ground and disappear, the law of Buddha will come to an end.' The figure at the south angle is now up to its breast."[68]

The idea of an image standing for the state of Buddhism is plainly expressed in the Sandalwood Buddha story known in many places in Buddhist Asia.[69] The story relates that when the Buddha first saw the statue, it attempted to rise to honor him, but the Buddha told the statue to remain seated, as it would carry on the *sāsana* after the Buddha's *parinibbāna*. In Lanna versions of the story, the Buddha specifically states that the statue will take care of the *sāsana* for five thousand years; likewise, in a Lankan version the Buddha urges the statue "to endure five thousand years."[70]

As we shall see, Lanna projects of different eras reflect this need to slow the decline of Buddhism and promote its security, and, consistent with the Sukhothai inscription, the imperative for people to accumulate merit to ensure rebirth during the time of the next Buddha. The marking of the two thousandth anniversary in the mid-fifteenth century may well have supplied a pressing motivation for more intensive output of Buddhist art and literature. Yet this motive in itself does not explain why the different projects took the specific forms they did. In the present case, why would Lanna people believe that the writing and copying of stories with certain subjects and themes would contribute to the security of the *sāsana*? A further look at the historical situation of the time may help to answer this question.

Buddha Images and Monastic-Lay Relations

Modern scholars have attempted to relate the historical circumstances of Lanna during its "golden age" to the structure and themes of *tamnan*. Such investigation has focused on political systems and events, which seems like a natural starting point in view of the prominent role of kings in many chronicles.

The texts relate how each ruler in turn obtained a statue through his extraordinary merit. In the Sihing chronicle, King Mahābrahma of Chiang Rai, after installing the image in his city, boasted that his possession of the Sihing Buddha confirmed the superiority of his merit over all other kings.[71] In the story of the Sikhi Buddha images, King Anawrahta of Bagan sent one Sikhi image to Queen Cāmadevī of Haripuñjaya because he learned of the prosperity of the *sāsana* in her kingdom, and this reflected her high merit.[72] As noted earlier, in the chronicles merit is typically linked to military strength; the threat of war enabled kings of great merit to overpower other kings to get hold of famous Buddha images, and the possession of a statue was a signal that could broadcast a king's power far and wide. In the chronicle of the Sandalwood Buddha, envoys from "the south" (the kingdom of Ayutthaya) who came to make an alliance with King Kaeo paid homage to the image during their visit to Chiang Mai.[73]

Moreover, Buddha images and other kinds of relics were regarded as powerful objects, and only a ruler of great merit would risk interacting with them. Handling relics was an act by which a ruler demonstrated his confidence and asserted his right to rule.[74] The travelling images, as objects associated with prestigious rulers and other famous figures, affirmed the status of the rulers and polities that possessed them.[75] At the same time, by worshipping these powerful images, a king could benefit his people by sharing his merit with them.

Promoting the prestige of certain Buddha images could have supported political objectives of the kings of Lanna. During the late fourteenth and fifteenth centuries, when some travelling image chronicles may have first been written, Lanna did not have a centralized political structure; each local polity had its own ruler, who did not always obey the wishes of the king of Lanna. The kings' efforts at centralized control were further challenged by the region's geography of chains of mountains and rivers running north to south and diverse local dialects and ethnicities;[76] kings sought to spread Buddhism as a way to bring together the disparate peoples. Relic enshrinement and monastic land donation were tactics by which King Tilok projected his authority over his territories.[77] Tilok and other kings of Chiang Mai in the fourteenth and fifteenth centuries targeted towns for visits, during which they would listen to sermons and make donations at local monasteries.[78] Chiang Mai, the capital during the golden age, plays a prominent role in the travelling image chronicles: the Emerald Buddha was installed by Tilok in the Chedi Luang in the middle of Chiang Mai; the Sandalwood Buddha was established at the Asoka Monastery to the east of the capital. The presence of these statues attested to the extraordinary merit of the king, encouraging his subjects and lesser rulers to back him. The statue and the spread of its story could have served to proclaim to others the superior moral and physical force of the king.

The worship of images and other relics also could have enabled kings to assert power over divided local interests in another way. As Dhida Saraya has pointed out, Buddhist relics were positioned as a higher authority over the territorial powers of local and ancestral guardian deities. In this way Buddhism could transcend the fragmented landscape of localized, clan-based polities.[79] At the same time, in Thailand and elsewhere statues of the Buddha were sometimes viewed as inhabited by guardian spirits. Such spirits were not merely housed within or associated with the material but were equivalent to, or as one with, the material itself. When the material was formed into a Buddha statue, the spirit continued to be present; the transformation of the material into a Buddha image subsumed the spirit to Buddhism and made it the guardian of the image. For example, Robert Lingat has noted that the story of the Sikhi images being carved from a rock on which the Buddha had sat may be an explanation for how a rock worshipped by local people as an animist spirit was changed into a monument by a pious Buddhist; likewise, the Emerald Buddha could perhaps have been sculpted from some particularly sacred green stone.[80]

A variety of possible divinely linked symbolisms may be expressed by the Emerald Buddha, particularly through its material as well as the roles of deities in its history. The statue is apparently not made of emerald but a green stone resembling jade or jasper. King Rama IV (r. 1851–1868), one of the few individuals able to closely examine the Emerald Buddha, wrote that its surface was unmarked by tools and polished to a smoothness and luster "like the fur of a cat." He suggested that the stone had been mined around the northern Thai border area with China, though he had never seen any material exactly like it.[81] Even as emeralds are not found in any significant deposit in Southeast Asia, they probably became familiar to local people through trade and transmission of cultural values from ancient India. Known for their green color, emeralds are correlated with the god Indra (also called Sakka), as well as with fertility and wealth, in Thai and other cultures. The Emerald Buddha, through its connections to Indra and other associations, was perhaps connected with celestial power, while the Sihing Buddha was associated with underworld powers symbolized by the snake god upon which it was modelled.[82]

Many Buddha images, of diverse materials, were and continue to be seen to have wish-granting and protective powers to serve the well-being of the communities in which they reside, enhancing the protective role of rulers. Proper veneration of the statues is frequently considered to bring prosperity. According to its chronicle, the Sandalwood image, after receiving tremendous homage from the people of Phrae, caused rain to fall over the whole city.[83] The Emerald Buddha chronicle notes that during the statue's two-hundred-year stay on Lanka, all of the wishes of the island's inhabitants were granted.[84] The Sihing was seen to have especially strong protective powers; it became associated with a Pali phrase, a restatement of the Four Noble Truths, known as the Sihing Buddha image *gāthā* (Thai: *khatha Phra Phuttha Sihing*).[85] Both the Sihing and Emerald Buddha images were apparently charged with protective responsibilities over the towns where they were enshrined. The Sihing was positioned at the Chedi Luang in the heart of Chiang Mai during the late fourteenth century and later at the *uposatha* (Thai: *ubosot*) hall (ordination hall) of Wat Phra Sing in the late eighteenth century, where it was placed to face the spirit door (Thai: *pratu phi*) in the city wall of Chiang Mai and guard against any evil forces that might try to breach its threshold. Likewise, the Emerald Buddha, when it was placed in the *uposatha* hall at Wat Phra Sri Ratanasadaram in the late eighteenth century, was oriented to face the city of Bangkok's spirit door.[86]

At the same time, the fact that the centuries-long journeys of the Sihing, Emerald, and other images and relics culminate in their enshrinement in Lanna characterizes Lanna as a place of special significance in Buddhism; indeed, it designates the region as the leading center for the practice and support of the *sāsana*. Through their lineages of people and places, the statues integrate local society into a larger and deeper Buddhist world and history. The presence of the statues evidenced the high merit and potential for spiritual advancement of the people of Lanna. In the historical circumstances of the early sixteenth century, the need to position Lanna as the leading Buddhist center may have taken on a special urgency. During this time Lanna and its rival, the kingdom of Ayutthaya, battled in the territories of the former kingdom of Sukhothai in central Thailand as well as farther north. Between 1510 and 1515, Lanna attacked the Ayutthayan territories of Chaliang, Kamphaeng Phet, and Sukhothai. Ayutthaya retaliated by seizing Lampang, and from then on kept Lanna on the defensive. After the death of King Kaeo in 1525, Lanna faced a series of internal and external problems and its weakness caught the attention of its rivals.[87] Thus Justin T. McDaniel has proposed that the *JKM*, written in Lanna during this difficult period, "can be read as creating a local identity [for Lanna] by establishing uniqueness in relation to its expansionist neighbor [Ayutthaya] and cohesiveness with the larger *sāsana*."[88] In this view, the people of Lanna, faced with a serious external threat, were attempting to deploy not only military force but also ideological force, constructing an image of Lanna as a Buddhist territory in which superior merit should be equated to transcendent political power. Lanna's claim for special religious authority was linked to its assertion to political authority in the face of threats from Ayutthaya.

This view emphasizes how the political interests of rulers were reflected in *tamnan;* it seems plausible, though, that the motivations behind *tamnan* were multiple, with the chronicles representing not only the interests of Lanna's rulers but of the monkhood as well. All (or nearly all) *tamnan* were written and copied by members of the *saṅgha*. A recent study of Pali manuscripts predating the end of Lanna's independence in 1558 (when it was conquered by the Burmese) found that over 90 percent of manuscripts that state the name of the scribe note that he was a monk or novice. Furthermore, based on information contained in colophons, about half of the patrons seem to have been monks and the other half laypeople.[89] The *saṅgha* no doubt shared certain common objectives with their most powerful patrons, the ruling class. For donors and writers, composing or copying a chronicle was a meritorious act. Both kings and monks wanted to encourage adherence to the *sāsana,* and the writing of chronicles, which were meant to be preached, was one way to indoctrinate the people and bolster their faith.

However, it should be noted that while the monkhood was politically and economically dependent on the ruling class for its survival, it was not necessarily beholden to it; the survival of the *saṅgha* also depended on the assertion of its own form of sovereignty over people and places. The agendas of monarchs and monks were not always identical. King Tilok attempted to restrain the power of the *saṅgha* through reforms to "purify" the monkhood and by measures that restricted land donation to it.[90] By returning to the texts themselves, we should attempt to consider how the agency of the chronicle writers—the members of the *saṅgha*—is reflected in them.

Indeed, the chronicles may be understood as means for the monkhood to present models of patronage to the lay community, and especially its most powerful patrons, monarchs. Legendary rulers such as Cāmadevī, Mangrai, and Ruang may have been associated in the texts with Buddha images in order to appeal to other rulers to become an image's patron and imitate the abundance of offerings that these rulers lavished on images. The chronicles have a repetitive structure in which a ruler, stereotypically described as having a huge army and exceptional merit, wisdom, and cleverness, obtained the Buddha image and then constantly venerated it with various offerings in large quantities. This pattern was reiterated throughout the chronicles in order to demonstrate how possession of a special Buddha image was directly correlated with a ruler's superiority. Moreover, by venerating one of the travelling images, Lanna's rulers could attach themselves to prestigious lineages that incorporated them into a deeper history and the broader landscape of mainland Southeast Asia and the larger Buddhist world.

Communicating to lay devotees a link between large donations and the superiority of the donor would also have been in line with supporting the *saṅgha*'s interest in inspiring people to donate. Near the end of the Sihing chronicle, King Kli (Kuena) is said to have thought, "Oh, this wealth, when we are alive, it belongs to us. When we have died, it will belong to someone else. Let that not happen. We must make it such that it will be ours in the next world also." The king then embarked on a series of merit-generating donations for the *sāsana,* such as the building of monastic shrines and halls.[91] Here the chronicle writer clearly suggests an incentive—other than interests in current prestige or legitimacy—for a ruler to make gifts for the *sāsana:* maintaining his royal status and wealth in the next life.

The chronicles were probably written not only with rulers in mind as a potential audience; the writers referred to common people frequently in connection with the images. For example, in the story of the Sandalwood image, villagers spirited the statue to safety when there was war in the area.[92] In many chronicles, the entire populations of various towns were described as participating in consecrations and other occasions of worship and being filled with happiness upon glimpsing the images. In the Emerald Buddha chronicle, it is noted that, after the statue was created, "[t]he people at that time had faith in the Buddha image, which contained supreme, excellent relics, and worshipped greatly. When they died from this world, they went to a joyful heaven full of hosts of divinities. The *arahants* at that time, free from desire, did not hold onto anything, but wanted to make the *sāsana* flourishing, had faith in the Buddha image containing excellent relics, exclaimed, "*Sādhu*" [good], and each attained *nibbāna.*"[93] In part such descriptions were probably meant to show rulers the popular unity and virtue that could be achieved by establishing the worship of Buddha images. Nonetheless, the connection between veneration and reward is a lesson that the *saṅgha* would have wanted to convey to lay devotees of any social rank.

As Gregory Schopen has shown, the ability of monks to successfully appeal to donors on an ongoing basis has been essential to the stability of Buddhist monasteries since the first durable monastic structures were erected in ancient India. To ensure the permanence of a monastery, monks had to acquire and manage land, buildings, money, and labor and obtain steady donation of these items. For example, evidence that monks were cultivating long-term donations in the form of perpetual endowments is already present in northern Indian monastic texts that may date to the early centuries of the Christian era. To survive, monks had to be skillful in managing relations with donors.[94]

Buddha images may have been especially preferred by the *saṅgha* in Lanna as objects of patronage. They were easier to obtain than other kinds of memorials to the Buddha—his bodily relics (*sārīrikacetiya*) and items used by him (*pāribhogikacetiya*), which would by definition be limited in supply. Images could be produced from a wide range of materials, enabling lay devotees of both modest means and greater resources to sponsor them. A Buddha image also had a "donation-multiplying" effect, because while an image itself was a donation, it attracted a range of further donations such as an image hall, offering vessels, jewels, other decorative items, and money. Ceremonies were also held for its consecration and periodic ritual washing, and these attracted more donations for the monastery. Laborers and land might be given by rulers for the maintenance of the image, and copies of the image made on various occasions. The statue might also attract pilgrims, both lay and monastic. For monastic schools, relics and images were "the main form of advertisement"; monastic teachers and students were drawn to monasteries where they could be in the presence of these objects.[95] Thus, for various reasons the *saṅgha* may have been particularly enthusiastic about disseminating stories that communicated the special qualities of Buddha statues. That this monastic orientation towards images is not new or unique to Lanna is demonstrated by Schopen's evidence that monks of medieval northern India regarded images as a significant source of income; they even promulgated guidelines for increasing the images' fund-raising potential through advertising campaigns and processions in towns.[96]

It is also notable that the journeys of the travelling images covered a wide geographic area that was not limited by political divisions. This understanding of the landscape may be reflected in the nature of monastic travel in and around early Lanna. McDaniel has noted that monastic schools comprised a "loose network of open campuses that shared teachers, texts, and students across the larger Tai-speaking world of eastern Burma, Laos, parts of southwest China, and Northern Thailand. These networks, while certainly affected by the economy and warfare, were generally independent of the machinations of leaders and borders."[97] In the fifteenth and sixteenth centuries, the Pa Daeng order was active not only in Lanna but also in Ayutthayan territories. There was at times fierce competition between monastic orders during that period for lay patronage in Tai territories, as we will see in more detail in chapter 3.

The peripatetic travels of the images probably reflect how Buddhist orders actively endeavored to expand their presence across the region by cultivating wealthy and powerful patrons wherever such persons lived. In the travelling image chronicles, the rotating designation of meritorious leaders in a repetitive pattern reflects the realities of death and political succession and the *saṅgha*'s changing relations with different leaders over time. The repetitive lineage structure emphasizes the ongoing "lives" or presence of the statues despite patrons dying or losing the statues in different places. This also appears to be evidenced by the insertion of the travelling image stories into the *JKM*, causing the text to shift between narrative viewpoints, one centered around monarchs and the other around Buddha images. The histories of four important images were significant enough to the author that he related them outside of the succession of Chiang Mai monarchs.

In each travelling image chronicle, the lives of the royal patrons are aligned—indeed, conformed—to the life of a Buddha image, and the text contains few if any details of a king's reign outside of his interaction with the travelling image. Through the chronicles, the *saṅgha* promoted the veneration of certain Buddha statues, a practice supporting both religious and politico-economic objectives, by situating the practice within a distinct historical and territorial context that combined local conceptions of landscape, ancestral lineage, and monarchy.

That this conception of history—with its themes of lineage and place, its appeal to both selflessness and self-glorification, its integration of the mundane and the transcendent, and its visions of power and wealth—was successfully received among both priestly and lay communities is indicated by the continuing popularity of the travelling images and the copying of images and image chronicles around the region over hundreds of years.

The successful reception among Lanna devotees of the travelling image chronicles is also indicated by the later composition of *tamnan* with similar structures and themes. The chronicle of Phra Sila, the Stone Buddha image (Thai: Phra Sila or Phra Hin On; Pali: Silābimba), currently enshrined in Wat Chiang Man, Chiang Mai, was apparently written in 1785.[98] The text recounts that the Buddha image was sculpted shortly after the Buddha's *parinibbāna* by King Ajātasattu (Thai: Achatasatturat) in Rājagaha, India. The chronicle goes on to narrate the image's sojourns with different patrons in Lampang, Lanka, Sachanalai, and other places before its enshrinement in Chiang Mai by

King Tilok. As in the travelling image chronicles, the patrons of the Buddha image are said to have wisdom and great merit. Wherever it arrived, Phra Sila received great veneration from the populace, for whose benefit the image performed miracles of flying and causing rainfall.[99] The Phra Sila image is among the most famous Buddha images in Chiang Mai today.

Chapter Three

BUDDHA IMAGES AND THE MONKHOOD

Monastic Political Power beyond the Cloister

In chapter 2 we saw how the travelling image chronicles depicted Buddha statues as objects that not only integrated the Buddha into Lanna society but also mediated relations between lay patrons and monks. This chapter turns to another set of chronicles that provide a different insight into the interaction of lay and monastic agencies in Lanna. This set of chronicles, typically entitled *Mūlasāsanā* (*Root of the Religion*), narrates the history of the spread of two monastic orders around the Lanna region and particularly in the cities of Chiang Mai and Chiang Tung. The latter, also known as Keng Tung or Jeng Tung, became part of Lanna in the fourteenth century but is today in Shan State, Myanmar (Burma). The *Mūlasāsanā* chronicles are particularly interesting because they describe a furious feud between the two orders, called the Flower Garden and the Redwood Grove, both sects with links to Lanka. A number of examples of patronage in light of this feud highlight the power-inflected relationships that existed between lay patrons and monks. Though Gregory Schopen's work has demonstrated that managing relationships with donors was a common preoccupation of monks in early medieval India,[1] this sense of monastic power shaping and directing acts of Buddhist patronage has been slow to influence scholarship on Thai Buddhism, which has emphasized the donor as the principal agent in acts of patronage. Indeed, the chronicles show that monastic claims to power could extend beyond the cloister to assert authority over the lay political order. Buddha statues were deployed as monastic agents, reflecting the status of the Buddha image as both the Buddha himself and an object subject to human manipulation.

This sense of the image is also found in Burmese stories, which we will also examine.

In this chapter we will consider two versions of the *Mūlasāsanā*. One version was disseminated by the order of the Flower Garden Monastery (Thai: Suan Dok or Suan Dokmai; Tai Khoen, the language of Chiang Tung: Sōn Dôk; Pali: Pupphārāma). The other version of history is that of the Redwood Grove Monastery (Thai: Pa Daeng; Tai Khoen: P̱ā Daeng; Pali: Sīhaḷarattārāma, Rattārāma, or Mahāvana). Studied in this chapter are two versions by the Flower Garden order and three by the Redwood Grove order.[2]

The initial composition of the *Mūlasāsanā* of the Flower Garden by an unnamed author is estimated to have occurred between the mid-fifteenth and early sixteenth centuries.[3] Prasert na Nagara hypothesized that Wat Suan Dokmai in Chiang Mai produced the *Mūlasāsanā* and Wat Pa Daeng of Chiang Mai created the *Jinakālamālīpakaraṇaṁ* (*JKM*), the *tamnan* (chronicle) of Buddhist history, in response to the dreaded two thousandth anniversary of Buddhism in the mid-fifteenth century.[4]

The Redwood Grove or Pa Daeng version of *Mūlasāsanā* does not provide textual clues to dating, as the Flower Garden version does, but it seems to date to around the same period; there is "a credible level of idiosyncratic detail and direct observation" in the account of the fifteenth to sixteenth centuries, which takes up most of the text.[5]

Mortal Risks of Monastic Patronage amidst a Sectarian Feud

The Redwood Grove order was founded in the mid-fifteenth century by a disaffected Flower Garden monk in Chiang Mai named Ñāṇagambhīra.[6] According to the Redwood Grove version of history, Ñāṇagambhīra suspected that certain practices of the Flower Garden order, such as language usage and the handling of property and money, were not consistent with the *dhamma vinaya*, or teachings and standards of monastic discipline, of the Buddha. Ñāṇagambhīra journeyed with several monks and laymen to Rohaṇa country on the island of Lanka, where monks confirmed his suspicions that the practices in Chiang Mai were ridden with errors. Ñāṇagambhīra disrobed and was reordained in Lanka. After a period of study there, he returned to his homeland and established a new sect that came to be known as the

Redwood Grove order. He also declared that the monks of the Flower Garden order were not actually monks due to their incorrect practices.

The version of history written by the Redwood Grove order is essentially an account of the righteous and glorious establishment of the order in what are now Myanmar and Thailand by Ñāṇagambhīra and his followers. By contrast, the version of history written by the Flower Garden order depicts Ñāṇagambhīra not as the hero of a triumphal journey but as a rascal on the lam, conducting a cross-regional smear campaign against the Flower Garden.

Modern scholars have mined these texts as sources for factual information such as monastic rules on matters such as the pronunciation of Pali, the mode of robe wearing, and the handling of money in the fifteenth century.[7]

The texts have also been examined to delineate the history of the monastic orders in Lanna and the associations of particular orders with local rulers. Studies have focused on rulers and how their political power was abetted or impeded by supporting the monastic orders.[8] In a similar vein, scholarship on Buddhist patronage has tended to focus on donations to the *sāsana* (Buddhist thought and practice) as means by which lay patrons asserted their political, social, and economic status. Such conceptions are also common in ancient texts: for instance, monastic accounts of the distribution of the Buddha's relics by Asoka, the monarch who set the model for later Buddhist rulers, have tended to portray the monks as "adornments to the king and/or facilitators of the royal vision, rather than independent focal points of devotion."[9] In the travelling image chronicles, monks were presented as collaborating with lay patrons in the production of images by conducting consecrations, handling relics, and making predictions. Yet as the examples of the *Mūlasāsanā* chronicles illustrate, there were accounts in which monks asserted themselves to be far more than "adornments" or collaborators to their powerful patrons.

The Redwood Grove order's chronicles relate that when Ñāṇagambhīra and his entourage were in Lanka and had completed their studies there, the Lankan monks gave the foreign visitors parting words of advice, which included a warning:

> If monks do not follow the correct language, the *dhammapiṭaka* [teachings of the Buddha] will be distorted. If the *dhammapiṭaka* is corrupted, the monastic rules will be also; the monks' behavior will not

> be in conformity to the *vinaya*. . . . In the countries where the rulers, ministers, and officials revere such improper monks as good and well versed in the *dhammapiṭaka,* there will be no peace and happiness. Hardships will occur and later greater catastrophes, until the order of the government and the *saṅgha* [community of monks] is lost. Finally, that country will be destroyed because the religion of the guardians of the four quarters and the *devatā* [gods] of the world is ill-founded.[10]

In other words, communities that supported monks of "faulty" practices such as those of the Flower Garden order would be planting the seeds of their own destruction. It is probably not coincidental that the list of afflictions evokes the prophecy of societal breakdown associated with the decline of the *sāsana.*

Traditionally, magical powers were seen to be the result of advanced spiritual practices, so the wielding of such powers was seen as evidence of a monk's superior practices and state of being. Redwood Grove monks presented in their version of history a series of examples demonstrating their miraculous ability to protect the city of Chiang Tung. Their text relates that after Ñāṇagambhīra left Lanka by ship, he and his disciples landed at Mergui and Tenasserim (today the Burmese towns of Myeik and Tanintharyi, respectively) and then went on to Ayutthaya, Chiang Mai, Chiang Rai, Chiang Saen, Chiang Tung, Lampang, Lamphun, Mueang Wang, Phayao, Phitsanulok, and Sukhothai. In every place the monks gained the support of local rulers and established monasteries. In Chiang Tung, Redwood Grove monks proved their value to the king by ridding his palace of demons who were haunting it. This accomplishment also represented a triumph over the Flower Garden monks, because the latter had been incapable of exorcising the demons; naturally the Redwood Grove monks blamed this failure on their rivals' incorrect customs. After the cleansing of the palace, a fire broke out in a valley near Chiang Tung, smothering the city in smoke. The king again called for the Redwood Grove monks, who chanted *suttas* (texts containing the words of the Buddha), and the fire died away. Not long afterwards, a torrential rain fell and nearly submerged the city. The Redwood Grove monks recited a *sutta,* and after a day the rain stopped.[11] Later, Wat Pa Daeng was established in Chiang Tung as a monastery for the Redwood Grove order. One day there was a fierce storm of wind and rain that took down many trees and smashed houses, but Wat Pa Daeng was completely undamaged. From then on, the halls there were called the iron pavilion and the brass pavilion.[12]

The Redwood Grove monks emphasized the importance of the monkhood to the welfare of communities through other kinds of accounts. Their chronicle recounts several acts of patronage which we might describe as cautionary tales for would-be patrons. One section of the chronicle is a list of the days that the king must avoid when selecting the date for the annual *mahākaṭhina*, or gift of robes to the monks of Wat Pa Daeng. The types of days that are inauspicious are determined through elements of astrology, local tales, and traditional Buddhist stories; these days are to be avoided due to "ancient tradition." In the text the list of days is followed by six examples of Chiang Tung rulers between the fifteenth and eighteenth centuries who failed to pay attention to the list. All of the would-be patrons met with calamity. To give one example,

> Brayā Kænarindā [1560–1597] gave *dāna* [a donation] on Pükseḍ day 7 of red sky, day of death after secret burial, the great ghost was in the east. The astrologers said, "Today if lord of earth leaves the palace and proceeds toward the south, then turns north and only then enters the monastery, there should be no trouble." It was also said that nothing should matter about going to perform meritorious deeds. That day, after having given *dāna*, lord of earth emerged to ride on an elephant. At that time Tīnp̱ā was on fire [and] people stampeded. The elephant was afraid of the fire and became alarmed and greatly maddened. Lord of earth fell from the elephant and suffered greatly; this turned into a serious illness, [and he] lived for seven months and died there.[13]

The death of Brayā Kænarindā illustrates the result of disregarding the monastery's injunction that *dāna* must not be given on the "day of death after secret burial," a day rendered inauspicious because of a tragic episode in which a husband murdered his wife's lover, and when the wife tried to clandestinely bury her lover's body, she was killed by her husband. Regarding Brayā Kænarindā, the chronicle indicates that the king's meritorious intentions, his political authority, and the high accumulation of merit suggested by his royal status could not save him from the mortal danger resulting from disregarding the advice of the Redwood Grove monks.

The Redwood Grove order also emphasized the threat to devotees whose patronage was guided by monks of irregular practices—that is, the monks of the Flower Garden order. The Redwood Grove text recounts the story of a nobleman called Samavan who went to

Wat In, a monastery of the Flower Garden order in Chiang Tung, and there with a "devout intention" built a large Buddha image, leaving the top half of the head unfinished. The next day, however, the image miraculously appeared complete, and the local people suggested that the god Indra must have come and worked on it overnight. Not long afterwards, though, the noble Samavan and the monk residing at Wat In both died.[14] As in the account of the king who tumbled from the elephant, this story also sends the message that virtuous intentions are not sufficient in themselves; the patron must observe certain rules or face consequences.

The Redwood Grove text also recounts that in the sixteenth century, Brayā Kæu Phāpbhummin, king of Chiang Tung (r. 1560–1597), decided to investigate the conflict between the two monastic orders and brought them together in a joint assembly. A debate between the two orders was held, and the Flower Garden order lost. The king was from then on reluctant to support Wat Yang Gong, the Flower Garden's main monastery. But the king's younger brother, Indadhara, married a woman from the village of Yang Gong, and the two had a son who eventually was ordained at Wat Yang Gong. Indadhara donated a "big" *stūpa* and a "great" Buddha statue to the monastery and asked Brayā Kæu Phāpbhummin to consecrate them. The king reluctantly carried out his brother's wish. He also dedicated rice fields for the upkeep of the image and the *stūpa,* again at his brother's request. After that the abbot and other monks of Wat Yang Gong disrobed, saying they wanted to serve the Buddha image and the *stūpa,* even though they could have served them while still monks. The abbot explained, "The fruit of bad *kamma* [Sanskrit: *karma*] has not yet come to an end."[15] In other words, he left because the Flower Garden's history of bad practices was still haunting it. The account suggests that the eminence of the patrons, a king and his brother, and the lavishness of the donations were insufficient to support the prosperity of a monastery where the monks were of inferior qualifications. The ultimate upholder of the *sāsana* is indicated to be the monkhood, not the lay community, so acts of patronage were to be directed to the right sort of monks.

The Flower Garden order, for its part, also told stories emphasizing the danger to patrons who support the wrong monks. The Flower Garden chronicles relate that in Songkhwae (Phitsanulok, in north central Thailand), the local ruler gave his support to Ñāṇagambhīra of the Redwood Grove order. Subsequently, the ruler fell off his boat, both his royal elephant and his son died, and the ruler himself developed leprosy.[16] Later, in Chaliang, when there was a terrible drought, Ñāṇagambhīra's followers failed to induce rain to fall; the Flower Garden monks, on the other hand, being "most excellent in truth," caused the rain to pour down day and night.[17]

These cautionary tales recounted in the Redwood Grove and Flower Garden chronicles resonate with an old belief in Lanna and elsewhere that the truth in itself has the potency to instigate concrete action. According to the tradition of *saccakiriyā* (the "act of truth"), when truthful words are spoken, they set in motion extraordinary power. Uttering a true statement, even something as prosaic as "the sun has rays," can cause the action expressed in a wish, "May your head split into seven pieces," to miraculously occur.[18] True statements were deployed in various contexts as forces to protect oneself and one's interests. In acts of Buddhist donation, true words were stated for the purpose of generating power to safeguard the use of the donation. For instance, on the gateway of Stūpa No. 1 of Sāñcī, built by Asoka in the third century BCE, an inscription warns that anyone who "dismantles or causes to be dismantled" the *stūpa* will "go to the [same terrible] state as those who commit the five sins that have immediate retribution." True statements elsewhere in the inscription are the fuel for the power to enact the punishment.[19] In Lanna, similar imprecations appear in inscriptions made in the past few centuries in which devotees express the wish that their buildings, land, laborers, and other kinds of Buddhist donations be kept intact and that retribution be visited upon anyone trying to divert the assets dedicated by the donation.[20] In this context of true statements as magically potent forces, the stories composed by the Redwood Grove and Flower Garden monks may be understood as accounts of the power that is wielded by monks who have access to the truth. The chronicles may then themselves be extensions of the supranormal capabilities of the monks, as the truthful words in the manuscripts are vested with the power to punish future wrongdoers.

The stories of patronage thwarted because of donors' failure to obey the monks' injunctions present a striking contrast to the description of acts of patronage in the *JKM*, the northern Thai historical chronicle most frequently cited by scholars. That text, believed to have been composed by a Redwood Grove monk of Chiang Mai in the early sixteenth century, dedicates many pages to describing the acts of patronage of Lanna kings. Its recounting of the Mangrai dynasty from the late thirteenth to the early sixteenth centuries is essentially a listing of acts of patronage by different monarchs; there are very few, if any, other kinds of events described in each king's reign. The text emphasizes the royal lay patrons' accumulation of merit through donations and how their donations caused the religion to prosper greatly. In a similar way, the travelling image chronicles underscored patrons' veneration of the Buddha images and the benefits which thereby accrued to the patrons. The Redwood Grove and Flower Garden *Mūlasāsanā* chronicles, on the other hand, draw attention to the crucial role of the *saṅgha* in the welfare of Buddhism. The texts demonstrated why the sectarian dispute should have been a matter of concern to the lay community by showing how the state of the monkhood affected lay patrons. The lesson that lay patronage must be guided by appropriate monks was a very significant directive, carrying the suggestion that one's act of donation could potentially be totally worthless, failing to support the stability of the five-thousand-year life of Buddha Gotama's *sāsana* or to add merit to ensure one's rebirth during the future period of Maitreya's *sāsana*.

In contrast to the *JKM* and travelling image chronicles, the Redwood Grove and Flower Garden chronicles expose how, in each act of patronage, different expressions of power may be brought into the encounter of lay devotee and *saṅgha*. Although the *saṅgha* may be the beneficiary of the patronage, this does not necessarily mean it yields power to the donating party; the *saṅgha* attempts to control the form, structure, and style of discussion of patronage. Contradicting Weberian visions of monks as spiritually focused renunciants withdrawn from the political and economic machinations of the wider world, the texts show that the various arguments and tactics that the rival monks fired off against each other were deliberately aimed at embroiling the lay community and its political order.[21]

The Role of Statues of the Buddha in the Feud

The process of manufacture and consecration of a Buddha image entails the interaction of agencies of multiple parties: lay patrons, the Buddha, craftsmen, and monks, as well as other images. During the consecration ritual, notes Stanley J. Tambiah, "frequently a famous lay sponsor (or sponsors) is integrally involved, not only as the provider of the material assets to make the statues, but also as a ritual participant himself whose 'merit' and achievements are also transferred to the statue."[22] Moreover, Buddha images are imbued with "some portion of the virtues and powers of an already installed historic Buddha statue" and the "psychic energies" of "monks sitting in meditation."[23] The image channels the qualities of the Buddha himself, through the intermediation of monks, and it also resonates with the inputs of the lay and monastic communities.

In the sectarian dispute, one of the Redwood Grove order's main criticisms of the Flower Garden order centered on the proper use of a Buddha image. The Redwood Grove chronicles claimed that the founder of the Flower Garden, the monk Sumana (or Matima, depending on the version), journeyed from Phan (near Mottama or Martaban in present-day Myanmar) to the island of Lanka to study at a monastery there. Upon the completion of his studies, he and four other monks boarded a ship to return to Phan. While at sea, one of the monks died. In order to have the requisite five monks to perform ordinations, Sumana ordained a lay pupil aboard the ship using a Buddha statue to stand in as a fifth monk. The Redwood Grove order alleged that the substitution of the image for a monk was a violation of the *vinaya,* or rules of discipline for monks: because of this, the lay pupil could not have been truly ordained and therefore nor were the men whom the five ordained after they reached Phan. Hence, none within the lineage of monks of the Flower Garden order was a true monk, according to Ñāṇagambhīra and the Redwood Grove order.[24]

During the consecration of a Buddha image, at least as it is practiced in modern times in northern Thailand, the image is ritually imbued with the biography of the Buddha.[25] Indeed, the image is often treated by worshippers as if it were a living incarnation of the Buddha. The Sandalwood Buddha image, according to Buddhist tradition the first Buddha image ever made, was treated by the Buddha as an equal and tasked with carrying on his *sāsana* by the Buddha himself. Nonetheless, in the story above, the Redwood Grove order asserted that such a statue may not substitute for a human monk for the purposes of monastic ordination. The rationale behind the Redwood Grove order's objection is little elaborated, at least in the versions of Redwood Grove chronicles considered here, beyond noting that Sumana's act contravened the Lankan monastery's monastic rules. One might think it obvious, perhaps, that what was at issue for the Redwood Grove order was the physical materiality of the manufactured object, which makes a statue unlike both the Buddha himself and a flesh-and-blood, chanting monk.[26]

Another account involving Buddha images in the Redwood Grove chronicle is also interesting in this regard. During the sixteenth-century debate between the Redwood Grove and Flower Garden orders in Chiang Tung, a Redwood Grove abbot told the following story.

A king of Haṃsāvatī (present-day Bago, in Myanmar) was being advised by a heretic, who convinced the king to dispose of all of the Buddha images in the kingdom, but a certain Lady Subhadrā (or Saddhacittā, in some texts) remained devoted to the *sāsana*. One day a deity informed her that "an object of miraculous powers" had been thrown away and was submerged at the bottom of a river. Whoever retrieved and venerated it "would be protected from all dangers, namely sticks, staves, rocks, spears, and swords, and will not perish by water or fire." She salvaged the image, cleaned it, and paid homage to it. A servant of the king saw her and reported to the king, who then had Subhadrā brought to the palace. To punish her, he had a fierce elephant come and try to gore her, but she turned her thoughts to the Buddha and the Buddha image, and the elephant was unable to attack. After her miraculous survival, Subhadrā had the king write the name of her guru, Lord Gotama Buddha, and the name of the king's guru, the heretic, on separate palm leaves and drop them into a fire. The leaf with the heretic's name was completely burned up while the leaf with the Buddha's name remained fresh and unsinged.

After hearing this story, the king of Chiang Tung's officials had palm leaves inscribed with the names of the gurus of the Redwood Grove and Flower Garden sects. The leaf with the Flower Garden name was totally incinerated. The leaf with the Redwood Grove name, Ñāṇagambhīra, did not burn at all.[27] Thus victory drums were beaten for the Redwood Grove monks and they returned to their monasteries.[28]

It is interesting that in at least two versions of the story, it is specified that Subhadrā was saved from the elephant's attack because she turned her thoughts to both the Buddha and his image.[29] If the image had been understood only as a duplicate, substitute, or symbol of the Buddha, then it would have been redundant to name both the statue and the Buddha. Was there a differentiation she perceived between the Buddha and his image? Did Subhadrā hope that the statue, which she had "saved" and worshipped, would reciprocate and rescue her? According to the Sandalwood image chronicle, the first Buddha statue ever made miraculously moved its limbs, to rise from its seat to greet the Buddha, suggesting its investment with the power of Buddhahood. At the same time, the statue was a discrete entity that was not fully contiguous with the Buddha, as he ordered it to sit and commanded it to protect the *sāsana* after his *parinibbāna* (death). A Buddha statue is frequently said to be the Buddha and honored as if it is, but the fact that it is not the Buddha is what drives the need to empower it. The distinction between the Buddha and his image has opened the way for the proliferation of images and the different ways statues participate in the societies of their worshippers, each image indeed able to become distinctive to the Buddha and to other Buddha statues.

The story of Subhadrā is also interesting from a present-day standpoint, as it provides an example of how actual Buddhist practices may reflect beliefs that contradict certain modern scholarly presentations that characterize worship of Buddha images as a form of "psychological relief" for devotees. These have been based on the claim that, from a doctrinal view, the Buddha no longer has any presence in the world, even in his images. On the other hand, this story reflects the belief, at least among people of the past, that someone who demonstrates devotion to the Buddha may profit from the direct intervention of the power of the Buddha despite the Buddha's long-ago *parinibbāna*, and this power is closely linked to, or even vested in, an image.[30]

The Flower Garden order's chronicles do not mention the episode of the seagoing ordination using a Buddha image. But the Flower Garden monks spread their own allegations about the Redwood Grove order's attitude towards Buddha images; they claimed that Ñāṇagambhīra and his followers travelled to Chiang Rai, Chiang Saen, Chiang Tung, and Phayao and in each of those places tried to destroy the Flower Garden order by urging people to throw away their Buddha statues. The Flower Garden monks accused Ñāṇagambhīra and his disciples of spreading word that the Buddha had not authorized the veneration of images and that since the Flower Garden monks were not really monks, paying homage to images consecrated by them would bring no merit whatsoever. The Flower Garden monks said that people who were "foolish" obeyed the Redwood Grove order and burned, buried, or threw Buddha images into watercourses, while those possessed of "wisdom" retrieved the images and venerated them.[31]

It is unknown whether this iconoclasm actually occurred, but it seems possible in view of the fact that Buddha images are often closely associated with the monasteries in which they reside; some monasteries even take their names from the famous Buddha statues enshrined on their premises. In addition, given the role of Buddha images in the support of the five-thousand-year life of the *sāsana,* the Redwood Grove order's desecration of images may have been presented by the Flower Garden as a metaphor for the Redwood Grove order inflicting damage on the *sāsana* itself.

Moreover, the allegation in the story that Buddha images are worthless if the monks who consecrated them are not true monks underscores the importance of the role of monks in the creation of Buddha images; in fact, here the agency of monks is depicted as the most significant factor in determining whether an object may actually be defined as an image of the Buddha, apparently overriding other factors such as the resemblance of the images to the Buddha and the insertion of Buddhist relics in the images. The agency of monks is emphasized to the extent that the iconoclasts draw an analogy between monks and Buddha images. The disposal of images by burial, burning, and submersion in water evoke the putting to death of living beings. Eric Reinders has noted that an early Buddhist text found in China indeed makes an analogy between the crafting of monks and of Buddhist objects, depicting a monk's body as iron to be forged, once the impurities are cast out, into a "vessel (*qi*) of the Dharma-body." Likewise, during imperially ordered anti-Buddhist persecutions during the Tang dynasty, the melting down of Buddha images into coins and weapons paralleled the disrobing of monastics to convert them into farmers and soldiers.[32]

At the same time, the Flower Garden order's broadcasting of the Redwood Grove order's iconoclasm was apparently meant to incite lay outrage against the latter. A Buddha image was the ideal choice to entangle the lay community in the dispute. It is created from the agencies of the Buddha, monks, lay devotees, and craftsmen, and is thus connected to all of them. The image is the venerable Buddha, while simultaneously persistently remaining a thing closely connected to its audiences and vulnerable to their conceptual and physical manipulations over time.

In the next section, we will consider examples of Burmese stories of Buddha images that illustrate how the agencies of images may be directed for unexpected purposes.

Burmese Stories of Buddha Statues: Exploiting the Agencies of Buddha Images

Chronicles and inscriptions record many examples of interaction between Lanna and Burmese areas—particularly the Mon region of contemporary Lower Myanmar. Monks travelled between the regions at least from the time of Sumana in the fourteenth century and likely much earlier. Relations between the two regions probably existed for a number of centuries through connections of trade as well as of religion, heritage, and language. Haripuñjaya is said to have been established by Queen Cāmadevī as an outpost of the Dvāravati city of Lopburi in the late eighth century;[33] the *JKM* describes Cāmadevī as "the queen of a vassal state of the Mon kingdom."[34] The *Cāmadevīvaṁsa* (*Chronicle of Queen Cāma*) reports that about two and a half centuries after the founding of Haripuñjaya, a severe cholera epidemic struck the city. The survivors abandoned their homes and fled to the area which is now Lower Myanmar, first to Sudhamma (probably contemporary Thaton) and then to Haṃsāvatī (Bago), where they were welcomed: "The inhabitants of Haripuñjaya and of Haṃsāvatī came to know and love one another. Even their languages were the same." After six years the epidemic subsided, and some of the people of Haripuñjaya returned home, while others remained; "[t]he people of Haṃsāvatī, who still loved their friends and relatives in Haripuñjaya often visited them, bearing many letters."[35] A royal connection between Lanna and Lower Myanmar in the early fourteenth century is also noted in the *Chiang Mai Chronicle:* Mangrai took his army to Haṃsāvatī; the king of Haṃsāvatī, wishing to avoid the enmity of Mangrai, gave the latter his daughter, Lady Phai Kho, to be his wife.[36] It seems probable that the exchange of stories between Burmese and Lanna people increased during the more than two hundred years of Burmese suzerainty over Lanna from the mid-sixteenth to late eighteenth centuries.

The *Glass Palace Chronicle of the Kings of Burma* (1923) is the English translation by the great Burmese scholar Pe Maung Tin of the portion of the *Hmannan Mahayazawindawgyi* that covers the history of the three kingdoms of Tagaung, Śrī Kṣetra (Tharehkittara or Prome), and Bagan. The *Hmannan Mahayazawindawgyi* is a history of Myanmar from its origins in the distant past up until 1821; it was written in 1829, at the command of King Bagyidaw (r. 1819–1837), by a committee of monks, ministers, and Brahmans who compiled it by comparing the *Great Chronicle,* written by Maung Kala in the early eighteenth century, with various other inscriptions and manuscripts.

The *Glass Palace Chronicle* contains numerous accounts about relics and several Buddha images; the accounts vary in length from cursory mentions to elaborate stories, and include examples in which the agencies of statues are enlisted by patrons for their own purposes.

The *Glass Palace Chronicle*'s account of the history of Śrī Kṣetra reports that in the late first century, a king named Nagarachinna led his army in an invasion of the Kanyan country. There they discovered a solid gold Buddha statue eighty-eight cubits in height. The king, filled with faith, began to worship it nonstop, day and night. After three years of this, Nagarachinna's ministers advised the king that it was time he returned home. Nagarachinna agreed, but was determined to take the image with him. He told the ministers to assemble a big raft to float the statue back to Śrī Kṣetra. The ministers saw this as a hopeless task given the image's tremendous heaviness—"it weighed tens and hundreds of crores of viss of gold"—and despaired that they would never see their families again. They then dug a hole under the statue and it fell in. Nagarachinna asked the ministers why the statue had fallen in, and they claimed that it had "entered *parinirvana.*" The ministers then ignited a flame under the image. When Nagarachinna inquired about this, they replied that "the spirits are holding the cremation ceremony." Nagarachinna knew that they were insincere; he felt sad, but said nothing. The ministers became concerned that the king might be angry, so they used some of the gold from the giant statue to make seated Buddha images, each one cubit in height, and presented twenty-eight of them to the king. They also retained some of the gold images for themselves. The king and his entourage then returned to Śrī Kṣetra, but "when these vessels were used by the people, this noble kingdom, albeit it was founded by the Seven Exalted Ones, became disordered and ungovernable, infested with thieves, robbers, plunderers, and cut-throats." Later the people broke up into three groups—Burmans, Kanyans, and Pyus, and the king fell sick and died.[37]

In this story the ministers, lacking Nagarachinna's piety but recognizing its intensity, attempted to justify their destruction of the giant image by casting their handiwork in terms of the Buddha's death and cremation. In this attempt to pass an explanation to the king, they invoked the representation of Buddha images that equates the Buddha to his statues. Their objective was not to reverence the image but to ruin it. In their view the statue was just an accumulation of its gleaming, precious material: gold. Even though they molded smaller Buddha images, their intention was to appease their sovereign, not to serve virtue. The Buddha images, embodying nonpious intentions, then caused the ruin of their homeland.

The story suggests the ease with which Buddha statues may be conscripted as agents in the schemes of human weakness. It is a cautionary tale that warns devotees that the improper use of Buddha images will lead to suffering.

The *Glass Palace Chronicle* describes another instance in which the agency of a Buddha statue was deployed to support the power of one party versus another.

The story begins with King Narapatisithu (r. 1174–1211) discovering a shining ruby in a hollow and forcing the people to fill the hollow so that the Sulamani Temple could be built on the spot. The elder Panthagu Ngaswèshin warned the king that the building was not an act of merit but in fact a demerit. The two argued, and the monk, feeling offended, declared that he would leave the kingdom and go to Lanka. At that time an ogre appeared on the Tharaba Gate of Bagan and refused to move. The king's advisers interpreted this as a consequence of the offense paid to the elder Panthagu. The king then dispatched his ministers to invite the elder to come to the palace, but the elder declined, saying he was off to Lanka. The king then summoned a clever minister, Turinkapyissi, "a man full of seeing and hearing," and ordered him to find the monk and get him to return to Bagan. Turinkapyissi loaded a gold-covered Buddha image onto the royal boat, which was then paddled down the river towards the harbor where the ships to Lanka were moored. En route he caught up with the elder. Turinkapyissi said, "Great master, the Lord Omniscient hath visited this port. I pray thee come!" The elder, knowing it would be unmeritorious to decline to honor the Lord, boarded the royal boat and paid homage to the gold Buddha statue. While the elder was thus occupied, the boat was turned and paddled back towards Bagan. Turinkapyissi made a string of appeals to Panthagu to support the *sāsana,* which the elder could not refuse because it concerned the religion, and the boat carried them all the way back to Bagan. There the king received the elder with reverence, and the ogre climbed down from the gate. The king announced, "Great master! Henceforth from thee I take my doctrine!" He also offered his five sons to be Panthagu's disciples.[38]

In this story, Turinkapyissi realized that by invoking the Buddha's agency in the image, he could compel the monk to follow him.

Turinkapyissi took advantage of the Buddha image's status as both an object, which he could place on a ship, and as the Buddha. As in the story of King Nagarachinna and the giant gold statue, this story involves a man using the discourse of Buddha images to further a personal objective. The difference between the two stories lies in the intentions of the persons who attempted to direct the image's agency. Nagarachinna exemplified the proper relationship between devotees and images through his great veneration for the image, and his ministers demonstrated an improper relationship to the image. Having utilized the agency of the Buddha in the image in order to disrupt the king's relationship with it, they created small Buddha images that became agents of their ill intentions. Turinkapyissi, on the other hand, served as the agent of a pious devotee with a virtuous intention: the king who realized his error and wanted to honor Panthagu. Turnikapyissi's actions exemplified an appropriate deployment by devotees of the agency of the image.

The complexity of relations among the Buddha, his images, and his devotees (both lay and monastic) were apparently familiar to the authors of Burmese and Lanna chronicles. The statue, though subject to a confined iconography, consecratory rituals, and conventions of display, was still exposed to manipulation by devotees and monks. Monastic stories about images may be viewed from one angle as an attempt to control these agencies by communicating what relations are seen as righteous among the Buddha, the image, and the devotees. These stories challenge contemporary conventional perceptions in which the Buddha image is merely a production of merit or a religious symbol. It is through narrative that the image is empowered.

Chapter Four

Buddha Images and Place

Materializing the Buddha's Agency in the Landscape

In the *tamnan* (chronicles of Buddhist history), Lanna was not merely a stage backdrop against which the sagas of Buddha images and their worshippers played out. The statues were depicted as being specifically drawn to Lanna, a place crucial to the ongoing welfare of Buddhism. In this chapter we will consider another set of chronicles in which the significance of Lanna to the future of Buddhist thought and practice (*sāsana*) is more profoundly developed through a focus on the crucial relationship of Buddha images to their places of enshrinement.

Canonical Buddhist texts do not mention the Buddha ever visiting Southeast Asia himself. Nonetheless, many Lanna *tamnan* claim that he did. They recount that the Buddha summoned the superior powers he earned through enlightenment to glide through the air from India, along with hundreds of his disciples, alighting in Lanna and then making an expedition around the region. The Buddha preached to local people and left them with relics with which to remember him, such as strands of his hair and imprints of the soles of his feet on rocks; he also commanded the creation of statues of himself or predicted where images would be made in the future. These accounts insert Lanna into the biography of the Buddha and confirm for his devotees the deep historical significance of Lanna's towns. The establishment of Buddha images and relics across the region mark out Lanna as what Donald K. Swearer has termed a "*buddhadesa*" (Buddha-land): a place given identity, order, and meaning by the presence of the Buddha and his material representations.[1]

As we will see, the chronicles do not depict Lanna as an untamed territory remade or transformed thanks to the Buddha, as Swearer's description might imply. Instead it is presented as a special place that through the ages has been a source of attraction and inspiration to Buddhas. Lanna's towns, lakes, and hills are shown playing a distinctive role in Buddhist history: they are the channels that enable the ongoing agency of the Buddhas. Buddha statues were created in these places to mark these channels that are crucial to the prosperity of the world.

In what follows, we will look at three examples of Lanna chronicles of such Buddha statues, which I call images in place. Then we will consider the themes, motifs, and relations of agency in the texts and how they relate to or differ from examples from Burmese, classical Pali, and Lankan traditions.

Chronicles of Lanna's Site-Specific Buddha Statues

The *Chronicle of the Buddha Image Lying on a Mango-Tree Log:* Connecting Lanna and Ancient India

The *Chronicle of the Buddha Image Lying on a Mango-Tree Log* (*Tamnan Phra Non Khon Muang*) relates the origin of a statue of the Buddha recumbent on his right side (fig. 4.1), enshrined at Wat Phra Non Khon Muang, a monastery in the Mae Rim district of Chiang Mai.[2] Udom Rungrueangsi has pointed out that the statue is associated with King Kawila (r. 1782–1816). The chronicle's dating is suggested by documentary clues. A version of this chronicle is embedded in the *Chiang Mai Chronicle,* which states that eight brothers will be born and that the city of Chiang Mai will be founded in 1796;[3] this seems to refer to the Chao Chet Ton, the collective name for King Kawila and his brothers, who led the final battles that ended over two centuries of Burmese suzerainty in Lanna. In 1796 Kawila resettled the city of Chiang Mai, which had been abandoned twenty years earlier following a siege by the Burmese. The *Chronicle of the Buddha Image Lying on a Mango-Tree Log* is situated in the text of the *Chiang Mai Chronicle* just after the death of Kawila in 1816.[4] According to another source, Kawila made repairs to the monastery and its name was changed from Wat Phra Non Mae Cha Yueang, the name given to it by local villagers, to Wat Phra Non Khon Muang.[5] In 1958, the monastery itself printed a booklet containing a version of the *tamnan;*

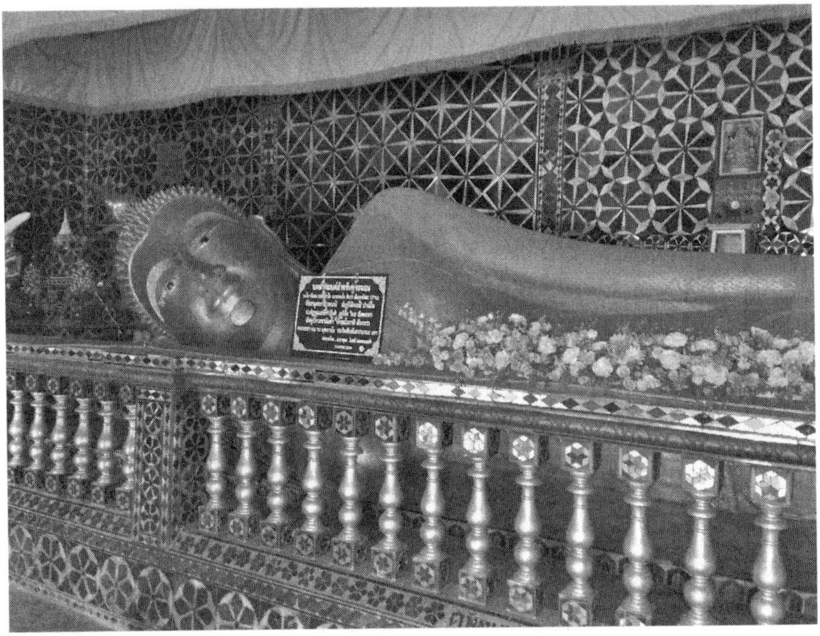

Fig. 4.1. Phra Non Khon Muang (Buddha Image Reclining on a Mango-Tree Log), Wat Phra Non Khon Muang, Chiang Mai.

this version closes with the year 1816.[6] Thus the composition of the *tamnan* seems likely to date to the early nineteenth century.

The chronicle describes a visit by the Buddha during his lifetime to the area that would eventually become Chiang Mai. The Buddha, flying from India, arrived at the Ping River. He thought, "[The previous Buddha] Lord Kassapa in the past came to the base of the great mango tree here. And now I should go there." By that time the tree had been there a long time, had fallen down, and was lying on the ground. The Buddha was feeling ill after eating some bad pork, so he lay down on top of the log. The *arahants* in his entourage said, "Venerable Sir, this place is extremely loathsome. Why does the Lord Buddha come to lie down here?" The Buddha replied, "Monks, when Lord Kassapa became enlightened in the past, he also came here. Because of that, the Tathāgata comes here also." The Buddha then declared that his instruction to them in the *dhamma* (Buddhist teachings) was complete (1A–1B). An ogre (Sanskrit: *yakṣa;* Thai: *yak*) guarding the spot approached, and Gotama performed a miracle for the ogre to prove that he was a Buddha. He then bestowed a hair relic on the ogre to install in the same place where the ogre had previously installed a hair relic of Kassapa (1B–2B). The Buddha then recounted past events in that same place: long ago, the mango tree had grown from a seed that a king had given his gardener to plant; the king later passed the gardener a trove of silver and gold that the gardener buried by the tree (2B–3B). The Buddha noted that the king who planted the mango seed was a past incarnation of one of his disciples, while the gardener was an earlier incarnation of the ogre. The Buddha also recounted that the Buddha Kassapa had come to the mango tree and granted a hair relic to the ogre to install at the spot; this was the same ogre who now approached Gotama at the mango-tree log (3B–4B). The Buddha predicted that eight hundred years after his death, or *parinibbāna,* great monks would bring his ashes and install them on that spot and that an image of the Buddha lying on the mango-tree log would be built there by the king who had been the gardener in a past life. The Buddha also predicted the founding of Chiang Mai at that place, a prediction that triggered uproarious rejoicing by the gods. He assigned the god Indra to watch over the *sāsana* there (5A–5B). And the Buddha's predictions all came to pass (7B–10A).

This chronicle is titled for the so-named Buddha Image Lying on a Mango-Tree Log, suggesting that the chronicle's subject is the famous Buddha statue related to the log, a "relic of use." Yet the chronicle could perhaps be more fittingly described as the history of a particular place, the spot where the log had fallen and upon which Chiang Mai would later be built. Notably, the place is described as being "extremely loathsome," but the Buddha determined that he must stay there because Kassapa had been there previously. The repeated installation of relics and precious materials, and the cycles of devotees' rebirths that circulated around the spot, confirmed the place's special character. Like the structure of a *jātaka,* or story of one of the Buddha's previous lives, the narrative begins "in the present," with a situation prompting the Buddha to recollect an incident from the past that involves previous rebirths of himself and others. This structure as deployed in the chronicle weaves together threads of past and future to create a multitemporal resonance of agencies centered on the place.

This chronicle echoes some events recounted in the *Mahāparinibbāna Sutta,* the classical text recording the Buddha's final moments before his death. In both the chronicle and the *sutta,* the Buddha paused to repose in the vicinity of mango trees: near Chiang Mai in the *tamnan,* and at the mango grove of Cunda the smith near Pāvā in the

Mahāparinibbāna Sutta. In both accounts, the Buddha fell ill after eating some sort of pig-related alms food; he also informed his disciples that he had nothing further to teach them. He lay down in a place which the *arahants* felt was unsuitable for him. In the *Mahāparinibbāna Sutta,* the Buddha's chief attendant, Ānanda, entreated his teacher, "Lord, may the Blessed Lord not pass away in this miserable little town of wattle-and-daub, right in the jungle in the back of beyond!" The Buddha explained that the village, Kusinārā, was once a great capital called Kusāvatī ruled by King Mahāsudassana, a "wheel-turning monarch" (Pali: *cakkavatti*).[7] The *Mahāsudassana Sutta* reveals that the Buddha was King Mahāsudassana in one of his past lives—in fact, the last of seven rebirths he had had in that same locale.[8] The connection of the Buddha to the seemingly wretched place is hence through his illustrious past life. In the *Chronicle of the Buddha Image Lying on a Mango-Tree Log,* the Buddha is linked to the place because one of his predecessors in the lineage of Buddhas had visited there.

Both the *Chronicle of the Buddha Image Lying on a Mango-Tree Log* and the *Mahāparinibbāna Sutta* depict agencies arising from the distant past affecting the Buddha in place. In the Lanna chronicle, the Buddha Gotama arrived at the Ping River and then realized the former presence there of Kassapa, prompting Gotama to also perform actions at that site. In other words, it was upon the Buddha's perception of the place that the past action of Kassapa was then revealed. The actions of the past resonated into subsequent time periods via the location; place had the role of enabling the ongoing agency of the Buddhas. The narrative driver of the *tamnan* is the theme of the relationship between Buddha relic and place. Even the founding of Chiang Mai was presented as a case of appropriate emplacement—that is, as a response to a site in which the agencies of Buddhas and their relics were activated. It is notable that there is no mention of King Mangrai, who built Chiang Mai in 1296 and founded the Lanna royal dynasty.

The statue is not depicted as an active agent in the travelling image mode by which a statue attracts powerful devotions across various towns through time. The statue is connected to the Buddha himself as the subject of a prediction and is a portrait of him in a specific local episode. The image is what we might call site-specific in that its production is intimately linked with one particular place.

The Buddha Image Lying on a Mango-Tree Log is also interesting in view of its iconography. The posture of the image of the Buddha, lying on his right side with legs straightened and aligned one atop the other, is according to contemporary art historical iconography typically meant to depict the Buddha's death scene at Kusinārā. In traditional Thai iconography, it also presents the Buddha reclining, one of his "four postures" (Pali: *iriyāpatha;* Thai: *iriyabot*), along with sitting, standing, and walking. As will be discussed further below, the reclining posture of the Buddha Image Lying on a Mango-Tree Log evokes both meanings while inserting the Buddha into a local episode. The application of a local meaning to a statue in reclining posture is also found in other *tamnan,* such as the *Chronicle of Water Basin Mountain* (*Tamnan Ang Salung*), recounted in a manuscript transcribed in 1944 found at Wat San Pa Khoi in Chiang Mai. That story tells of the Buddha travelling around Lanna and, upon arriving at the Ping River near present-day Chiang Mai, receiving a gift of a honeycomb from a *nāga* (snake god) king. The Buddha's chief attendant Ānanda arranged a pallet by the edge of the forest, and the Buddha rested upon it. The Buddha granted permission to the *nāga* to make a reclining Buddha image, which he predicted would be known as the Reclining Buddha Image of the Honey Inlet (Thai: Phra Non Nong Phueng).[9]

Lanna accounts evoking the *paranibbāna* while depicting the Buddha in local situations give the Buddha's biography a multitemporal and multispatial extension, which is materialized by the statue installed in Lanna.

The *Chronicle of the Grand Lord:* Buddha Integrated with Place

The *Chronicle of the Grand Lord* (*Tamnan Phra Chao Ton Luang*) recounts the origins of a statue called the Grand Lord or Grand Lord of Myna Bird Pond (Phra Chao Ton Luang or Phra Chao Ton Luang Nong Eiang), which is still very popularly revered today at Wat Sri Khom Kham in Phayao (fig. 4.2).[10] The image is eighteen meters in height and probably the largest Buddha statue in Lanna; it is said to have been built in 1491.[11] The statue may be the one described in a deteriorated inscription on stone found in an abandoned monastery in Phayao and now in the collection of the Hariphunchai National Museum in Lamphun. Thought to date to 1524, the inscription lists the characteristics and proportions of a huge Buddha image in Lanna.[12] A clue to the possible dating of the chronicle is that the action of the story ends with a note that the people of Phayao were swept up and

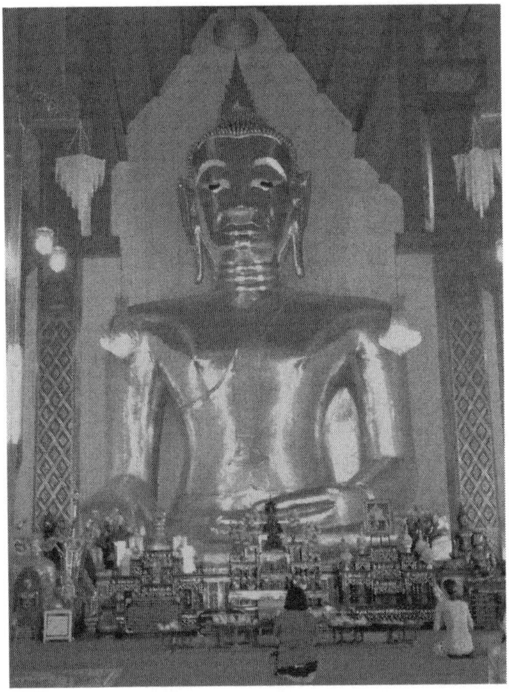

Fig. 4.2. Phra Chao Ton Luang, Wat Sri Khom Kham, Phayao.

exiled by the Burmese to Vientiane, and they subsequently had the chronicle of the statue written to educate people to venerate the Grand Lord they had left behind. Perhaps, then, the story was written down sometime after Burma's takeover of Lanna in the middle of the sixteenth century.

The chronicle relates that the Buddha Gotama, with his entourage of *arahants* and lay disciples, including King Asoka, travelled around the Lanna area teaching, receiving alms, distributing hair relics, and impressing footprints. In the Phayao area, the Buddha was offered alms of betel by an elderly couple and then alms of rice by a metal craftsman, leading him to comment to his attendant, "Ānanda, it is very good here." Then Ānanda, King Asoka, and the metal craftsman together enshrined a hair relic of the Buddha in a deep cavern nearby. The Buddha asked Ānanda to fetch some water from a nearby pond; this turned out to be the dwelling place of a *nāga* king with a head adorned with a flame-like crest. The *nāga* covered the pond with a blanket of smoke, causing Ānanda to flee (1A–2B).

The Buddha used his powers of access to "divine knowledge" and realized that in the past, the previous Buddhas Konāgamana and Kassapa had come to take a meal at the pond. He also knew that in the future the *sāsana* would be established in the middle of the pond for five thousand years, at the end of which the next Buddha would come to the spot. The *nāga,* upon seeing the Buddha, expressed skepticism that the Buddha was of the same class of being as Konāgamana and Kassapa because the Buddha seemed so puny compared to them, so the Buddha magically transformed himself to the height of Konāgamana, thirty-two *sok* (about fourteen meters) tall, and stamped on the *nāga*'s head so hard the snake god sank into the pond. Now convinced, the *nāga* went home and retrieved a rock on which the two previous Buddhas had sat. The Buddha rested upon it and drank water. He said, "Ānanda, the two Lords of the past came to drink water here, indeed, and although they were rather aged they came here. The Tathāgata is rather aged and so has come here. Here there is a very wide and deep pond. The *sāsana* should not be established here [now]." He then foretold that in the future, the pond would disappear, as the old couple who had given him betel would in a later rebirth drain the water and build a statue of the Buddha the same size as Konāgamana. The Buddha, upon making this prediction, commanded Indra and the *nāga* that in the future they should pass gold from the *nāga* country to the couple to meet the expenses for the making of the statue (2B–4A).

When 2,031 years had passed since the Buddha's *parinibbāna,* the couple was indeed dwelling near the pond, making a living by raising ducks and geese. The *nāga* assumed the guise of a man clad in white cloth and turned up at their house in the middle of the night. He told them of the Buddha's order, showed them the load of gold, and to illustrate the project, magically transformed himself into a likeness of the Buddha Konāgamana. He also carried up from the *nāga* country the rock on which the Buddha had sat (4B–5A).

The couple was delighted upon learning of the mission and hauled the gold into the house. They then filled in the pond and began the multiyear process of making the statue, including molding bricks, hiring craftsmen, and buying materials such as lacquer and lime with the *nāga*'s gold. Indra himself descended from heaven to help shape the statue's facial features. The old husband and wife eventually became sick and died, and both were reborn in heaven (5A–5B).

Meanwhile, the ruler of Phayao offered a portion of the field of merit from the production of the Buddha image to King Mueangkaeo

(r. 1495–1525) in Chiang Mai, who then donated gold for the building of a *vihāra* and pledged the territory surrounding a nearby village (Pali: *gāmakhetta*) and families to support the monastery (5B–6A).

Later, after the Burmese takeover of Lanna, Phayao was vanquished, and its people, including the families dedicated to the monastery, were exiled to Chanthaburi (probably Vientiane). The Phayao people lost the *tamnan* of the Grand Lord in the chaos and worried about the statue. They wrote a chronicle and asked Muen Uttama, a man from Chiang Khong, to take it and show it to people near Phayao to promote the image's veneration (6A–6B).

The story concludes with a listing of the impressively large measurements of the image, as well as three examples of people who offered banners to the Grand Lord and to other Buddhist monuments and thereby enjoyed favorable rebirths despite having led lives dedicated to sin (6B–7B).

As in the *Chronicle of the Buddha Image Lying on a Mango-Tree Log*, the *Chronicle of the Grand Lord* begins with the Buddha travelling around Lanna, arriving at a certain place, and then realizing that it is a special place. The place derives significance from the past, as a site visited by the previous Buddhas Konāgamana and Kassapa, and will have importance in the future as an eventual dwelling place of the *sāsana*.

In the *Chronicle of the Grand Lord*, the Buddha points out that the *sāsana* should not be established immediately while he is visiting there but that it should be established in the future with the building of the giant statue. In a practical turn, the Buddha orders the *nāga* to supply the gold to pay for the creation of the image. The provision of funding for the construction of the statue is indispensable indeed, for unlike in the travelling image chronicles, the makers of the statue, the old couple, are neither royals nor influential monastics but poultry farmers. They have earned the opportunity to make the image because in a past existence they had given alms to the Buddha during his visit to the Phayao area. Their agency is now rewarded by their becoming patients of the Buddha. Unnamed and only cursorily described, the donors are rather anonymous executors of the Buddha's command.

The depiction of the unassuming lay devotees draws attention to the prime role of the Buddha in the production of this statue. Like the *Chronicle of the Buddha Image on a Mango-Tree Log*, the *Chronicle of the Grand Lord* integrates the agency of the Buddhas with a specific place that has significance for Buddhas over multiple time periods.

The *sāsana,* the Buddha declares, will be established when the Grand Lord is built in that particular spot at a specific time; the statue materializes the arising of the Buddha's agency in Chiang Mai.

The *Chronicle of the Monastery of the Emerald Buddha Image of Don Tao Wiang Din:* Place and Issues of Gender in Patronage

The *Chronicle of the Monastery of the Emerald Buddha Image of Don Tao Wiang Din* (*Tamnan Wat Phra Kaeo Don Tao Wiang Din*) describes the history of Wat Phra Kaeo Don Tao, a monastery that traces its foundations to the year 680 during the reign of one of the sons of Queen Cāmadevī of Haripuñjaya.[13] Since 1984, the *wat* (monastery) has been combined with a small adjoining monastery, Wat Suchadaram, and the enlarged compound named Wat Phra Kaeo Don Tao Suchadaram. Wat Suchadaram is thought to have been initially erected in the early nineteenth century.[14]

Wat Phra Kaeo Don Tao is said to have hosted the Emerald Buddha during its two-decade residence in Lampang before it was moved to Chiang Mai in the fifteenth century. The *Chronicle of the Monastery of the Emerald Buddha Image of Don Tao Wiang Din* makes the claim that a "Jewel Buddha image" (Phra Kaeo) was carved in Lampang from a large emerald found by Nang Sujātā (Thai: Suchada), for whom Wat Suchadaram is named. This contradicts both the *Chronicle of the Emerald Buddha Image* and the *Jinakālamālīpakaraṇaṁ* (*JKM*), the *tamnan* of Buddhist history, both of which ascribe the creation of the esteemed statue to Nāgasena in ancient India. Other sources say that during the time the Emerald Buddha image stayed in Lampang, it was safeguarded in the palace of the ruler of Lampang while another statue was enthroned in Wat Phra Kaeo Don Tao and eventually sent to Chiang Mai; thus the original Emerald Buddha remained in Lampang.[15] The *Chronicle of the Monastery of the Emerald Buddha Image of Don Tao Wiang Din* does say that the image was removed from Lampang, however, and that the city subsequently fell into decline. After that the text goes on to narrate, in a very vague fashion, the city's subsequent history up to the year 1918. Notably, it does not seem to mention King Kawila and his brothers, whose hometown was Lampang. It would appear that the *Chronicle of the Monastery of the Emerald Buddha Image of Don Tao Wiang Din* consists of an older chronicle which a later author has sketchily brought up to date in the early twentieth century. Assuming that Wat Suchadaram was named to honor Nang Sujātā in the early nineteenth century, the story of Lampang's Emerald Buddha should date at least from that time.

Here let us focus on the narrative up to the point of the Emerald Buddha's departure from Lampang. The chronicle begins with the Buddha, accompanied by fifteen-hundred monks, travelling to a place where he had lived in a previous life. There he subdued a country of ogres and preached to them and other divine beings. He informed the assembled deities that in this "extremely excellent place," Don Tao, all of the previous Buddhas of this era had accumulated merit: Kakusandha had brought eight strands of hair to establish there; Konāgamana, twelve strands of hair; and Kassapa, thirty-two strands of hair (1A-2B). Moreover, after the *parinibbāna* of each of these Buddhas, their bodily relics were conveyed to the spot by their foremost disciples. After recounting these past enshrinements, Gotama plucked a strand of hair from his head, and the gods and monks buried it deep in the earth, ensconced in a huge quantity of treasures (2B–3B).

The Buddha then launched into an extended prediction about the future history of the place, particularly in respect of the fortunes of rice-growing and of the *sāsana*. He also highlighted the attentiveness of local people to the making of Buddha images and the veneration of Buddha relics (3B–4B).

The Buddha predicted that in the third millennium of the *sāsana* (which would begin in the mid-fifteenth century), a goddess would be born in the town as a laywoman named Nang Sujātā who would take care of the Great Relic (the hairs of the Buddhas) at Don Tao. She and a *mahāthera* (senior monk) also living there would decide to build a Buddha image. They would obtain a piece of red sandalwood but would be unable to find anyone to carve it. Nonetheless, they would continue to hope to make a Buddha statue some day. Then a *nāga* in the river nearby would take an emerald and insert it into a melon in Nang Sujātā's garden. She would notice the unusually beautiful melon and bring it to the *mahāthera,* who would split the rind with a knife, see the emerald, and again go out in search of someone to carve a Buddha image (5A–5B). The *mahāthera* would be unable to find anyone, but then the god Indra would come, disguised as an old man, and sculpt the jewel into a statue of the Buddha. Ecstatic, the *mahāthera* and Nang Sujātā would then spread the word about the Buddha image, causing crowds to come to the monastery, which would be dubbed Wat Phra Kaeo, or Monastery of the Jewel Image (5B–6B).

Unfortunately, people would spread false rumors that Nang Sujātā and the *mahāthera* were misbehaving together, and the local ruler, a sinful person, would condemn her to death. Upon being forced to the execution site at the riverbank, Nang Sujātā would resolve, "If I misbehaved with the *mahāthera,* may my blood fall on the earth. If I did not misbehave, may my blood gush upwards." Indeed, upon the sword's blow, Nang Sujātā's blood would surge into the air. Indra would catch the blood in a golden bowl and place it in the compound of the Cūḷāmaṇi (the *stūpa* in heaven that enshrines the hair of Prince Siddhattha, the future Buddha Gotama, when he cut it to become an ascetic). The sinful local ruler would die and fall into hell, and Nang Sujātā would be reborn in Tāvatiṁsa heaven. After that, the town would be afflicted with drought and famine; people would flee, Wat Phra Kaeo would become abandoned, and Indra would transfer the Emerald Buddha image to a distant place. The rulers of the town would fail to venerate and maintain the Great Relic of Don Tao (6B–8A).

After making this detailed prediction, the Buddha then listed potential acts of renovation to the compound of the Great Relic and the rewards that would accrue to sponsors of each, proclaiming that "whichever person, whichever *thao phraya* ruling the country, whichever official, whichever Brahman, householder, rich merchant, renunciant or Brahman [*sic*] who comes to build up the site of the Great Relic, who builds halls or walls, builds a *nāga*-lined staircase from the top of Don Tao here on 3 sides, on 1 side or 2 sides or 3 sides, when he dies from human existence he will be born in the Tāvatiṁsa heaven of the gods, have a golden mansion 3,000 *yojanas* [48,000 kilometers] high, and have angels surrounding as an entourage, 130,000 of them" (8A–9A). After supplying a few similar examples of wondrous rewards, the Buddha then continued predicting the history of the place, noting that the town would prosper during the times when the compound of the Great Relic would be built up and maintained (9A–12A).

This *tamnan* accounts for the Buddha statue as one representation of the Buddha amidst a series of installations of relics interred at the same site, emphasizing the multiplicity of Buddha interactions over time in one place. The image and relics are means by which the Buddha is unified with place, thereby exalting Lampang.

This story is also especially interesting because one of the sponsors of the Buddha image is a mere laywoman. As we have seen, the patrons of other famous Buddha images are typically kings who are described in exemplary terms as endowed with tremendous merit and

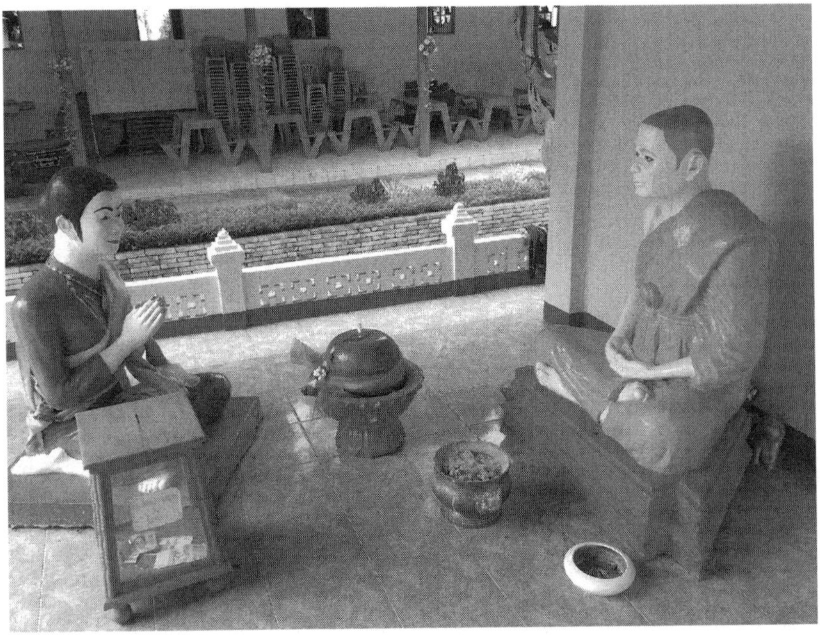

Fig. 4.3. Sculptures showing Nang Sujāta offering the melon to the monk, Wat Phra Kaeo Don Tao Suchadaram, Lampang.

monarchical virtues such as wisdom, generosity, and military prowess; their admirable characteristics and behavior entitle them to be associated with powerful Buddha images. Even as such sponsors express their superiority through the creation of powerful images, famous images likewise require powerful creators: *tamnan* idealize or glorify the sponsors of Buddha statues that became famous. In this context, Nang Sujātā is also presented in the *tamnan* as a quintessential laywoman. Upon finding the beautiful melon in her garden, she immediately donates it to the monk, a moment commemorated by slightly larger than life-size cement statues at the *wat* today (fig. 4.3). She also devotes her time and effort to taking care of him and the monastery. Nang Sujātā is in fact the namesake of the laywoman who played a limited but key role in the Buddha's life prior to his enlightenment in ancient India, a rich laywoman named Sujātā who presented Siddhattha with a bowl of milk rice, a meal that powered him through the enlightenment and for forty days afterwards.

Following this earlier Sujātā's example, women in Tai and other Buddhist cultures have traditionally provided food, labor, and other support to monasteries so that monks could attend to their spiritual growth. This nurturing role is closely connected to a focus in Buddhist text and imagery on women as mothers: in traditional belief in Thailand and elsewhere in mainland Southeast Asia, motherhood has been the attribute for which women are most highly valued.[16] Sujātā who donated the milk rice was also a mother; the reason behind her offering was to give thanks to the Buddha-to-be (whom she mistook for a tree god) that she had given birth to a son.

The northern Thai story of Nang Sujātā contains references to her reproductive capacity. The emerald nestled in the melon evokes a fetus inside the womb. The imagery also echoes Southeast Asian myths that say that the first humans emerged from a large gourd. There is something resembling a mother and father in the pairing of Nang Sujātā and the monk. While she is not only the donor who made the Emerald Buddha image possible, the chronicle seems to suggest that she is the image's symbolic mother. Nang Sujātā appears to reflect a conception in Buddhism, described by Charles Keyes, of motherhood as entailing not only the support of a child but of Buddhism itself.[17]

In Buddhism, mothers are honored for their child-raising role; when a novice monk is ordained, it is believed that great merit accrues to the young man's mother. In becoming ordained, the son repays the debt owed to his mother for her nurturing.[18] During his lifetime, the Buddha is said to have travelled to heaven specifically to preach to his mother.[19] Nonetheless, mothers are also perceived as potential obstacles to a monk's spiritual progress, as they are "attachments" from which monks must distance themselves. The Buddha's mother, Māyā, died seven days after giving birth to him. In fact, the mothers of all of the Buddhas throughout history are said to have had the same fate—that is, dying on the seventh day and being reborn as a god.[20]

Among the chronicles of famous Buddha images, there is only one named female patron, Queen Cāmadevī. As we shall see in chapter 6, inscriptions provide evidence that women have also been frequent donors of Buddha statues. Nonetheless, traditional and official Thai Buddhist hierarchy has privileged—and continues to privilege—men while providing no clear path to authority for women, who are unable to become ordained; they lack a secure position in monastery compounds despite their significance to the survival of monastic life. The scarcity of women identified as the sponsors of famous Buddha images may be an example of what Alan Sponberg has labeled "institutional androcentrism," the structuring of Buddhist community to elevate men as superior and thus subordinate women.[21] In the *Chronicle of the Monastery of the Emerald Buddha Image of Don Tao Wiang Din,* the *mahāthera,* who is unnamed in the story, apparently goes unpunished, even though sexual misbehavior is grounds for formal disrobing and lifelong expulsion from the order. By contrast, Nang Sujātā, though ultimately glorified, pays with her bloody execution. The male sponsors of famous Buddha images did not have to die to demonstrate their piety and virtuousness. Perhaps it is the instability of the status and authority of women in Thai Buddhism that made the death and deification of Nang Sujātā necessary to demonstrate her rectitude.

In understanding the fate of Nang Sujātā, the lineage structure of travelling image chronicles must also be considered. As Ashley Thompson has observed, the history of communities is built with the family unit as its basic element, and thus we must take into account how differentiation of gender roles influences the development of tradition and its genealogy.[22] The lineages of travelling images imitate the chronological recounting of members of dynasties and of monastic orders but provide an alternative vision of history centered on a Buddha statue instead of a royal progenitor or a sectarian leader. The Buddha statue also provides a link between royal and monastic lines, as kings sponsored the creation and worship of the image while monks consecrated and cared for it. These lineages, which entailed the positioning of members as heirs to political and religious power, are genealogies constructed with almost no women.

The depiction of a statue as the head of a lineage also draws attention to the Buddha image's nature as an object to which personhood is attributed. Through consecration a statue becomes the Buddha, and the chronicles recount how they are addressed and treated as if each was the Buddha. The Emerald Buddha of Don Tao originated as a gem ensconced in the rounded form of a melon, like the baby Buddha in his mother's womb. If a statue is indeed the Buddha, is it then enmeshed in hierarchies, social relationships, and protocols as if it were the Buddha himself? If the answer is yes, then the death of Nang Sujātā appears as necessary as that of Māyā, the Buddha's mother. And the distancing of Nang Sujātā from the statue may reflect the distance between monks and their biological families, as upon ordination monks' allegiance to biological lineage is displaced by dedication to monastic lineage.[23]

In the following sections we will consider contemporary scholarly and classical Buddhist writings focusing on the significance of place, the main theme of these Lanna stories of images in place.

The Relationship between the Buddha, Place, and His Representations

John S. Strong has noted how relics are "*extensions* of the Buddha's biography" that "do not just recall events from his life, but have adventures on their own. They travel to distant countries, to heavens and *nāga* worlds. They help legitimate empires here on earth and they further spread the dharma to places that the living Buddha never visited."[24] King Asoka "centripetalized" the relics, "distribut[ing] them outward in a way that allows them to exist locally, while at the same time emphasizing their ongoing ties to the center, their ultimate unity and interconnection."[25] Strong has shown how relics defeat the problem of the physical absence of the Buddha by giving him a presence across space and time. Relics mark the territorial spread of the *dhamma*, the range of "conquest" of the *sāsana*.

The theme of Buddhist domination of the territory is also reflected in Donald Swearer's presentation of how images and relics made Lanna into a "*buddhadesa*."[26] In a similar vein, Juliane Schober has written of the spread of the "cultural hegemony" of Theravāda Buddhism in Burma and elsewhere through discourses attributing power to those who control and patronize places where the Buddha's remains are enshrined.[27]

The interpretations of Strong, Swearer, and Schober emphasize the transformational effect of the presence of Buddha relics and statues on the places where they are established. Their scholarship emphasizes the impact of Buddha agency upon new lands. As we have seen, the *tamnan* illustrate how the Lanna localities did not perceive themselves merely as the passive or fortunate recipients of relics. The texts do not present the conquest of place by another agency, nor are these cases of ordinary or unworthy places being transformed into unusual or worthy ones. In the *tamnan*, the Buddha was moved to travel to Lanna. The statues and relics are presented as confirming or adding to the places' significance. One could say that the creation of Swearer's "*buddhadesa*" is the identification of the places in which Buddha agency is reanimated. Mircea Eliade elaborated the concept of the hierophany, which is "the act of manifestation of the sacred."[28] The *tamnan* explain the existence of each hierophany in Lanna as occurring in a sometimes unexpected place that enabled the activation of agencies over time. In these chronicles, the Buddha discovered in the landscapes of Lanna the past activities of other Buddhas and the future histories of the great Lanna cities. Gotama's perception of the past was based on place, thereby linking history of place to the Buddha. In turn, memory stimulated action. The collaborative power arising from the interaction of place and memory expressed in the chronicles fits well with Edward S. Casey's observation that "the functions of memory and place are strikingly parallel. They accomplish a similar task at a quite basic level. This task is that of congealing the disparate into a provisional unity."[29] The installation of statues and relics confirmed the unity of Buddha, time, and place in Lanna.

Étienne Lamotte was inclined to see the discourse of previous Buddhas having visited some place as part of a propagandizing effort by Buddhist missionaries. Strong has pointed out that, in fact, claiming that the sacred sites of non-Buddhist cultures are associated with past Buddhas "would seem to be have been an ideal way for incorporating non-Buddhist, pre-Buddhist, or Brahmanical elements into the Buddhist fold."[30] He observes that the Chinese pilgrims Faxian and Xuanzang reported seeing in ancient India *stūpas* marking sites where the Buddha Gotama's physical remains were buried adjacent to *stūpas* identifying places where previous Buddhas had meditated or preached. This conjunction of multiple Buddhas, he notes, "served to give layers of sacrality and antiquity to a particular site."[31] From the standpoint of the Lanna chronicles, sacrality would seem to refer to the degree of access to divine powers. The overlapping of Buddha interactions at a single site affirms the long-standing capacity of that site to draw in and channel the sources of such powers.

Elizabeth H. Moore has noted that chronicles about ancient Buddhist sites in Burma represent, in her view, "deliberate choices reflecting deeply rooted collective or social memory" and so provide "evidence [that] needs to be documented alongside empirical data."[32] The sacrality of sites often predated the establishment of Buddhist monuments upon them: the "recognition of 'super-natural' elements of the terrain and embedding new objects into the land brought local chthonic beliefs into Buddhist administrative frameworks."[33] Similarly, H. L. Shorto has suggested that in early Mon history, *stūpas* may have been built over the earthen homes of local cadastral deities in order to subsume them into Buddhism.[34] The establishment of reliquaries on mountains may indicate that Buddhism was fitted into a preexisting orientation to the local landscape.

The significant role of gods in many chronicles may also reflect the submission of local divinities to the Buddha. Indra (Sakka) features in multiple stories assisting humans to consecrate statues and enshrine relics. Divinities are described as celebrating enshrinements. *Yakṣas* (ogres) and *nāgas* (snake gods) are depicted being converted by Gotama to his teachings and then acting as guardians of relics and images. It may be that the presentation of ogres and snake gods in Lanna echoes their untamed personas as depicted in other Buddhist stories, such as the Lankan account of the Buddha's preparing Lanka Island for Buddhism by subduing the ogres and snake gods who inhabited it.[35] Another example of the connection of divinities to place appears in the *Mahāparinibbāna Sutta:* in the last days before his *parinibbāna,* the Buddha visited the town of Pāṭaligāma, which at that time was being fortified by Magadhan ministers. Through his advanced power of sight, the Buddha could observe many thousands of deities moving into Pāṭaligāma to settle because the town would eventually become the great city of Pāṭaliputta. This suggests the power of place—or, more specifically, the future of a place—to attract divine forces. Moreover, the deities' settlement pattern influenced that of the human residents moving into the city: the most powerful deities caused the minds of the most powerful royal officials to choose homes where those deities dwelt, while the middle- and lower-ranking deities caused royal officials of parallel status to pick residences near to them.[36] The greatness of deities and people is correlated to the greatness of their place of dwelling. The *Mahāparinibbāna Sutta* also relates that during the Buddha's final days, he rested at the Cāpāla Shrine and then praised as "delightful" several others—the Bahuputta ("Many Sons") Shrine, the Gotamaka Shrine, the Sattambaka ("Seven Mangoes") Shrine, and the Udena Shrine—as well as the Cāpāla Shrine. These seem to have been shrines for the worship of divinities,[37] and this episode apparently evidences the Buddha's approval of the veneration of deities at local sites.

As we have seen, the location that turns out to be a statue's place of establishment may not always have been a local sacred site, as such places were often described as unremarkable or even repellant. Perhaps this trope reflects a strategy of Buddhist partisans: because the significant sites of local Buddhist history were said to be those which did not seem obviously distinctive or attractive, any place in Lanna could then potentially be declared part of the domain of Buddhism.

Place and the Life of the Buddha

The role of place in the Lanna stories of images in place—and of relics, as we shall see in chapter 5—may have been inspired by the sense of place found in stories about the Buddha Gotama arising from classical Pali sources. Perhaps most famously, according to the *Mahāparinibbāna Sutta,* just before his death the Buddha named his places of birth, enlightenment, first sermon, and *parinibbāna* as sites of pilgrimage, indicating a powerful relation between the Buddha's actions and place.[38] Other examples in canonical texts suggest the significance attributed to place. Here let us look briefly at the *Nidānakathā* of the *Jātakaṭṭhakathā,* traditionally said to have been written by Buddhaghosa in the fifth century and now found as the introduction to the collection of *Jātakas.* The *Nidānakathā* narrates the career of the Buddha Gotama beginning many lifetimes ago, with his resolve to achieve Buddhahood, through his birth as Prince Siddhattha, his enlightenment, and his life up until the donation of the Jetavana Monastery. His career is marked by interactions with specific places. For instance, prior to his enlightenment, Siddhattha received the offering of milk rice in a golden bowl from Sujātā. He consumed the rice and walked to the Nerañjara River, descending the ford through which previous Buddhas-to-be had also stepped on the days of their enlightenment. He laid the golden bowl on the surface of the water, and it floated against the current and then dived to nestle under the bowls of the three previous Buddhas that were stacked on the river bottom.[39] Repeating the actions of his predecessors at specific places, Siddhattha was fitted into the lineage of Buddhas.

Ascending from the riverbank, Siddhattha then proceeded to the bodhi tree. The *Nidānakathā* recounts that the Bodhisatta, or Buddha-to-be, stood at three different sides of the tree in turn, and determined that each was not the place of enlightenment. Finally, at the eastern side, he found the spot that "trembles not and shakes not," where all previous Buddhas had meditated. The Bodhisatta Siddhattha "realized that that was the stable place, never forsaken by any of the Buddhas, the seat for the destruction of the aggregate of defilements."[40] He then proceeded to attain enlightenment despite a barrage of attacks by the god Māra and his army. Māra called out, "Rise, Siddhattha, from that seat. It is not meant for you. It goes to me." The Bodhisatta replied that Māra had not completed the perfections and other achievements, and so, "This seat is not meant for you. I alone have the right to it."[41] The seat thus metaphorically represented the accomplishments of the Buddha-to-be over numerous existences. The strength and stability of the seat may also refer to the importance of supporting the stability of the Buddha *sāsana* itself.

The seat is not only symbolic; it is also presented as a specific physical place, one carefully selected by the Bodhisatta. The reliable stability of the location turned out to be necessary to help Siddhattha to withstand the onslaught of swords, hot ash, mud, and other substances Māra launched at the meditating sage. The Bodhisatta achieved his objective without being disturbed. This unification of Buddha and seat, of person and place, supported the powerful process of his enlightenment. Indeed, after the Buddha's success, the *Nidānakathā* reports that he announced, "This, my throne of victory is a unique throne. Whilst seated here all my aspirations have come to pass; and I will not rise from it yet." The Buddha continued to stay there for such a long time that some deities suspected that he had "not yet given up his attachment to the throne of victory"; to dispel the misimpression, the Buddha performed a miracle of double appearances,[42] in which he caused flames or lights to shoot from the upper part of his body while streams of water poured from the lower part.

Classical Buddhist texts also highlight the seats of enlightenment of the previous Buddhas. In reviewing descriptions of their enlightenments as recounted in various canonical Pali texts, I. B. Horner has observed,

> This *bodhi-pallaṅka* position is uniform for all Buddhas and it is obligatory for them to sit in the same place, *ekasmiṃ yeva ṭhāne*. It is the only one able to support the weight of a Buddha's attainment, the *jaya-pallaṅka* (cross-legged position for victory) of all Buddhas, the navel of the earth. No one, not even Sakka himself, can pass over the *Bodhi-maṇḍa* (ground, circuit, platform or dais round a Bodhi-tree) whether a Tree be growing there at the time or not, for here it is that all Buddhas have routed all the defilements.[43]

Each Buddha's achievement of enlightenment was made possible by a specific place, and without a singular combination of person and place, the enlightenment could not have occurred. Enlightenment is an experience of place as well as person. The significance of the places continued to exert power even after the Buddhas had completed their transformations, as Sakka, the king of the gods, continued to honor these channels for Buddhahood.

The importance of specific sites for enabling a Buddha's achievements is also reflected in Xuanzang's account of his travels in ancient India. Xuanzang provided a more elaborate account of how Siddhattha discovered the seat of enlightenment, explaining that the Bodhisatta, after consuming the milk rice from Sujātā, headed northeast and climbed a "secluded and dark" mountain called Prâgbôdhi. At the summit, however, a god told him, "This mountain is not the fortunate spot for attaining supreme wisdom. If here you stop and engage in the '*Samadhi* of diamond,' the earth will quake and gape and the mountain be overthrown upon you." The Bodhisatta then started back down, and on the slope, encountered a spacious cavern. Taking a seat within, he heard a god call out that this was not the place of enlightenment—instead, it was a "diamond throne" under a pippala tree. Xuanzang reported that at the time of his visit, the spots on the mountain traversed by Siddhattha were marked with posts and *stūpas* erected by Asoka.[44]

Xuanzang also recalled visiting a *stūpa* that marked the spot where Gotama in a distant past life first made a vow to become a Buddha in a future life. At that time the Buddha-to-be was a deerskin-clad ascetic named Sumedha. He lay down in the mud so that the Buddha Dīpaṃkara could cross unsullied by treading on Sumedha's long locks of hair. Because this crucial event occurred at a previous time that was distant beyond counting, Xuanzang asked a local monk how the place had managed to survive the multiple obliterations and reconstructions of the cosmos that had occurred in the intervening period. The monk answered that "when the world was destroyed, this spot was also destroyed, but when the world was reconstructed, the spot also reappeared at its original place where it was before. . . . As this is a holy place, why should it not have the potency to emerge again?" As Strong has observed, "it is quite clear that what is being commemorated is the place—or even more abstractly, the space—where an event happened, but there is no question of the *bodhisattva*'s hair or deerskin garb still being there."[45]

In the next section we will consider stories of Buddha images from two other traditions—the Lankan and the Burmese/Mon. These have been selected because they have a history of sharing of Buddhist practices with the Lanna Tai. The comparison here is based only on examples published in English translation that enable productive comparisons to the Lanna stories discussed. As we shall see, while today these cultures are often categorized together as Theravāda Buddhist and have shared many aspects of belief and custom, the themes and motifs of the stories reflect differences in context of the roles of representations of the Buddha.

The Lankan Chronicles: Dimensions of Time

It is interesting to note that Buddha images do not seem to have been a major source of inspiration for Lanka's monastic authors. A version of the story of the Sandalwood Buddha image appears in the *Kosala-Bimba-Vaṇṇanā* (*Laudatory Account of the Kosalan Image*), a Pali text of Lanka that may date to the thirteenth or fourteenth century and which also inspired multiple adaptations in Sinhalese.[46] Other than the Sandalwood image, the origins and history of statues seem to have been only sporadically recorded in Lankan manuscripts. Wilhelm Geiger, translator of the *Mahāvaṃsa,* has observed that in that chronicle there are references to specific, named Buddha statues, but only in brief. The *Mahāvaṃsa* mentions images such as a "Golden Image," a "Kholakkhiyabuddha," and an "Abhisekabuddha." The information on these statues is limited to mentions of occasions when the statues were honored by kings through the donation of adornments, shrines, and festivals. The most famous image was apparently one made of stone (called Silāsaṃbuddha, among other names) said to have been placed in the third century BCE in the Thūpārāma in Anurādhapura by King Devānaṃpiyatissa. In the *Mahāvaṃsa*'s accounts of later reigns in the fourth through tenth centuries, the stone statue is mentioned at the times when it was transferred, installed in a new shrine, and decorated. This image was apparently held in some importance through many centuries, but no history of the statue was apparently written, even as Lankans composed histories of many bodily relics and relics of items used by the Buddha. Geiger notes that there are no mentions in the *Mahāvaṃsa* of these named Buddha images after the Coḷa invasion of Lanka in the eleventh century, suggesting perhaps an effect of the turmoil of that time.[47] There has not yet been any evidence found that Lanna's Sihing Buddha image was made or known in Lanka, despite the claim of the Lanna chronicle and a name that suggests a Sinhala association. Lanna stories of Buddha images seem to have no direct parallel in Lanka.

At the same time, it seems likely that the multitemporal approach found in the Lanna stories was inspired by Lankan narratives. Buddhas, people, ogres, and gods encounter each other repeatedly across lifetimes in the *tamnan*. Jonathan S. Walters has suggested that such associated existences, which feature in classical Buddhist texts and Lankan *vaṃsas*, entail the intertwining of two dimensions of time. One dimension of time is "calculable" (Pali: *saṅkheyya*), which includes historic events such as the reigns of specific kings and the birth and deaths of particular Buddhas. The other dimension of time is "incalculable" (*asaṅkheyya*), referring to circumstances beyond reckoning, such as kings who lived before the first king and places that existed before the creation of the world. The Lankan chronicles present each circumstance in "calculable" time and show how it echoes the deep tradition of "incalculable" time. For instance, the enshrining of relics and building of monasteries by a Lankan king are depicted as actions by a particular individual who has been accumulating merit over numerous lifetimes and as the reiteration of virtuous monarchical practices in infinite, cosmic tradition. The "calculable" event is thus linked to the "incalculable" through the operation of karma. Through this interpretation of the karmic resonance of present circumstances, the *Dīpavaṃsa* and *Mahāvaṃsa* depict Lankan kings as especially empowered to support the people of Lanka in their individual journeys toward Buddhahood.[48] The Lanna chronicles highlight that to Walters' insight it should be added that multitemporality via karmic connection occurs through place. It is in place—Anurādhapura, Chiang Mai, Phayao—that the interweaving of strands of time is manifested in present circumstances.

Myanmar's Mahāmuni Buddha Image: The Buddha's "Brother" in Arakan

Perhaps the most famous Buddha image in Myanmar is the Mahāmuni, a large statue currently enshrined in Mandalay in what is known as the Paya-gyi (Big Pagoda) or Rakhine Pagoda. This statue of Buddha Gotama is in a seated posture with right hand extended down over the knee (in "earth-touching" gesture). The image measures about 3.8 meters high and 1.8 meters from shoulder to shoulder. It is apparently made of brass but is covered all over, except on the face, with what seems to be a thick layer of countless small pieces of gold leaf donated by devotees, making its body appear as if encased in a lumpy shell.[49] Devotees consider the Mahāmuni especially deserving of veneration because it is said to have been created in Arakan (present-day Rakhine) when the Buddha himself visited there during his lifetime.

The creation of the Mahāmuni is recounted in local texts including the *Mahāmuni thamein* and the *Sappadānapakaraṇa,* the latter "an ancient Arakanese manuscript of great value" that was partially translated into English by Emanuel Forchhammer in the late nineteenth century.[50] His translation is summarized as follows.

The action begins in the past, when the Buddha Gotama was alive and teaching in Sāvatthī in ancient India. King Candrasuriya of Dhānyavatī in Arakan learned of the Great Teacher and expressed a strong wish to venerate him. Through his divine power, the Buddha became aware of the thought of Candrasuriya; he flew to Arakan, accompanied by Ānanda and five hundred *arahants,* and they landed on top of Selagīri Hill. There the Buddha pointed out to Ānanda and the other disciples the different places in Arakan where he had resided during many past lives and where his relics would also be enshrined in the future; for example, he declared, "On the western side of the Mallayu (or Rammamallayu) River, and close to the ocean, there is a range of hills known as the Kāsinapabbata; there I formerly spent a life as the king of the peacocks. On my death my neckbone will be discovered and enshrined in a pagoda to be called the Līyodawcetī."

King Candrasuriya travelled to see the Buddha at Selagīri Hill and accepted the Buddha's Ten Precepts. He asked the Buddha to visit Dhānyavatī. The Buddha assented and stayed and taught the people of the city for seven days.

When the Buddha was about to depart, the king commented that in the Buddha's absence they would have no one to venerate, and thus requested an image of him. The Buddha thought to himself that this country "is more excellent than the rest of the 84,000 countries," and it had been his home in many previous existences; he consented to the king's request. The king assembled nine *kutis* worth of treasures. The Buddha then issued an order to the gods Sakka and Vissakamma: "Take these treasures and with them make an image of me which shall not vary from the actual size of my body even by the breadth of a hair."[51]

When the gods completed the statue, the Buddha breathed upon it and it became so lifelike that it was like a twin of the Buddha. The king and courtiers paid homage to the image with various kinds of offerings and mounted it on a jewelled throne. As the Buddha regarded the statue, it rose to honor him. The Buddha raised his right hand and said to the image, "Younger brother, do not stand up. I shall enter Nirvāna in my eightieth year; but you, endowed with the supernatural powers of a Buddha, shall exist for five thousand years, which I have prescribed to be the limit of my religion; you shall be the means of working the salvation of men and *nats* [local deities]." The Buddha then predicted that the statue would eventually suffer the results (Pali: *kammavipāka*) of two evil acts that the Buddha had committed in a former life: when he had been a king on Cheduba Island, he had broken a gardener's thigh bone and cut off flesh from a prince's back.

The Buddha then noted that his "preceding elder brothers," the Buddhas Kakusandha, Konāgamana, and Kassapa, had called this place Dhaññavatī (grain-blessed), and so it would continue to be called. He and his disciples then flew off to a hill now called Tantawmutaung. There the Buddha spoke to Ānanda about his former lives spent in places in that area and enumerated which of his relics would be established in each place after his *parinibbāna*. Then the Buddha flew towards Śrī Kṣetra.

At the same time, back in Dhānyavatī, King Candrasuriya and his people were holding festivities all day and night to worship the Mahāmuni image. Nine miracles were manifested in the image hall. For example, the image emitted six-colored rays, which flashed like lightning when the faithful approached but faded away when heretics drew near, and the trees around the image house angled their leaves and branches towards the building.

The discussion of the Mahāmuni in the *Sappadānapakaraṇa* concludes here. Other accounts of the Mahāmuni, as far as the statue's history is concerned, also seem to end at this point: there is no further mention found in Burmese historiography of the Mahāmuni statue until the year 789, when inscriptions note that King Mahātaingcandra rebuilt the Mahāmuni image house on two occasions and set up a new stone altar there. It was said that while consecrating the image the king miraculously received the Areindama lance, the divine "spear of victory."[52] The statue was an important object of homage in Arakan and elsewhere; successive kings of Arakan journeyed to worship the Mahāmuni even when the capital was moved elsewhere.[53] Other documents record interventions from the ninth through eighteenth centuries by other kingdoms (Amarapura, Bagan, Bago, and Śrī Kṣetra) and ethnic groups (Burmese, Chin, Mon, Pyu, and Shan, among others) who variously venerated, renovated, raided, or destroyed the Mahāmuni image and/or its shrine.[54] In 1103, Mon and Pyu soldiers, who had been fighting on behalf of the king of Arakan, are said to have paid a visit to the Mahāmuni shrine and ended up looting and wrecking it. Pyu troops hacked out most of the statue's back, while Mons chopped off the right leg. The Buddha's prediction was thereby said to have been fulfilled.[55]

The famous statue inspired outsiders to attempt to carry it off to their own countries. None succeeded in achieving this until the Burmese King Bodawpaya (r. 1782–1819) conquered Arakan in 1784. His army managed to transport the Mahāmuni to a shrine near his capital city of Amarapura, now part of Mandalay, where it has resided ever since. The Burmese celebrated Bodawpaya's seizure of the Mahāmuni in their books and inscriptions, but for the Arakanese it was a grievous loss; some even claimed that the statue actually fell into the river on the way and that a copy was enshrined by Bodawpaya instead.[56] Today there are a number of images that are related to the Mahāmuni: copies, as well as a group of statues (between three and five, according to different accounts) called the "brothers" of the Mahāmuni which were said to have been formed using the metal left over from the casting of the original. As Pyi Phyo Kyaw and Kate Crosby have noted, these statues that are now enshrined in various sites in what are now Bangladesh and Myanmar are in some cases linked to nationalistic Arakanese or Burmese senses of patriotic identity, but at least one is more closely linked to the local community in which it resides. As a set, the Mahāmuni images exemplify how Buddha statues may be engaged in political claims across borders while also developing the presence of the Buddha in local communities.[57]

The story of the origination of the Mahāmuni shares similarities with that of the Sandalwood Buddha image. As mentioned in chapter 2, the story of the Sandalwood Buddha appears in many Buddhist traditions around Asia. It was recounted by the Chinese traveller Faxian, who visited ancient India in the fourth century and observed, "This image, as it was the very first made of all the figures of the Buddha, is the one which all subsequent ages have followed as a model."[58] Thus, by Faxian's time, images were already being described as copies of one initial Buddha image. A version of the story, as mentioned in chapter 2, appears in Lankan manuscripts. Lanna people incorporated the Sandalwood image story into the *Vaṭṭaṅgulirāja Jātaka,* part of a collection of nonclassical Pali *jātakas* (*Paññāsa-jātakā*), accounts of the Buddha's past lives.[59] The Sandalwood Buddha story was also extended by Lanna people into a travelling image chronicle to claim that the image was transferred from ancient India to Lanna, where it passed through the domains of many patrons. In the sixteenth century this story was summarized in the *JKM*. We can probably assume that some form of the account of the Sandalwood image was in circulation from a very early time and that it inspired whoever composed the Mahāmuni story.

Both the Sandalwood and Mahāmuni images were created after a pious king entreated the Buddha to permit a statue to be made to enable veneration when the Buddha was not available in person. In both stories the statue, once produced, was said to become magically alive thanks to the power of the Buddha. In the case of the Sandalwood image, the Buddha gazed upon it, while for the Mahāmuni, the Buddha breathed on it and then gazed at it. Both stories recount that subsequently the statue miraculously moved to pay its respects to the Buddha. This prompted the Buddha to indicate to the statue that it need not pay homage to him, as it would carry on the *sāsana* after the Buddha's death.

Historically, apart from its important role in Buddhist devotion in Arakan, the Mahāmuni also became an important object of legitimation for Arakanese kings. The historian Jacques Leider has described an Arakanese manuscript found in Sittway, probably composed in the eighteenth century, that recounts the Buddha's visit to Arakan. The manuscript tells of the Buddha's production of the Mahāmuni image and purports that the Buddha made a number of predictions about Arakan's kings, capitals, and pagodas.[60] Thus from the mouth of the Buddha the dynastic history of Arakan was delineated; this emphasizes the Buddha's link to Arakan.

The connection between the Buddha and the Mahāmuni is also indicated in an early nineteenth-century palm leaf manuscript in which a royal official extolled Bodawpaya's glorious virtues and works of merit and depicted his kingship as a stage on his path to Buddhahood;[61] among the examples of evidence of Bodawpaya's greatness is his acquisition of the Mahāmuni. The manuscript notes that even the eleventh-century Anawrahta of Bagan, still today one of Myanmar's most honored kings, had not been able to obtain the Mahāmuni: Anawrahta journeyed to Arakan, but while there had a dream in which the Mahāmuni declared that only "Metteyya who has been my elder brother" would eventually take the Mahāmuni away; Anawrahta therefore relinquished his quest and returned to Bagan. The text then notes the triumphant arrival of the Mahāmuni to Amarapura, confirming that Bodawpaya is the statue's "elder brother," the future Buddha Metteyya.[62] The recognition in Myanmar of the authenticity and authority of the Mahāmuni as a representative of the Buddha is the basis for the prestige and gravity of this account.

It is telling that after King Bodawpaya installed the Mahāmuni near his capital he did not treat it as his kingdom's palladium.[63] The statue is part of the collection of Buddhist relics, statues, and other items that Bodawpaya, like other Burmese kings, accumulated during the expansion of his empire and deposited in his home capital to demonstrate and enhance the meritorious power of himself and his city. Like the Grand Lord, the Mahāmuni is an image in place. Its chronicle was not extended to include the statue's history beyond the time of its creation; the text's emphasis is on the connection of the statue to the Buddha in a particular site.

It is also interesting that the Mahāmuni story involves previous lives of the Buddha; these did not feature in the Lanna stories, whose authors apparently preferred to invoke past Buddhas to enhance the historic depth and significance of their accounts. The prediction that the Mahāmuni would be damaged as a karmic consequence of the Buddha's actions in a previous life also emphasizes the statue's correspondence to the Buddha. This contrasts with the explanation for damage given in the chronicle of the Sihing image: when the image was being cast, a king struck one of the craftsmen on the hand, and when the statue was removed from the mold, it was found to have a broken finger.[64] The Sihing story linked the defect to the patrons. In the Mahāmuni story, it is the agency of the Buddha that was reflected in the image. An image in place, the Mahāmuni embodied the integration of the Buddha, in past, present, and future, with its site of establishment, Arakan.

The stories from Lanna and Myanmar discussed in this chapter present Buddha images as more than just memorials of the Buddha's presence at specific places. The statues integrated Buddha agency with each place. The Buddha was often personally involved in the creation of the statues, either by giving his permission for their creation or making predictions. Place inspired the Buddha's actions; it was not the passive recipient of his agency but the crucial conduit for its realization through time. In a nutshell, one might say that the images in place are unifications of Buddha and place, while travelling images are unifications of Buddha and persons. Because Buddha images integrated the Buddha with cities, mountains, and famous kings—all significant sites of power and identity—they assisted the incorporation of the Buddha into the Lanna world.

Chapter Five

Buddha Images and Relics

Form, Place, and History

In the final moments of the Buddha's life, as he lay on a bed set up in a grove of trees outside the modest village of Kusinārā, he exchanged final words with his followers, reassuring them that though his existence was at an end, his *dhamma* would continue as their teacher. When his attendant Ānanda inquired what should be done with the Buddha's remains, the Buddha instructed that they should be treated like those of a "wheel-turning monarch" (Pali: *cakkavatti*)—that is, wrapped in cloths, encased in iron containers, and cremated on a pyre with various perfumes. Then, a "stupa should be erected at the crossroads for the Tathāgata. And whoever lays wreaths or puts sweet perfumes and colors there with a devout heart will reap benefit and happiness for a long time."[1] These words have since encouraged generations of devotees to venerate the Buddha's remains (Pali: *dhātu;* Thai: *that*).

The Buddha's funeral at Kusinārā ended with the division and distribution of his remains to royal families of ancient India, as well as to the gods in heaven and to *nāga* (snake god) kings who also sought relics for their personal worship. Two hundred years later, the great Buddhist king Asoka is said to have gathered up the relics from the various shrines and then redistributed them to *stūpas* he constructed in 84,000 locations across Asia, establishing monuments of the *sāsana* (Buddhist thought and practice) far and wide.

Lanna people have understood the presence of many relics now in Lanna as part of Asoka's dissemination of the relics. As we saw in chapter 4, they also have traditional stories of the Buddha himself visiting Lanna and distributing relics as well as commanding or predicting the creation of statues in his likeness. In Thailand, statues and bodily relics, together with his teachings (*dhamma*), are considered types of reminders or shrines of the Buddha, *chedi* (Pali: *cetiya*). Images are often categorized together with relics, despite their differences as physical objects. How did devotees of the past distinguish them?

The Relationship between Buddha Images and Bodily Relics

According to the Buddha's guidance on sites of commemoration or veneration as expounded in the *Kāliṅgabodhijātaka,* he identified three kinds of shrines: those for a bodily relic (Pali: *sarīrikacetiya*), those for a relic of use (*paribhogacetiya*), and those for commemoration or indication (*uddesikacetiya*). This last type, he added, are "lacking in foundation" because they "are a matter of mind only." As *uddesikacetiya* is often thought to mean an image, this account has sometimes been interpreted to discredit the image as a valid representation of the Buddha. Nonetheless, the text seems to have hardly diminished the enthusiasm of Buddhists around the world for images. At the same time, unlike the bodily relics and relics of items used by the Buddha, statues of him are only recognized as valid representations of the Buddha after they are consecrated. It is notable that even as consecration would seem to authoritatively invest any particular image made at any time as the Buddha, the authors of the Lanna *tamnan* (chronicles) discussed in chapter 4 deliberately declared direct connections between specific statues and the Buddha himself. The making of the statues came from the Buddha's command or prediction. Some were also modelled on specific Buddhas: for example, in facial features and body size, the Grand Lord was designed to resemble Konāgamana. These images do not all house bodily relics per se, but they are linked to the Buddha's person through his speech or appearance. Did such stories reflect some sense of insecurity about the validity of statues versus other kinds of relics as representations of the Buddha?

The installation of relics inside of statues was a common practice that may also have enhanced the connection of a statue to the Buddha. Steven Collins has posited that "statues of the Buddha, although allowing him to be 'seen' in a rather obvious way, in fact are usually thought only to mediate his presence in a stronger sense if they contain relics."[2] As we saw in chapter 2, Nāgasena had seven relics of the

Buddha embedded in the Emerald Buddha. Likewise, the Setangkhamani Buddha is said to contain five relics bestowed by the king of the gods. The Sikhi images were carved from a stone on which the Buddha had sat while preaching; this stone could be classed as a *pāribhogikacetiya*, or item used by the Buddha.

The images did not derive their power only from relics, if any, enshrined within them, however. The Emerald Buddha chronicle states that the image performed miracles and was venerated by onlookers *before* the relics were installed. When the sculpting was finished, Nāgasena enthroned the statue in a beautiful image hall, and gods, *arahants* (enlightened persons), the king, and laypeople streamed in from all directions to pay homage to it. While the offerings were being presented, the statue performed miracles "as if it were alive" for seven days and seven nights. During this time both gods and humans worshipped it with an abundance of offerings, including thousands of umbrellas, flags, and lotus flowers; with exclamations of joy; and with the playing of thousands of musical instruments such that "the earth was as if it was going to collapse with the sound of music and shouts of approval resounding." After this, the relics were installed in the statue, and there was further rejoicing.[3]

In the Sihing Buddha chronicle, there is no indication of relics being associated with the statue at all. The image was at a thirdhand remove from the Buddha: it was created by craftsmen who were told what the image looked like by kings and *arahants* based on their recollection of the image generated by the *nāga* (snake god). There is no mention of relics entering the statue during consecration. Considering the evidence from the Lanna *tamnan*, then, Collins' claim that images containing relics more strongly mediate the Buddha is subject to notable exceptions in the eyes of devotees.

Collins' remark that the image enabled the Buddha "to be 'seen' in a rather obvious way" points to the difference in form between relics and images, as well as to the importance of *darśana,* the Indic ritual practice of seeing a revered being. In view of this, it is well to consider the question Robert Sharf has raised, of why splinters of bone and ash, plucked from the remains of the funeral fire, are worshipped at all. He suggests that the relics, despite their dirt-like appearance, derive allure and power from their condition as essence, a "pure corporeality," the ultimate reduction of the substance of the person that persistently asserts existence even in the absence of figural form. The relic *is* the Buddha. It is physical evidence; the image on the other hand is representational and dependent on conceptual acceptance. Nonetheless, as Sharf observes, due to the relic's uncharismatic appearance, it requires some kind of "frame" to indicate its sacred status. Thus it is housed in reliquaries and *stūpas,* as well as inserted into statues.[4]

As Ashley Thompson has noted, the *stūpa* is a form that stands for the absent Buddha without anthropomorphic representation; through this framing, the relic enters the realm of representation, and therefore into proximity to the image.[5] Relics are also framed through discursive means. As we will see in this chapter, relics are described in the chronicles of Lanna (and elsewhere) as emitting rays of colored light and flying. These descriptions confirm that the relics are indeed remains of the Buddha invested with his supernatural potency. The descriptions also endow relics with a visual imagery, generating a mental picture of relics, ordinarily covered from view by monuments, while displacing the relics' dusty reality and, in a sense, allowing for the possibility of *darśana.* Through discursive imagery not only statues but relics, too, were "a matter of mind." If visuality was an important means by which the authenticity of any representation of the Buddha was attested, these descriptions of the appearance of relics were not merely decorative but essential.

In the Lanna stories, bodily relics, often more than one, were enshrined on the same site as a Buddha image; does this reflect a sense of insufficiency of the image alone? There may have been contexts in which this was the case, but the enshrinements depicted in *tamnan*—whether of a relic added to a site where an image is established, or of an image added to a place enshrining a relic—are not presented as entailing the replacing or surpassing of other objects but as being additions that further emphasize the significance to Buddhism of particular places.

Images and relics were not always considered mutually exclusive types, either physically or conceptually. As we shall see in this chapter, Burmese accounts describe a fungibility between the two; for example, in one account, a relic of use, the branch of a tree that shaded the Buddha, is carved into a Buddha statue. Some stories even describe bodily relics as if they are portraits of the figure of the Buddha, complete with robes. A contemporary wall painting in Dawei (Tavoy) in Lower Myanmar illustrates a bodily relic in the form of a statue of the seated Buddha, the most common posture for Burmese Buddha images (fig. 5.1). In this case, has the imperative of *darśana* meant that it is the image that is the preferred form of representation of the Buddha, and not the relic?

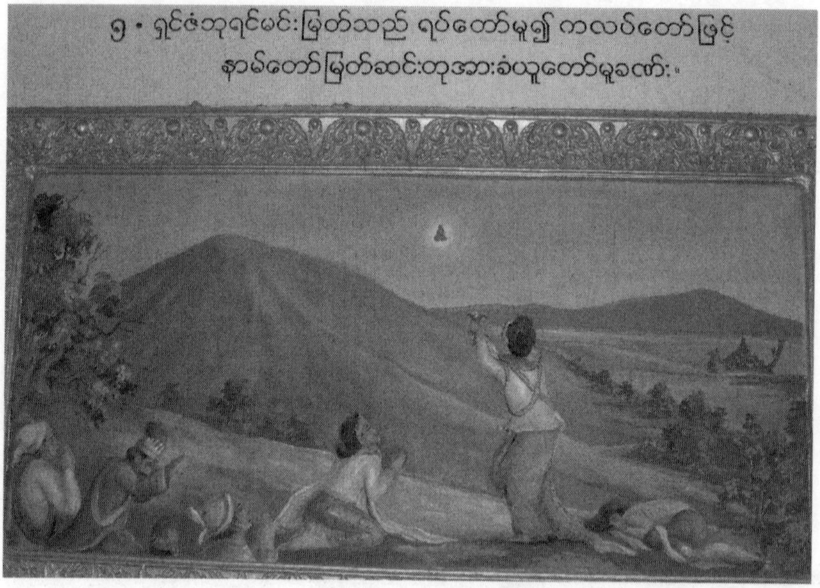

Fig. 5.1. Painting at Yat Kan Taung Monastery, Dawei, Myanmar. The caption indicates that Shin Zan is receiving a relic on a small, stemmed, circular tray. Photograph by Elizabeth H. Moore.

The presentation of the relic as Buddha figure may be an echo of what is perhaps the most striking visual image associated with relics, a description found in the narrative of the event known as the final *nibbāna* (nirvana) of the Buddha or the *nibbāna* of the relics. According to Buddhaghosa's *Manorathapūraṇī,* in the moments before the end of the five-thousand-year period of the *sāsana,* all of the Buddha's relics, incandescent with a glow of six hues, will soar up from their shrines and amass at the Mahābodhi throne at Bodh Gaya, the site where the Buddha attained enlightenment. There, "[t]aking on the form of the Buddha, they will display the glory of the Buddha's body seated cross-legged on the throne of awakening. They will manifest the thirty-two major and eighty minor marks of the great man" and reenact the twin miracle of Sāvatthi, shooting flames from his upper body and streams of water from his lower. "Then, from the relic-body, a fire will leap up, and that body will become non-existent." This will mark the end of the *sāsana.*[6]

The final *nibbāna* reverses the process of the dispersal of Buddha relics as each fragment retakes its position in the Buddha's body, even as the Buddha long ago enacted his *nibbāna,* and his body was obliterated in the cremation fire and cannot be re-created. The relics form an image of the Buddha that is not the Buddha who existed previously but is lifelike enough to perform the Buddha's double miracle. The relic-merged body thus incorporates, like Buddha statues, both the demise of a particular Buddha and his era and an enduring power of Buddhahood or Buddhism. Relics, as well as images, can therefore tread the line between permanence and impermanence of the Buddha; as Thompson has observed, the relics generated at the Buddha's funeral are the product of the rendering of the transient body of the Buddha into the lasting, institutional body of Buddhism.[7] The incorporation by relics and images of both the impermanent and the permanent, of personhood and the institutional, opens up the range of possibilities for devotees to create frames for them. As facsimiles of the Buddha, which are not identical to him, relics and images can draw on his power and aspects of his biography while becoming integrated into new social configurations and power structures. As we saw in chapter 2, the *Chronicle of the Sihing Buddha* stated that "the Buddha image Sihing has no life but has power through the strength of the resolution [Thai: *athitthan;* Sanskrit: *adhiṣṭhāna*] of the *arahants,* the strength of the resolution of the Lankan king, and the strength of the *sāsana* of the Fully Enlightened One. It is not the image itself alone."[8] The representations of the Buddha, the author seems to acknowledge, are productions shaped by the frames assembled by devotees.

As we shall see below, relics in Lanna are framed by stories that focus on the significance of place. As John Strong has noted, the Buddha's relics were "centripetalized" out from ancient India. The devotees of Lanna understood this as a set of meaningful journeys undertaken by the relics, which came deliberately to Lanna, and their enduring installation in particular places in Lanna testifies to the lasting importance of those sites. This theme is shared with chronicles about images; any movements of both types of objects were not only miraculous but purposeful and deliberate. At the same time, the Lanna chronicles do not depict relics as journeying, as the travelling images do. There is a sense here of the relics as undetachable from their places of enshrinement, and perhaps as a consequence, that their ideal state is to be hidden from view, as they typically are in Lanna. The image is modelled on human form, designed for ritual viewing and seemingly capable of interactive exchange and spontaneous movement.

The Chronicles of Relics of Lanna: Honoring the Relic in Its Place of Enshrinement

Tamnan explain how specific relics came from the Buddha's person to points far from India. The fact that such accounts exist raises the question of whether the authenticity of particular relics was at one time or another subject to doubt. These Lanna stories spell out the precise link between particular relics and the Buddha and thereby legitimize or glorify particular relics. At the same time, the bulk of these texts is given to narrating the history of the relics while they were in Lanna. In other words, the chronicles are as much statements of the relics' authenticity as histories of the relics and their relationship to local communities. Like the stories of images in place, the Lanna accounts of relics persistently emphasize their sites of enshrinement. The *tamnan* focus on the association of relics with their place (Thai: *thi, than,* or *sthan*), the site where devotees installed or established the relics (*wai, tang, sthapna, praju,* or *banju*) or enshrined them (*pratitthan*). Often the place was a mountain, in which devotees commonly buried the relics deep in the ground and built a *stūpa* on top of the spot. The construction of the monument is usually minimally described; in these chronicles, the emphasis is on the movement of the relics. Below we will first look at some Lanna chronicles about relics, and then consider Burmese and Lankan relic stories.

The *Chronicle of the Flower Garden Monastery:* Relics Go towards Their Destination, Borne by Kings and Monks

As an example, let us consider the *Chronicle of the Flower Garden Monastery* (*Tamnan Wat Suan Dok*), which recounts the history of Wat Suan Dok in Chiang Mai, particularly the discovery of relics and their later enshrinement by the monk Sumana and King Kuena (r. 1355–1385) at the site of Wat Suan Dok and on a nearby mountain, Doi Suthep (Pali: Ucchupabbata).[9] Sumana, as mentioned in chapter 3, was a monk whose career is described at length in chronicles such as the *Mūlasāsanā* and the *Jinakālamālīpakaraṇaṁ* (*JKM*), the *tamnan* of Buddhist history;[10] he is credited with establishing the Lankan Buddhist tradition in the Tai territories and particularly the monastic order of Wat Suan Dok. Notably, the *JKM* mentions the enshrinement of a relic at Wat Suan Dok in 1373,[11] but not the relic installation on Mount Suthep. This suggests that perhaps at the time the *JKM* was

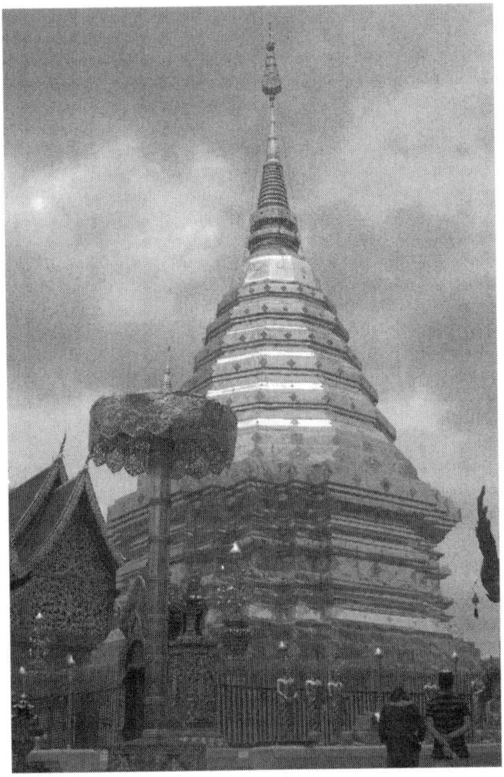

Fig. 5.2. Chedi Phra That Doi Suthep, Wat Phra That Doi Suthep, Chiang Mai.

written, between 1516 and 1527, the relic had not yet been enshrined on Suthep. The *Chronicle of the Flower Garden Monastery* refers to the Emerald and Sihing Buddhas enshrined in Chiang Mai;[12] as the Emerald Buddha was present there from 1468 to 1548, the chronicle may have been composed not long after the reign of Phraya Kaeo (1495–1525).

The main part of the *Chronicle of the Flower Garden Monastery* is taken up by the account of Sumana's discovery of a Buddha relic and his transport of it from Sachanalai to Sukhothai and then to Chiang Mai. Here follows a summary.

Acting on hints he received from a god, Sumana uncovered a relic in an abandoned *stūpa* in Sachanalai. The relic performed the miracle of emitting rays of light throughout a whole night. (4A–5B). Sumana brought the relic to Dhammarāja, the ruler of Sukhothai, but the relic did not perform miracles "because Sukhothai was not the place of establishment of the most excellent relic" (5B). Sumana carried the relic back to his monastery. Later he was invited to go to Chiang Mai by the ruler there, King Kuena (6A–6B), and Sumana took the relic with him. Kuena had a prophetic dream that spurred him to build a monastery (Wat Suan Dok) in his royal flower garden. He and Sumana then "invited" the relic to enter a golden vessel to be installed in a *stūpa* at the monastery. The relic performed miracles, floating in the air and shining luminously. It then multiplied itself, becoming two, three, and then many relics. When the relics returned to their container, Sumana found that there were two of them. One had its typical gleam, but the other looked less lustrous. He invited the one with normal brightness to be established at the *stūpa* (7B–8B). Later, contemplating what to do with the other relic, Kuena and Sumana said, "There has not yet been a good sign given to us of where the relic of the excellent Lord Buddha should be installed. We resolve to leave the identification of the location to the gods by putting an auspicious elephant to use" (9A–9B). The relic was then mounted on top of a magnificently decorated royal elephant (fig. 5.3). The elephant proceeded to climb mountains. At one point the large animal reached a summit so pleasant looking that Kuena and Sumana were prompted to say, "The place here is flat and extremely beautiful. We request the relic of

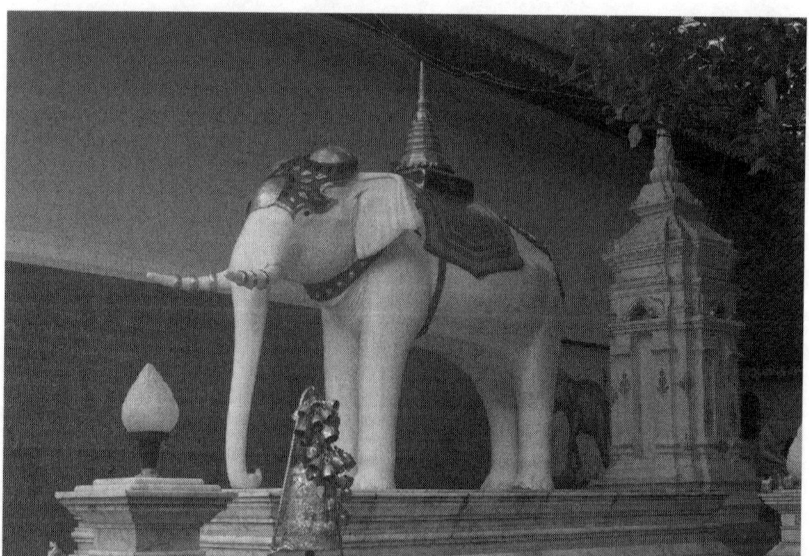

Fig. 5.3. Sculpture of relic-bearing elephant, Wat Phra That Doi Suthep, Chiang Mai.

the Lord Buddha to stay here" (9B–10A). But the elephant did not halt and continued on to Mount Suthep. There, on the stone peak, it cried out resoundingly three times, performed circumambulation three times, crouched on its four knees and, its mission completed, expired on the mountain. The relic was then installed in a hole dug into the peak, and a *stūpa* was built over it (10A–10B; fig. 5.2).

This story illustrates how a relic was constantly considered by devotees in relation to its place, and how its miracles were read by devotees as signs of the relic's satisfaction with its location. It is interesting that during the relic's journey on the back of an elephant, the elephant marched on even after King Kuena and Sumana pointed out that a certain summit looked like an appropriate residence for the relic. Even a relic's most devoted patrons could not decide where the relic should reside; the relic itself decided. The usual phrasing in *tamnan* for describing the transport and installation of a relic or a statue is to note that the object was "invited" (Thai: *anchoen* or *nimon*) to go, suggesting its assumed autonomy.

The *Chronicle of the Great Relic of Haripuñjaya:* The Relic's Residence Is Fixed, Even If It Is under a Toilet

The *Chronicle of the Great Relic of Haripuñjaya* (*Tamnan Phra That Hariphunchai*), which probably dates to the fifteenth century, concerns the founding of what has historically been one of Lanna's most highly venerated sites (fig. 5.4).[13] The reliquary was established by King Āditta (Thai: Athittarat), who was the thirty-third monarch in the dynasty founded by Queen Cāmadevī at Haripuñjaya. As recounted in the *Chronicle of the Relic of Lamphun and the Chronicle of Wat Ton Kaeo* (*Tamnan Phra That Chao Lamphun lae Tamnan Wat Ton Kaeo*),[14] the story begins with King Āditta moving into his newly built royal palace. He paid a visit to the palace privy to effect the royal bodily function. While there the king was attacked by a crow and discovered that a Buddha relic was buried beneath the toilet (21B–23A). The crow informed the king,

> Phraya White Crow, my grandfather, said that the Lord Buddha, when he was still alive, one day came to sit here and eat myrobalan [a kind of plum] and predicted that when the Tathāgata had gone to *nibbāna*, this place will be a great city called Haripuñjaya, indeed. The place where the Tathāgata was sitting will be the place of establishment of the Golden

> Stūpa [Pali: Suvaṇṇacetiya] of the Tathāgata's relic of the chestbone, the relic of the fingerbone and granular relics of the Tathāgata filling one bowl, which will be established here through Phraya Āditta. My grandfather then had me come here to guard and not let animals and people harm this place. (23A)

King Āditta was delighted by this news. He had the royal palace moved elsewhere, and with offerings and homage he together with his ministers and subjects invited the relics to come out of the ground. The relics emerged, performing miracles of flying and emitting rays of light of six colors for seven days; then they resubmerged themselves in the ground as before. The king had his people dig on the spot to retrieve them, but the more they dug, the farther down the relics dived. Halting the excavation, the king again performed veneration and acts of homage and entreated the relics to emerge. They did so, again flying and emitting light. The king had a casket of gold made to hold the relics and built for them a palace decorated with gold, silver, and jewels over the spot (24B–25B).

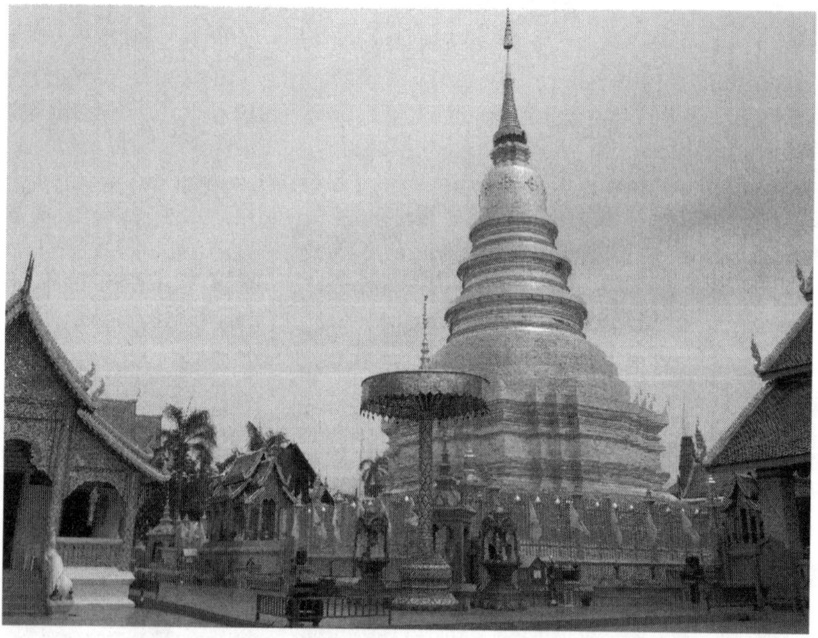

Fig. 5.4. Chedi Phra That Hariphunchai, Wat Phra That Hariphunchai, Lamphun.

The story dramatically and amusingly highlights how an unattractive place may still be a highly significant one, as the home of the Great Relic turns out to be directly underneath a toilet. In the end, the *Chronicle of the Great Relic* exalts the place where the relic persistently embedded itself: Haripuñjaya.

An interesting insight into this story has been offered by Donald K. Swearer. Together with Sommai Premchit, Swearer produced an English translation of the *Cāmadevīvaṃsa,* a longer chronicle about Queen Cāmadevī and her dynasty that includes the account of the Great Relic. Swearer also presented an illuminating analysis of motifs and themes of the chronicle.[15] He focused on the roles of the dramatis personae, whom he saw as representing various kinds of complementary and divergent powers that interact and ultimately actualize order, prosperity, and protection for Haripuñjaya under Buddhism. In the narrative, King Āditta is the protagonist who is foreseen by the Buddha as the one who will discover and enshrine the relic. Swearer suggests that it was through the king's interaction with the relic that "the world-renouncing power of the Buddha is conjoined with the sovereign power of the world-ruling king (*cakkavatti*)."[16]

Nonetheless, the story depicts Āditta's interaction with the relic as rather awkward: he had built an outhouse over the relic, and it is a crow that directs him to the relic's presence. The structure being a toilet emphasizes the king's lacking any power of insight that would have enabled him to notice the presence of the relic. The Buddha predicted not only that the relic would be honored by the king but also that it would be manifested in a particular place. The king's task was a specific one: to enshrine the relic in its dwelling place. Āditta was obliged to pack up and move the royal palace elsewhere. The narrative emphasizes that the king had to defer to the relic and did not in any way control it.

Thus, while, as Swearer observed, the story links the power of the Buddha with the power of the world-ruling monarch, it should be added that the connection of Buddha to king is realized only when the relic is enshrined by the king at its designated place of establishment.

The *Chronicle of the Hair Relics* of the Shwedagon: Relics and the Quest for the Place of Enshrinement

The *Chronicle of the Hair Relics* (*Tamnan Phra Kesa That*) extends an account found in both canonical and noncanonical texts across the

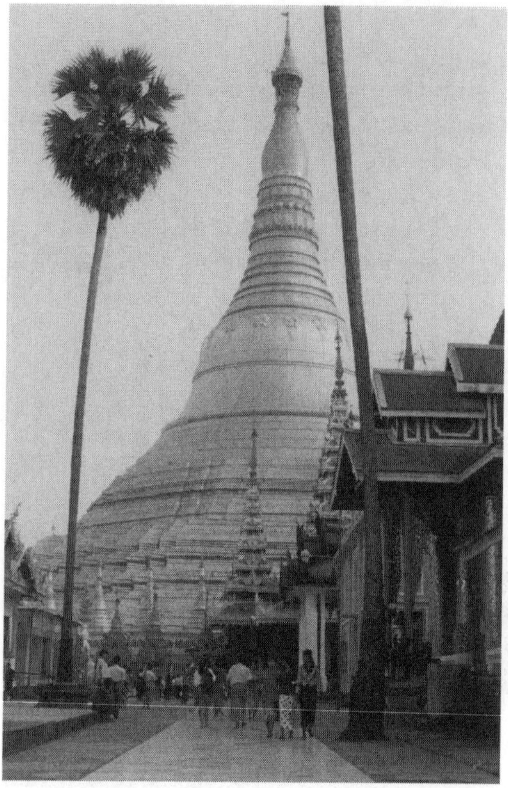

Fig. 5.5. Shwedagon, Yangon, Myanmar.

Buddhist world: the encounter between the Buddha and two merchants, Trapuṣa and Bhallika, who became his lay disciples.[17] A Burmese/Mon tradition elaborates the Pali account to claim that Trapuṣa and Bhallika hailed from Mon lands. The two were on their way to sell rice in a drought-ridden country when they met the Buddha, to whom they presented a meal of rice.[18] The Buddha taught them the *dhamma,* and then, running his hand over his head, extracted eight strands of his hair that he granted to them. Trapuṣa and Bhallika then travelled to Singuttara Hill, where they enshrined the hair relics; today the site is located in Myanmar's capital, Yangon. A massive, spectacular gold-covered *stūpa,* it is known as the Shwedagon and considered one of the country's most sacred monuments (fig. 5.5). The text of the *Chronicle of the Hair Relics* found in Chiang Mai is apparently based on this Burmese/Mon tradition, though it is not known when the tradition spread in Lanna in the form of Tai Yuan-language *tamnan.*

The reliquary site is not mentioned in the early sixteenth-century *JKM*, though Trapuṣa and Bhallika are; perhaps this story did not spread among the northern Thai until after the Burmese takeover of Lanna in the mid-sixteenth century.

The *Chronicle of the Hair Relics* recounts that at the moment when the Buddha passed the strands of hair to the merchants, the two asked him where the relics should be placed. The Buddha replied that they should be installed in the same place where the relics of the three previous Buddhas—Kakusandha, Konāgamana, and Kassapa—were installed on Mount Singuttara (6A–6B). The two merchants abandoned their original plan to sell rice and immediately set off on a quest to find the mountain, whose location was unknown to them. Along the way a king and a *nāga* each snatched away two strands of the hair relics for their personal devotions, leaving the merchants with only four strands (8A–8B), but the relics miraculously became eight again in the presence of the meritorious ruler of the city of Uparāpa (10A). The god Indra assisted the merchants in finding Mount Singuttara by having the divine civil engineer Vissakamma clear it of trees and scrub and transmit the location to the merchants via a dream (11A–11B). Indra further lent a divine helping hand by interrogating extremely aged gods who remembered the occasions when the previous Buddhas' relics were enshrined eons ago (13B–14B). When the merchants finally arrived at Mount Singuttara, many miracles were manifested. The hair relics flew up into the air and emitted light. People in the vicinity afflicted by blindness and deafness were miraculously able to see and hear. The earth shook, Mount Sineru (also Meru: center of the world) swayed, the oceans roared in tumult, and a huge downpour of rain fell. Trees suddenly sprouted flowers and fruit. A vast quantity of lotus flowers appeared. The relics were venerated by deities and humans and then ensconced in a vault in the mountain (15A–16B).

In this story, the fact that the merchants, upon receiving the relics, straightaway asked the Buddha where to establish them, reflects two assumptions: first, that for each relic there is a certain place where it should be enshrined; and second, that the location is not a matter that the recipients of the relic could decide by themselves. The Buddha's reply indicated a course of logic for determining relic placement. He ordered that the relics should be installed in the same place where the relics of the previous Buddhas had been installed. Kakusandha's water cup, Konāgamana's walking stick, and Kassapa's *saṅghāṭī* (robe) had been established at the same place at various times in the past by three different ogres who had at first hunted these Buddhas as prey but ultimately came to accept their teachings. The precedent of actions of earlier members of the lineage of Buddhas guided Gotama's bestowing of relics to Trapuṣa and Bhallika and the establishment of the relics.

The challenge to identifying the place where the relics should be installed drives the narrative of the chronicle. Mount Singuttara, despite the presence of three Buddha relics, was not obviously prominent. The difficulties encountered by the two merchants during their journey to find this place and the various kinds of assistance by the divinities take up the main part of the text and enhance the sense of the relics' arrival at Singuttara as an extraordinary occasion. The greatness of the relics' unity with their dwelling place was further amplified by the appearance of numerous miracles at the moment of enshrinement, while the flight and extraordinary luminescence of the relics themselves signalled the relics' approbation of the site. The power of the hairs to perform miracles demonstrated that the power of the Buddha himself was implanted in his relics.

The story culminated in the literal unification of relics with place through their interment. The description of lavish veneration and offerings given by the people and numerous deities who converged on the site emphasizes the unity of the various beings of the Buddhist world in a particular special place. The installation of the relics also creates a unity across time. The layering of multiple relics in one spot unifies the Buddha with his predecessors. The establishment of the relics was foretold by a distant past recovered through the Buddha's power to see across time and by the memory of the gods. At the same time, installations of hair relics while the Buddha was still alive foreshadowed the future distribution of all of the bodily relics in shrines after his death. The enshrinement of Buddha relics in their place is depicted as a cosmic event, as a coalescence of time, place, and being. We also encountered this sense of multitemporal action coming together in one location in the stories of images in place (see chapter 4). Attention was drawn to the images' resemblance to specific Buddhas and to their materials, but otherwise the stories of the images in place share the same spatial and temporal themes as those of bodily relics.

In the next sections, I will compare these Lanna relic stories to some Lankan and Burmese/Mon stories. This is not meant to provide a comprehensive overview of these traditions but to consider different ways in which relics were integrated by worshippers in three culturally related areas.

Lankan Stories about Relics: Social Role Models, Time, and Karma

Lankan literature about relics was a likely source of inspiration for many Lanna stories as it was for other literary traditions in Asia. Lankan accounts communicated model examples of devotion intended to influence the attitudes and actions of the devotees who heard them recited; as Stephen C. Berkwitz has suggested, late medieval Lankan literature "comprised a project for fashioning virtuous persons."[19] The Lanna relic chronicles also reflect awareness on the part of their authors of the power of historical narrative to transform perceptions and moral attitudes and inspire meritorious action.

Accounts of the coming of the relics to Lanka drawn from Lankan sources are embedded in the sixteenth-century Lanna chronicle the *JKM,* which, as noted in chapter 2, contains an account of the spread of Buddhism from India to Lanka and the expansion of Lankan Buddhism in Lanna.[20] The *JKM* includes a summary of the *Dāṭhāvaṃsa,* the Lankan *Chronicle of the Tooth Relic.* The Tooth Relic was boosted along its journey from India to Lanka Island by the magical faculties of an *arahant,* and Lanka's religious and political authority was buttressed by this account of the journey of the much-exalted relic to the Lankan king. This and other Lankan chronicles bridge temporal and geographic separations in order to make the Buddha "present" after his *parinibbāna* (death). The Lanna chronicles share this bridging function. Both Lankan and Lanna stories also explain how Buddha relics came to be established in specific localities: often the narratives involve a visit of the Buddha himself to a certain place, during which he made prophecies about his relics that were later fulfilled through the efforts of monks and lay devotees. In addition, the visits of the three previous Buddhas to Lanka and their depositing relics there is recounted in the earliest known Lankan chronicle, the fourth- or fifth-century *Dīpavaṃsa,*[21] as well as in the fifth- or sixth-century *Mahāvaṃsa.*[22]

It should be noted that the Lankan relic stories have a thematic emphasis that does not feature in the Lanna accounts we have reviewed. As Kevin Trainor has pointed out, the narratives from Lanka are structured to display exemplary roles for different social actors in the acquisition, handling, and veneration of relics. The accounts reflect a "hierarchy of possession," in which control of relics is directly correlated to devotees' attainment of the Buddhist ideal of nonattachment. In this way, it is the members of the *saṅgha* (community of monks) who are privileged as those who control access to relics.[23] Lankan stories of relics provide models for an ideal relationship between monarch and *saṅgha* "reflect[ing] the fundamental structural opposition between the *saṅgha* membership, which exemplifies separation from worldly concerns and attachments, and the laity, who are associated with mundane passions and attachments."[24]

For example, the thirteenth-century *Thūpavaṃsa,* the subject of which is the creation of the large reliquary monument called the Mahāthūpa, relates that King Duṭṭhagāmaṇi of Lanka requested the assistance of monks in obtaining various relics. The novice Soṇuttara entered the fourth level of trance and descended to the relic-blessed realm of the *nāga* king Mahākāḷa. The snake king's nephew tried to conceal the relics from the monk by swallowing them and hunkering down at the foot of Mount Meru. Not deceived, Soṇuttara extended his arm, stretching it long and thin to reach into the *nāga*'s stomach and retrieve the relics. He then handed them over to King Duṭṭhagāmaṇi for establishment in the Mahāthūpa at Anurādhapura.[25] Thus the extraordinary power of the monk was instrumental in obtaining the relics for establishment in Lanka.

The *Mahāvaṃsa*'s description of the creation of the *stūpa* at the Thūpārāma also can provide insight into the motifs of Lankan relic stories. This account, which is summarized in the *JKM,*[26] also serves as a productive comparison to Lanna relic stories. According to the Lankan history of the Thūpārāma, the monk Mahinda suggested to King Devānaṃpiyatissa that relics should be brought to Lanka. The king affirmed that he would build a *stūpa* and stated that Mahinda should find the relics. The novice Sumana was then dispatched to retrieve the Buddha's alms bowl, filled with relics, from his grandfather King Asoka in Pāṭaliputta, and the right-collarbone relic from Indra in the home of the gods. After Sumana had obtained the relics and delivered them to Lanka, they were mounted on the back of an elephant. The elephant walked to the site where a branch from the bodhi tree from India would someday be transplanted, and then pivoted to face towards the site where Mahinda had predicted the *stūpa* of the Thūpārāma would be built. The site was cleared of vegetation, and the construction of the *stūpa* began. The king returned to the city to plan the festival of celebration, while the monks withdrew to rest in a lovely grove. When the brickwork base of the *stūpa* reached knee's height, the elephant travelled around to various regions, drawing a great crowd to gather at the shrine. At the site, the relics soared up from the elephant's back and performed the miracle of double appearances. It was revealed that the relics' performance and their establishment in the *stūpa,* as well as the transplanting of the bodhi tree, had in fact all been predicted long ago by the Buddha himself while he was recumbent on his deathbed in Kusinārā. The relics came down from the air and landed on the head of the king, who then installed them in the shrine. At that moment the earth quaked, and the people experienced faith in the Buddha.[27]

This story emphasizes a Lankan interest in a clear division of labor between lay patron and *saṅgha,* with King Devānaṃpiyatissa responsible for the building of the monument and Mahinda and the monks in charge of obtaining the relics. In northern Thai stories, relics are also depicted as only being accessible to, and manageable by, persons of high karmic attainment. In the *Chronicle of the Flower Garden Monastery,* it was the monk Sumana who was the discoverer of a relic and who conveyed it to the kings of Sachanalai, Sukhothai, and Chiang Mai in turn. Sumana's training and virtuous practice are noted in the text, and he is prominently presented as the one who brings together relic and royalty, yet he hardly seems to have exerted any control over the relic's movement. The relationship between the extraordinary powers of a member of the *saṅgha* and the ability to handle a relic so vividly described in Lankan stories is not obvious in the depiction of Sumana's behavior. He was its caretaker and its "legs," being directed to carry the relic to different places by its miracle performances, of which he displayed no evident foreknowledge.

The enshrinement of a relic or a statue in Chiang Mai is in fact depicted as a cooperative effort among multiple agencies, without the clear separation of roles presented in Lankan stories. Sumana's initial discovery of the relic in Sachanalai was prompted by a message sent to him by deities. In Chiang Mai, the location for the reliquary was identified by King Kuena, who had received advice from gods that his garden was the appropriate home for the relic. Further, Sumana and King Kuena together mounted a relic on the back of a royal elephant that they hoped would be guided by divinities to the relic's dwelling place. Despite the urging of the king and monk that the relic be established in a particularly beautiful spot, the elephant instead kept moving until it reached the relic's desired destination. Other Lanna relic stories present examples of parties other than the *saṅgha* discovering and handling relics. The Great Relic of Haripuñjaya was discovered by King Āditta beneath the royal privy. Lanna chronicles seem to urge that all devotees—monks, kings, and deities—should ensure that relics are installed in their proper places of establishment.

It is also interesting that in the Lankan story the relics demonstrated the miracle of double appearances, replicating the display of supernatural power performed by the Buddha of emitting flames from the upper part of his body and streams of water from the lower. This performance would suggest that the relic took on the form of a human body. The relic here apparently becomes, at least visually, a portrait of the Buddha.

One final observation about the Lankan relic stories is that the identification of the relic's site of enshrinement is not the climax of the narrative, as it is in Lanna stories. This may be illustrated by the *Thūpavaṃsa,* which includes a lengthy description of the construction and the elaborate decoration of the relic chamber of the Mahāthūpa. The chamber includes statues crafted from precious materials representing the bodhi tree and the Buddha, as well as sets of images of divinities depicted in attitudes of paying homage to the relic. There are statues representing all of the *jātaka* stories (accounts of the Buddha's past lives) and murals showing scenes from the Buddha's life story. Strong has aptly described this artistic scheme as creating a "biorama" of the Buddha. The *stūpa* was built before the relics were obtained. Strong has compared the postconstruction emplacement of the relic with the ritual of consecrating a Buddha statue, in which the image's eyes are "opened" by painting them in or peeling away a layer of wax covering them; the insertion of the relic in the *stūpa* is an act that makes the biorama "come alive."[28] The site became appropriate for the deposit of the relic only after the changes made to it. In the Lanna stories, relics go to a certain spot, where typically they are interred deep in the ground, and a monument is constructed afterwards.

Burmese Stories about Relics: Victory Ground, Monarchy, and Relics that Speak

The idea that place is especially important for relics also features in the Burmese/Mon tradition. The story of the origin of the Shwedagon, the *Chronicle of the Hair Relics,* is in fact the most common manuscript that the manuscript collection team of the École française d'Extrême-Orient found in Lanna monastery libraries as of 2007.[29] This may well reflect the historical connections between the Buddhist traditions of the Lanna people and the Burmese and Mon. Moreover, the Shwedagon features in a northern Thai custom, according to which Buddhists are supposed to visit one of twelve Buddhist pilgrimage sites according to their years of birth in the Lanna twelve-year, zodiac animal cycle (Thai: *naksat pi*). The site associated with the year of the horse is the Shwedagon.[30]

As noted previously, the story of the enshrinement of hair relics in the Shwedagon is an expansion of accounts of Trapuṣa and Bhallika found in earlier Pali texts. In his 1934 article "The Shwe Dagon Pagoda," Pe Maung Tin traced these earlier accounts as well as provided English translations of excerpts from several different versions of the Burmese/Mon telling.

Pe Maung Tin's English version of the story compiled from Mon accounts is very similar to the *Chronicle of the Hair Relics* in the plot if not in all of the details, indicating that it is plausible that the Lanna story was based on some Burmese/Mon version(s). The latter, like the *tamnan,* emphasize the protracted search for Mount Singuttara, with at least two of the chronicles—the *Slapat Waṅ Dhat Kyuik Ceti Lagun* and the *Slapat Rājāwaṅ Datow Smi Roṅ*—noting that it took the merchants as long as three years to find the place.[31] The *Slapat Waṅ Dhat Kyuik Ceti Lagun* also relates some of the later history of the shrine, remarking that in the time of the Third Buddhist Council two centuries after the Buddha's *parinibbāna,* the shrine had been neglected and become overwhelmed by forest growth. King Asoka then searched for and found it, had the forest cut away, and constructed a golden monument on the spot. Other kings tried to unearth the hair relics to carry them off, but were thwarted; during the attempted excavation by King Anawrahta of Bagan, a "terrific whirlwind storm" whipped up as the king's men were digging and scared off the soldiers and attendants, obliging the king to scrap the plan and instead plant umbrellas and a ruby on the shrine as offerings.[32]

Pe Maung Tin quoted Buddhaghosa's statement in the *Manorathapūranī* that "in whatever place the relics do not get worship and honour, they go, by the power of the Buddhas' will, to a place where they get worship and honour."[33] In view of this, we could perhaps say that to date, despite the apparent abandonment of the hair relics during the time of Asoka, there has been no other place where the relics would have received greater honor than at Singuttara, which is why they have not been moved. The ongoing history as related in the Mon chronicles expressed the rather firm entrenchment of the relics in their residence, highlighting the endurance of this particular unification of Buddha and place.

The Burmese Idea of "Victory Ground"

A particular Burmese conception of place that seems to resonate with that found in the Lanna chronicles is the idea of "victory ground" (Burmese: *aungmyei* or *zeyabhumi;* Pali: *jayabhūmi*) or "strong earth." This concept was applied by the Burmese to determining appropriate sites for royal capitals. As Tun Aung Chain has observed, "Myanmar dynastic lines are traced, not on the basis of family, but of the city, and the royal city assumes a significance of its own." A city was not a worthy capital merely because of its antiquity; indeed, a royal capital was periodically moved on the understanding that each city had a limited lifespan. Each royal court needed to ensure that its capital was situated on a victory ground, a place of triumph, both in the past and in the future, of various kinds. For instance, King Alaungpaya (r. 1752–1760) described the royal city of Shwebo as "a victory ground where all enemies are overcome," noting with satisfaction that there his small band of fighters beat a much larger Mon army. The king's advisers then traced a parallel between Shwebo and Kapilavatthu, the capital of the Buddha Gotama's Sakyan clan. Thus the royal city of Shwebo was positioned alongside the important sites of ancient Buddhist India. In a like way, King Bagyidaw (r. 1819–1837) compared the royal city of Inwa with the site of the Buddha's enlightenment under the bodhi tree and declared that Inwa was "a true victory ground, proper for the Three Gems to reside and suitable, both by land and water, for the habitation of men and beings."[34] The idea of "victory ground" joined together the king, the capital, and *sāsana.*

Certain royal cities were asserted to have been the subject of prophecy by the Buddha Gotama himself, a claim made by successive royal courts in Burma beginning in the late eleventh or early twelfth centuries, or perhaps earlier.[35] As François Tainturier has highlighted, royal assertion of the venerable Buddhist history of the sites of royal cities became even more pronounced during the Konbaung period (1752–1885). For each Konbaung capital, court officials constructed a lineage associating it with the lineage of Buddhas; for example, for the capital of Amarapura, which was founded in 1783, they expounded a genealogy of the city that listed the names of cities on the same spot during each of the periods of the five Buddhas of the present era.[36]

While a prophecy of the Buddha might seem to guarantee that a royal city was indeed a victory ground, the Burmese royal courts undertook various actions, guided by astrological considerations, to furnish and configure the royal city to ensure auspiciousness.[37] The Burmese royal courts aggregated representations of the Buddha in different forms within the city. Buddha relics and images, prominent monks, and copies of the *Tipiṭaka* (the Buddhist canon) were ceremonially transferred from the previous royal city to the new one; the objective was to materialize the Triple Gem of Buddhism in the new capital. The presence of these many powerful entities moreover buttressed the authority of the king over the realm.[38] Royal courts also performed ceremonies to support the identification of the city as the capital. This included the ritual deposit in the city of portions of earth from previous royal cities and other symbolically significant places. For example, during the establishment of Amarapura in the late eighteenth century, officials collected earth from four each of lakes, islands, and hills and from sixteen former royal palaces in sites across the Konbaung Empire. The officials collected earth on two occasions. The first set of earth was mixed into the ground at the site of the future royal palace of Amarapura and, to the accompaniment of incantations, plowed in seven different patterns. The second set of earth was deposited, with fragrances and food items, in the holes for the posts of the royal palace. As Tainturier has pointed out, this aggregation of earth from noteworthy places could have suggested the intentional association of the significant cities of Burmese history with the sixteen Mahājanapadā, or polities of ancient Buddhist India. Another round of earth gathering also asserted the importance of the Burmese royal foundation to Buddhism: for the establishment of the throne at the royal palace, earth from twelve places connected with the life of the Buddha Gotama in India was collected, mixed with "untainted earth" and deposited under the "lion throne" of the king.[39] This connected the site chosen by the king to the seat of the Buddha's triumph under the bodhi tree.[40]

In my view, the elaborate execution of the collection of earth and thorough plowing suggest that the particles of earth themselves were understood to have a certain power that enhanced the quality of the ground at the site. As Juliane Schober has noted, present-day Burmese pilgrims who visit Shwebo, a site still associated with the Konbaung dynasty, ascribe protective powers to the area's ground and collect small amounts of earth in bottles to bring home and set on their own altars. "Strength of the locale," Schober observes, "is believed to be a significant factor in the ability to hold and contain sacred objects within one's sphere of influence and power."[41] While the presence of the Buddha's relics augmented the eminence of king and city, it was also believed that in order for relics to be firmly settled in any particular place, that place had to be robust enough to sustain them.

It is notable that in the earth gathering ritual for the establishment of Amarapura, included among the sixteen former royal palaces from which earth was gathered was the royal palace at Chiang Mai, called Zinme by the Burmese and at that time still considered by them a Burmese domain.[42] Thus, the meaning that the Burmese attached to the ground of significant places may have been familiar to Lanna people.

In Lanna *tamnan* we can find usage of the Pali term for "victory ground," *jayabhūmi* (Thai: *chaiyaphum*). For instance, the *Chiang Mai Chronicle,* a history of Chiang Mai compiled in the early nineteenth century from existing texts, describes Mangrai's identification in 1292 of a site as a *jayabhūmi* and a fitting place for the construction of his capital, Chiang Mai. The area was a "victory ground" because a pair of hog deer, a mother and fawn, defeated a pack of wolves on the spot. This is similar to Alaungpaya's view of Shwebo as being a *jayabhūmi* because an against-the-odds triumph occurred there. There is no apparent reference to the earth gathering ritual in this account of Chiang Mai's founding, however.[43]

There may be references to ritual earth gathering in other Lanna manuscripts. In the *Chronicle of the Buddha Image Seated on the Earth* (*Tamnan Phra Phuttha Rup Chao Nang Din*), it is recounted that the Buddha instructed a layman called Khamdaeng to make a Buddha statue and also deputed a delegation consisting of Indra, a *nāga* king, two *ṛṣis* (holy men), and five *arahants* to "go to get clay [or earth; Thai: *din*] from Lanka Island to build the Buddha image."[44]

A similar understanding of earth may perhaps be detected in Lankan chronicles. Both the *Mahāvaṃsa* and the later *Thūpavaṃsa* contain detailed descriptions of the laying of the foundation of the Great Stūpa.[45] The bottom layer of the *stūpa*'s foundation consisted of crushed stone pounded into the earth, and on top of this was spread a layer of "butter clay," described as clay from the place (in the Himalayas) where the divine River Ganges dropped down to the earth, a place "where varieties of rice of spontaneous growth arise."[46] This "butter clay" was collected from that spot and brought to Lanka by *arahants*. In the *stūpa*'s foundation, several other substances were also layered over this clay, including brick, cement, cinnabar, and iron, as well as *marumba*, "a sort of (sweet-scented) earth or sand" that monks transported from the Himalayas.[47]

The concept of certain granules of dirt having power is also found in Indic sources. A Hindu idea holds that the soil is the body, or the residence, of the goddess as mother.[48] There is also a sense of place similar to that of Lanna in Tamil stories that recount the histories of particular Hindu shrines in the area of what is today southern India. This tradition of literature had its golden age in the sixteenth century, though oral forms may antedate the written by many centuries. The affinities between Lanna and Tamil accounts are multiple: the discovery of a particular shrine is depicted as a miraculous event; the narrative highlights the benefits that accrued to gods, humans, and other beings who worshipped at the shrine; local idiosyncrasies of the site are explained; and the shrine is glorified above all others.[49] Tamil accounts also reflect "the Tamil belief in a rooted, totally localized godhead. . . . The god is essentially immovable—even when he has been 'imported' into the shrine from somewhere else (often the prestigious north)."[50] Each account asserted that its shrine is the center of the universe, the single point on earth that directly connects with heaven and the lower realms, and it is the one place that survives the cosmic flood that periodically destroys the universe at the end of each cycle of creation.[51] The stories endow the sites with wider and more powerful significance by ascribing cosmological and cosmogonic dimensions to them. Although it is impossible to state precisely whether and how Indic ideas of place influenced Lanna culture, the commonalities in concepts and discursive tactics raise the question of a sharing of the idea of the link between divinity and place among Asian cultures.

The Glass Palace Chronicle: Relics and Rulers in Symbiosis

Earlier I noted the belief that if a relic stays in a certain place and does not leave, then that land is robust enough to hold it. At the same time, as Buddhaghosa's writings indicated, it was believed that relics quit those places where they did not receive sufficient veneration and moved to places where they would. Thus, the presence of relics in any particular spot could be directly linked to the character of the place, which must first be "strong," and second be tended by a specific set of devotees (especially rulers) responsible for the relic's veneration. The effects of these two factors on the settlement or removal of relics are observable in the *Glass Palace Chronicle.* Most of the relic accounts in the text concern the category of bodily relics of the Buddha, as do the Lanna relic chronicles.

A story from the *Glass Palace Chronicle* involving King Anawrahta reflects an orientation to situating relics on "strong" land. When Anawrahta invaded the city of Śrī Kṣetra (Thayekhittaya), he bore a hole into a monument and pulled out the Buddha's frontlet (forehead bone; Pali: *unhissa*) relic, which he transported back to his capital of Bagan. After consulting with the eminent monk Shin Arahan, Anawrahta mounted the relic on the back of a jewelled white elephant and made a resolution that the elephant should kneel in whatever place the relic wished to rest. The elephant was then allowed to wander freely and eventually dropped to its knees on a sandbank. Upon seeing the chosen site, the king "was sorry, for he had thought the religion would last five full millennia. His heart was ill content that the white elephant knelt not upon natural soil, but on shifting sand." However, Indra (Sakra), king of the gods, appeared in Anawrahta's dreams that night and assured him that the *sāsana* would indeed endure for five thousand years; and "Sakra strengthened the ground with solid rock, two hundred and forty thousand times thicker than before, and clamped it all around with iron plates." Anawrahta then erected the Shwezigon Pagoda on the spot; the frontlet relic performed miracles before its enshrinement.[52]

The attitudes of Anawrahta and Indra point to the broader purpose of enshrining Buddha relics. As their words make clear, the lifespan of the *sāsana* depended on the sandbank. It is because the relic must be enshrined in its chosen place that Indra was obligated to undertake his feat of engineering. That the ground in this case is said to be sand clearly illustrates the point that, for the Burmese, the very physical state of the ground was essential to the prosperity of what rested upon it. A relic enshrined in its dwelling place became the material representation of the *sāsana* itself.

Upon its enshrinement, the frontlet relic displayed its satisfaction by miraculously flying and emitting light. The relic also demonstrated the power of speech, announcing, "In days of yore this king was a

Pulali elephant, and during the three months of rains once ministered to me. Now also he hath exalted my religion. In time to come he shall be Lord like me!"[53] This declaration reflects the high degree of merit associated with the enshrinement of a relic. A ruler who was able to undertake such an act demonstrated that he was a person of great merit with whom the relic had agreed to depart from its former home. At the same time, the ruler earned enormous merit because of the enshrinement of the relic in its new site of establishment. The relationship between ruler and relic is a merit-fuelled symbiosis in which both agencies are rewarded by the act of enshrinement.

Several stories recounted in the *Glass Palace Chronicle* suggest that at various times devotees considered Buddha images to be equivalent to or interchangeable with other kinds of relics of the Buddha. Materially the statues and relics were sometimes one and the same; they could also be physically integrated to become as one: stories present images as being formed out of relics or as being containers or carriers of relics.

This sense of interchangeability or fungibility is reflected in the account of King Anawrahta's visit to the Tarop country of the kingdom of Gandhala (probably located in modern-day Yunnan, China),[54] where he sought to obtain a tooth relic. Anawrahta balanced a jewelled casket upon his head, but the tooth, which was flying about in the sky above, did not deign to land in the casket. The ever-helpful Indra intervened, and then "Sakra, knowing [Anawrahta] was heartbroken, and that he would prove a firm upholder of the religion, brought an emerald image and caused it to pass to and fro with the sacred tooth and descend from the sky, and rest within the jewelled casket on the king's head."[55] Thus the Buddha image was a replacement for the relic. The image's airborne duet with the tooth and its subsequent descent to the casket intended for the tooth reflect the sense of equivalency between the image and the relic.

Anawrahta's grandson, King Alaungsithu, also received Buddha images—a pair—from Indra. The story of these images, named Shinbyu and Shinhla, are recounted at length in the *Glass Palace Chronicle*. The story is summarized as follows.

At one time Alaungsithu made a journey to venerate a golden rose-apple tree beneath which Buddhas had sat. Arriving there he saw the seat of the Buddhas, a shiny rock-mat at the root of the tree. Following the suggestion of his advisers, Alaungsithu set his headdress upon it and vowed that if that rock-mat was indeed the Buddhas' seat, the headdress should be incinerated "like a fowl's feather." When the headdress was forthwith reduced to ash, the king celebrated with a great festival for seven months. Indra observed Alaungsithu's piety and decided to consecrate him as king. He presented him with a new title, royal regalia, and two Buddha images. One of the images was sculpted out of the rock-mat of the Buddhas and was named Shinbyu; the other was chiseled from the lower branch of the golden rose-apple tree and called Shinhla. Later, when Alaungsithu, together with the images, was travelling by sea, the ship was suddenly jolted, pitching the Shinbyu image overboard. A pair of Brahmani ducks flying by caught the Shinbyu with their wings, and the image cried out, "Alaungsithu, take me!" The king accepted and venerated it. He was then known as Alaungsithu;[56] in Burmese, *Alaung* means "future Buddha" and *sithu* is "victorious hero."[57]

This episode describes an interchange among Alaungsithu, Indra, the relics, and the images that illustrates the symbiotic interrelationship between patrons and Buddha relics. First, Alaungsithu's subordination to the Buddha was demonstrated by the miraculous burning up of his headdress when it was laid on the Buddhas' seat. The king's pious reaction, sponsoring a massive festival, then earned him a divinely bestowed royal consecration. He was also rewarded with statues carved from relics of things used by the Buddha: the rock-mat and the tree. The relics continued to be relics, but they were detached from their original situation and transformed into the shape of images that facilitated their interaction with Alaungsithu. This new role was signalled by the assignment of the names Shinbyu and Shinhla, which distinguished them from their origins as relics of items used by the Buddha. In turn, it was because Alaungsithu accepted responsibility for Shinbyu that he received his own new name.

The story of Alaungsithu and the images continues further. The *Glass Palace Chronicle* recounts that one day the king thought, "It were better for the benefit of all beings to set the images of the Lord, Shinbyu and Shinhla images, where the Lord is fain to dwell than to keep them in the palace and worship them." Setting them on a raft, he headed upcountry by water. Above Sagaing at Gyaukma the Shinbyu image announced, "Let me ever abide in this chasm!" Alaungsithu placed the image on the back of a white elephant that was released to bring the image to its preferred dwelling place. The elephant walked to a riverbank and knelt. Alaungsithu thought that this was not an appropriate spot on which to build a pagoda and said, "Let it ascend to a high place and kneel!" The elephant climbed to the top of the bank and lowered its knees, and there the king built a *gu* (hollow temple) to enshrine the Shinbyu and Shinhla images.[58]

As in other relic stories, a devoted king allowed Buddha representations to go to their place of enshrinement by setting them on the back of an unfettered elephant. However, in this story, Alaungsithu got the elephant to move from the chosen site to a new one, and apparently rather easily at that.

Alaungsithu's unusual prerogative in moving the images differentiates him from other patrons featured in stories about relics and images who clearly did not have a choice in the location of the places of enshrinement. It may be that Alaungsithu's influence arose from the nature of his personal relationship with the pair of Buddha images. The two statues were gifted to him through divine intervention; it was Alaungsithu's strong piety that caused Indra to make and present them to the king. This is unlike a more typical depiction of image or relic acquisition in which a monarch initiated the making of a Buddha image, embarked on a journey, or undertook a war in order to obtain a Buddha representation. The Shinbyu and Shinhla images were created in order that Buddha agency in the shape of the transformed relics could become the recipient of Alaungsithu's agency.

An interesting aspect of relic stories in the *Glass Palace Chronicle* is the portrayal of relics appearing and behaving in humanlike ways. The accounts of relics in Lanna do not share this motif. In Burmese stories relics speak, as did the frontlet relic to Anawrahta. They could look like the Buddha himself: during a visit by Anawrahta to Lanka, "the holy tooth adorned itself with the thirty-two greater and eighty lesser signs and the six rays of noble men, and rose all-glorious with grace transcendent shouldering all the eight priestly requisites, and abode passing to and fro in the sky."[59] Three other accounts in the *Glass Palace Chronicle* describe relics taking on a similar anthropomorphic appearance.[60] The relic's ostensible form and appearance as a tooth has been replaced by a vision of it as the entire, iconographically complete body of the Buddha. The fact that the frame for the relic is visual may reflect exactly how compelling the practice of *darśana* was for devotees. The relics, transformed into statues, or encased within them, could enable *darśana*. The significance of visual imagery may suggest that at least at the time these stories were written, Buddha images were seen as no less directly mediating the Buddha's presence than relics, and perhaps even more so. This draws into question a typical scholarly assumption that images are inferior to relics as presences of the Buddha.

Historical Contexts of Burmese, Lankan, and Lanna Relic Chronicles

The sharing of themes and motifs in the Lanna chronicles with the other traditions seems to well reflect Peter Skilling's observation that in the early and premodern eras, texts arose within "cultural conversation" that was "multi-directional and multi-dimensional" between Tais and other people across Asia. Although there are Tai texts that are not known in the literature of other Theravādin areas, there was a complex Asian "intertextuality."[61] Justin T. McDaniel has characterized the culture of Lanna monastic manuscript production and consumption as forming "interpretive communities and reading cultures" that arose within "a loose network of open campuses" across the Tai-speaking region.[62] This chapter's study of relic stories in Burmese, Lankan, and Lanna traditions, though limited in scope, suggests this interplay of common regional themes and particular local interests in texts. The varying structures and themes of relic stories also reflect the different cultural and historical contexts in which they were written and distributed.

Trainor has proposed that in Lanka the focus on the social hierarchy of relic handling may have arisen from concerns on the part of the local *saṅgha,* especially the Mahāvihāra monastics who were active composers of chronicles. The chronicles helped to assert the Mahāvihārins' authority by emphasizing their link with the Buddha's first followers, a connection they claimed was evidenced by their adherence to the monastic code of discipline as well as by the presence of the Buddha's relics.[63]

Regarding Burmese texts, it is notable that the *Glass Palace Chronicle* was written in a period of intense political stress. King Bagyidaw ordered the composition in 1829, about five years after his kingdom's defeat by the British Indian Army in the First Anglo-Burmese War. This humiliating loss resulted in the Royal Court of Ava being forced to cede to British India the provinces of Arakan, Manipur, and Tennasserim; accept the exchange of diplomatic representatives; and pay an indemnity to the British of ten million rupees or one million pounds sterling.[64] Of this situation the historian Thant Myint-U has noted, "Defeat had made the Court of Ava anxious for the future of the kingdom. . . . Their home was the centre of an expanding empire, and their king a universal monarch, a *chakravati* over many subject peoples. . . . The defeat, the annexations and the indemnity, the sudden awareness of their inferiority in science and technology, threw the Burmese ruling class into confusion. One of their first responses was to write a new book of history, the *Hmannan Raza-windaw-gyi*, 'The Glass Palace Chronicle.'" Among other things, this chronicle for the first time delineated direct links between Bagyidaw's "somewhat upstart" Konbaung dynasty and the prestigious lineages of the kings of Bagan and of the Sakyas, the family of the Buddha Gotama.[65] The dissemination of stories about relics in Burma emphasized the Court of Ava's importance in a wider and venerable world of Buddhism. The presence of relics also represented a continuity through Burmese history, confirming the power and righteousness of monarchs and, significantly for the Burmese, of their capital cities. Because the text of the *Glass Palace Chronicle* was compiled by reviewing the eighteenth-century *Great Chronicle* and comparing it to other manuscripts and inscriptions, it seems plausible that this theme of interrelationship in relic stories existed previously in Burmese writings and that it was emphasized or adapted in the writing of Bagyidaw's chronicle in 1829 because it could serve well the objectives of the Burmese kingdom at that historical moment.

For the Lanna chronicles, the historical circumstances of composition are less well-documented than for Lankan and Burmese examples, and I have estimated for each chronicle when it might have been initially written. Perhaps it might be observed generally that the repetition of motifs and themes in the chronicles is neither a simple result of copying nor merely a reflection of Buddhist respect for tradition. After all, as we have found, the Lankan mode of relic story as model of societal hierarchy was not imitated in Lanna, even if Lankan monastic orders had increasing influence and numbers of adherents there, especially during the fifteenth century.

The spread of particular local motifs and themes reflects the fact that these modes of understanding and presenting knowledge were accepted and believed by Lanna people; had audiences rejected them, they would not have been repeated. We might then see the Burmese/Mon–originated *Chronicle of the Hair Relics* as having become popular because Lanna audiences appreciated the themes of the Shwedagon story, which had an affinity with their own relic stories. The account may also have stirred social memory of the Mon heritage of

Haripuñjaya. The later *Chronicle of the Buddha Image Lying on a Mango-Tree Log* of Kawila's time may demonstrate the enduring acceptance of the motifs and themes of the earlier chronicles in Lanna over hundreds of years.

These stories may then suggest how Buddhism was adopted by Lanna people. As we have seen, the interment of Buddha relics may have been a means to establish the legitimacy of the Buddha's claim to the top of the hierarchy of deities and in a parallel way the claim of Lanna kings to superiority over local polities. The Buddha was incorporated into the system of territorial jurisdiction of local divinities. This is a phenomenon that John Clifford Holt, drawing on the ideas of Paul Mus, has proposed was integral to the adoption of Buddhism in the culture of the Lao people. Holt has proposed that the most famous Lao Buddha image, the sixteenth-century Phra Bang, stood for the presence of the Buddha and was at the same time positioned as a pivot of political power analogous to the spirits of the polity.[66] The Phra Bang's association with Lao kingship and role as a palladium may be related conceptually to Lanna presentations of powerful Buddha statues, linked perhaps to cultural exchange with Lanna that intensified in the sixteenth century.

For much of its history, Lanna was not characterized by strong political centralization, even during its periods of expansion. The orientation to local interests was deeply held. For instance, during the period of Burmese suzerainty, each polity of Lanna acted on its own, fighting with the Burmese and with other Lanna territories. In the last hundred years of Burmese suzerainty, Burma's policy was to transfer officials frequently to keep them from building up too much personal power.[67] The chronicles' emphasis on the significance of specific places could have served to demonstrate how each site was constantly important and deserving of worship regardless of which parties wielded local political power at any particular moment. The sites are presented as having an innate significance apart from distant, fluctuating, and discontinuous lineages of political interests. The chronicles were meant to educate and spur patrons, existing and new, to venerate particular monuments. The manuscripts refer to this edifying function.[68] For instance, the *Chronicle of the Relic of Doi Tung* (*Tamnan Phra That Doi Tung*) may have been written, as Hans Penth suggested, to deliver information about the reliquary to a king. Penth estimated that the *tamnan* was composed between 1631 and 1812.[69] Given that for nearly all of that period the Burmese ruled Lanna, the ruler may have been a Burmese recently appointed to the post who was receiving a report about local history.

At the same time, glorification of local places would help attract donations and pilgrims, inspire local rulers to rule justly, and encourage inhabitants to follow the Buddhist precepts and not abandon the area. The various stories seem to have a competitive dimension, with each town trying to claim a more prestigious heritage than other towns. The production of what Donald K. Swearer has termed a "*buddhadesa*" (Buddha-land) probably arose just as much from competitive efforts as from concerted ones. Regarding the Tamil temple myths mentioned earlier, which I noted share several commonalities with the Lanna examples, Richard H. Davis suggests that the Tamil accounts proliferated in the sixteenth century due to a situation of disruption, and the stories were written to assert a sense of stability. Thus, for instance, the stories positioned the sites in mythic time, separating them from the ordinary disjunctures of everyday history.[70] One could speculate that some destabilizing event, such as a threat of war or change in political power, may have been the impetus at certain times for promoting particular shrines in Lanna. Relics and images may be framed and reframed by stories that devotees tell about them, enabling their integration into the histories and aspirations of their communities.

Chapter Six

Buddha Images as Objects of Donation

Intention, Wishes, and Economic Value in Inscriptions on the Bases of Images

This chapter turns to look at another type of text related to Buddha images: inscriptions cast or carved on the statues' bases. In the early 1970s, Hans Penth, the pioneering researcher of Lanna, began paying calls on the abbots of dozens of monasteries in Chiang Mai, his objective being to conduct a survey of all of the Buddha images bearing inscriptions in monasteries in the center of Lanna's capital. Penth and his assistants meticulously took photos and transcribed the often worn and lacquer-covered inscriptions on hundreds of wooden, metal, and cement statues. In 1976 he published the data in a Thai-language catalogue, *Khamcharuek thi Than Phra Phuttha Rup nai Nakhon Chiang Mai* (*Inscriptions on the Bases of Buddha Images in Chiang Mai*).

Penth's extraordinary work provides a rare and valuable record of images made from the fifteenth to the twentieth centuries in an area that is home to some of Chiang Mai's oldest and most prominent monasteries, including Wat Chedi Luang, Wat Chiang Man, and Wat Phra Sing. The inscriptions reveal the contributions of hundreds of donors, including kings, nobles, monks, and commoners. Alongside the *tamnan* (chronicles), they provide insight into the relationship of devotees to Buddha images.

Scholars have tended to discuss the data in a generalized fashion or to single out individual examples of inscriptions from Penth's catalogue to support particular research endeavors.[1] As far as I am aware, a detailed analysis of this treasury of information as a whole has never previously been undertaken. What do the inscriptions tell us about why people donated Buddha images? In what follows, we will consider various aspects of the inscriptions and the statues, including the donors' inscribed wishes; the types of donors, and the dating, materials, and iconography of the statues. As we shall see, Buddha images were often the result of collaboration between devotees, for whom a statue materialized a sociokarmic grouping and shared hopes and wishes. The inscriptions also reflect the importance of Buddha statues for the prosperity of Buddhism, positioning the images and their worshippers in the cosmic time and space of the *sāsana* (Buddhist thought and practice) at the time of their consecration. At the same time, the inscriptions also show how worshippers appreciated the materials and process of making images, underlining Buddha statues' condition as both sacred and as materials of commercial value in society beyond the monastery.

An Overview of the Inscriptions

Penth's survey covered thirty-nine monasteries in two *tambon* (subdistricts), Phra Sing and Si Phum. In these two *tambon* there was only one monastery, Wat Lam Chang, that declined to participate. In all, Penth and his team discovered 1,200 images, of which 350 bore inscriptions. Some wooden images were so decayed that their inscriptions were illegible, reducing the data set to 312 images. Of these, 303 are images of the Buddha, eight are images of disciples, and one is of a *paccekabuddha,* an enlightened being who does not pass on teachings. Among the total of 312, Penth selected eighty-five images for which he translated to central Thai the full text of the inscriptions. Penth explained that he selected these eighty-five because they are images that (1) are from the oldest period up until the Burmese takeover of Chiang Mai in 1558; (2) were made during the ten years following the end of Burmese suzerainty in 1774; or (3) have an "odd" appearance or an "interesting" inscription.[2] For the other 227 images, he did not provide the texts of the inscriptions, but does supply the name of the monastery (Thai: *wat*) in which the image was found; the year of inscription; the material, height, and posture of the image; the languages and scripts of the inscription; and a list of personal names cited in the inscription.

The inscriptions were typically made on the bases when the images were initially created. Between 1450 and 1550, a format for inscriptions came into common use that has been followed to the present day. First, the year of the production or repair of the statue is given, and then the names or positions of the donors, of which there are often more than one. This is followed by an explanation of why the donors sponsored the image and their wish or resolution regarding the benefit resulting from the gift. The inscription may include some or all of these items, and sometimes additional text.[3] The language is usually Tai Yuan, with a few words of Pali, in Tham script. The inscriptions vary in length, from a single word or number to dozens of lines of text wrapping around the surface of the base. Typically the year, which at times is the only information inscribed, is rendered according to the Cūlasakarāja (Thai: Chulasakarat) era, a calendar commonly used by Burmese, Thai, and other cultures from the thirteenth to nineteenth centuries. This era began March 22, 638.[4] Thus, to convert years in the Cūlasakarāja era (CS) to the Christian era (CE), one adds 638 to the CS figure, though it must be kept in mind that the final months of the CS year belong to the next CE year.

A typical inscription is that of Image No. 24, a one-meter-high seated Buddha image cast of bronze, topped by a wooden *rasmi* (flame finial), found at Wat Chai Phra Kiet:

> [Chula]sakarat 953 [1591 CE], year *ruang mao,* month 8, 5th night of the waxing moon; [according to the calculation method of the] Mon, day 6 [Friday]; [according to the calculation method of the] Thai, day *kat sai,* hour *klong ngai* [7:30–9:00 am], this Buddha image was cast. Chao Hua Muen Luang Dap Ruea Sai and his wife, father, mother, and children live in a house in front of Wat Chai Pha Kien [*sic*] and together built [this Buddha image] to be an object of homage for all humans and gods for five thousand *vassas* [rainy seasons].

The donors are a nobleman named by his official title and the members of his family, who are neighbors of the monastery. The objective of their donation is a common one, to create a Buddha image to support the *sāsana* for the duration of its five-thousand-year life. The image is a suitable gift to sustain the religion; worshipping the Buddha enables devotees to earn merit and to make spiritual progress by focusing their minds on the Buddha, the ideal model.[5]

The date of the inscription corresponds to April 26, 1591.[6] Like other Buddhist ritual activities, the creation of an image is timed to occur at a moment determined to be auspicious through calculations by an expert in astrology. The year, month, day, and hour are then inscribed on the image, according to the northern Thai calendar; the equivalent timing in the Mon and Khmer calendars may also be recorded.[7] Some inscriptions are also accompanied by a circular diagram called a *duang chata,* which indicates the positions of the sun, moon, and planets in the signs of the zodiac. Recording of the time in multiple formats memorializes the donation and endows it with a cosmic significance. Moreover, as the calendrical expert J. C. Eade has suggested, it may give the inscription a legal or authoritative cast.[8]

Dating the Images

The oldest image bearing a date in Penth's data set is Image No. 1, inscribed 827 CS (1465 CE), a 176-centimeter-high bronze standing Buddha image at Wat Chiang Man (figs. 6.1 and 6.2). The newest dated image is Image No. 246, made in 1971, a seated bronze Buddha image 51 centimeters in height at Wat Muen Ngoen Kong. There

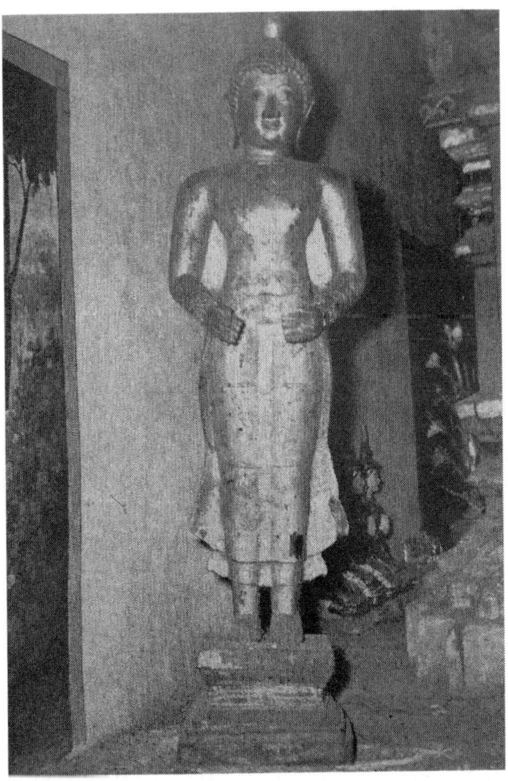

Fig. 6.1. Penth Image No. 1.

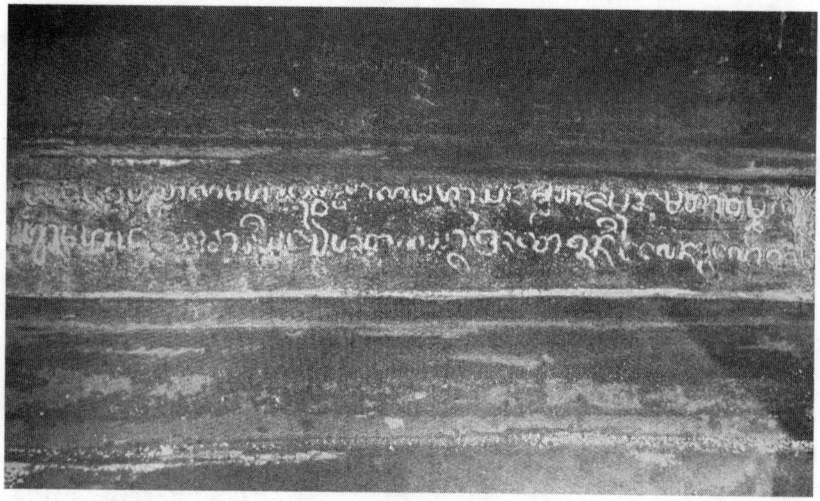

Fig. 6.2. Tai Yuan inscription on base of Penth Image No. 1.

are 248 images bearing a date (79 percent of the total 312) and sixty-four having no date (21 percent).

Notably, Penth and his team did not find any statues with an inscribed date during the period 1592–1782. Penth suggested that during that time few Buddha images were made because of the many battles with the Burmese.[9] Many statues were probably also destroyed or broken. Evidence of damage to statues in times of conflict is provided by the inscription for Image No. 22, a 241-centimeter-high bronze image named Phra Chao Mueangrai, after Mangrai, the founder of the Lanna dynasty. The large statue was cast jointly by the queen of Chiang Mai and the general of the occupying Burmese Army in 1566, in the early period of Burmese rule of Lanna, and commemorated with relatively lengthy inscriptions, one in Burmese and another in Tai Yuan. The latter inscription recounts that the lord general invited the queen "to jointly make merit, along with rulers, generals, ministers, monks and citizens by collecting Buddha images that were broken in turmoil to not allow their further ruin and to [melt and recast] them into a complete Buddha image as they had been originally." The ravages of battle scarred the city of Chiang Mai on multiple occasions over subsequent periods—most severely in 1763, when the Burmese Army demolished Chiang Mai and deported the entire population, and in 1776, when the Burmese again besieged the city, leading to its abandonment until 1796, when King Kawila revived the city as his capital. Nevertheless, it is hard to imagine a period of nearly two centuries in which Chiang Mai devotees produced almost no images. It seems quite possible that Buddha images were created in Chiang Mai but then destroyed, stolen, or moved to safety during the periods when the city was in disorder or abandoned.

Twenty-four images were produced in Lanna before 1774, the end of Burmese suzerainty, and survived at least to the time of Penth's survey. All are made of bronze, a material whose durability probably contributed to their survival. Four of the twenty-four images are inscribed with dates in the early period of Burmese suzerainty over Lanna (Nos. 21–24, dated 1563, 1566, 1590, and 1591, respectively). Beginning in 1774, King Kawila and other Lanna leaders pledged their loyalty to Siam and with Siam's support ejected the Burmese from Lanna. For the last two decades of the 1700s, there are four images (1 percent of the total) bearing a date (including the famous Phra Sila Buddha image, discussed further below); for the 1800s, 128 (41 percent), and for the 1900s, ninety-two (29 percent).

The chronological distribution of the images found by Penth reflects factors including chance, the hardiness of each image's material, and the continuity of worship of each image. The large number of images surviving from the nineteenth century may also perhaps reflect the improving economic and political situation of Chiang Mai following the rebuilding efforts by the Chao Chet Ton dynasty of Kawila in the early nineteenth century and the more peaceful state of the city since then.

The date distribution of the images in the data set contrasts sharply with the chronological scope of art historical research on northern Thailand, which has tended to focus on the period of the Mangrai dynasty of the fourteenth to sixteenth centuries. That era, regarded as the "classical" period of Lanna art, has benefited from a scholarly treatment that later periods are still waiting to receive. For example, Santi Leksukhum's *Sinlapa Phak Nuea [Art of the North]: Hariphunchai—Lanna* (1995), though illuminating and well-researched, does not discuss Lanna Buddha images after the sixteenth century. Carol Stratton's *Buddhist Sculpture of Northern Thailand* (2004), an otherwise extremely valuable encyclopedia of its subject, dedicates only fifteen pages to sixteenth- to twentieth-century Lanna Buddha images in contrast to 153 pages to those of the fourteenth to sixteenth centuries.[10] Likewise, scholarly treatment of the art of Thailand generally has until recently tended to underrepresent the art of the Ratanakosin period (1782 to the present). Penth's Chiang Mai catalogue reminds us that sculpture currently in monasteries consists mostly of more recent statues that may still be worthy of historical interest. Given that a number of these images are made from relatively vulnerable materials such as wood, research on these pieces should not be delayed for too long.[11]

Donor Wishes (Resolutions): Personal Intentions, Aspirations, and Merit

"Sacred sites," Donald Stadtner has observed, "offer a unique glimpse into the most cherished aspirations of a people."[12] Inscribing their images, Chiang Mai donors often expressed the impacts they hoped their gifts would have on themselves and others. Such wishes were meant to testify to the donors' virtuous intentions, thereby ensuring that the gifts would create merit. Over centuries, certain wishes, and the phrases used to express them, became conventional.[13]

The declaration of wishes reflects the hope, if not the belief, that the donors could determine the results of their deeds. Perhaps the making of the declaration in itself was seen as producing the desired result. As we saw in chapter 3, the traditional belief in the power of the truth meant that a linguistic expression could be a magical device, deployed to protect oneself and one's donation from meddling by future generations. In the inscriptions on the bases of the images, one may sense that the announcement of the donation of the image could potentially have been seen as the truth statement that magically empowered the donor's wish.

Magical force may also have been summoned through other kinds of language. As Penth observed, the oldest images he discovered were inscribed with the "Sihing Buddha image *gāthā*," a Pali phrase that is an expression of the Four Noble Truths. The phrase is not inscribed in full, but in abbreviated form on seven images, all of which seem to be in the robust-bodied Sihing or "lion" style and to date to the fifteenth to early sixteenth centuries.[14] This *gāthā* was mentioned in chapter 2 as having possible associations with perceived magical protective powers of the Sihing Buddha image. The *gāthā* may have been seen as potent because it reiterates the powerful words of the teaching of the Buddha. Donors may have aimed to activate its protective strength to support the durability of the Buddha *sāsana*.

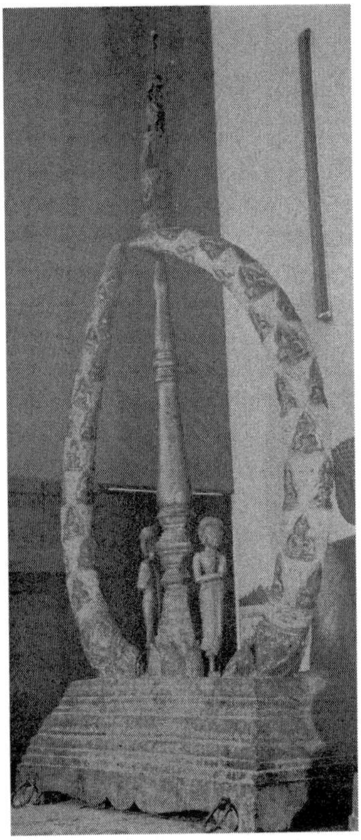

Fig. 6.3. Penth Image No. 252.

The wish to support the *sāsana* is the most typical aim expressed by donors in the data set. The inscription for Image No. 24, cited above, noted that the donors created the image "to be an object of homage for all humans and gods for five thousand *vassas*." Such a wish appears in thirteen inscriptions of the eighty-five for which Penth provides the full text, the earliest dating from 1470.[15] Later the similar wish that the donation will "support the *sāsana*" (for five thousand *vassas*) appeared, a phrasing used on the bases of twenty-six images, all from 1783 and later.[16] As in the *tamnan*, the inscriptions reflect the understanding that making and repairing Buddha statues is an important means to support the *sāsana* against forces of deterioration over the course of its lifespan.

One of the more visually striking sculptures catalogued by Penth is Image No. 252, found at Wat Chedi Luang; it consists of two elephant tusks that are mounted side by side on a single base, the points curving towards one another (fig. 6.3). The tusks are sculpted with many reliefs of seated Buddha images with a plant motif filling the interstices. Installed on the base between the tusks is a long, thin *stūpa* surmounted by a five-tiered umbrella. Two small statues of disciples or worshippers each stands with his back to the *stūpa* and facing a tusk with hands raised, palms together in veneration. The undated inscription is relatively long:

> The lords of great faith, with Mae Chao Kham Phaen as the leader, and Chao Nai Noi Maha Phrom Rachorot and Chao Nai Nan Maha Thep Rachabut, were the people, with chief wives, royal sons and daughters, grandsons and granddaughters, in whom arose a great faith [when] they saw the elephant, the Conqueror of Mueang Ma [Thai: Phu Prab Mueang Ma], the auspicious elephant of the country, who died and went to the next world. They thus together had the idea to carve Buddha images on the tusks of the elephant in order to support the *sāsana* of the Fully Enlightened Lord Buddha.
>
> We request [that the merit arising from the carving of the Buddha images] is a benefit that sticks to us going forward and is a means to support [us and] increase happiness and prosperity (?) [for all of us] . . . in this life and the next until we attain *nibbāna* [nirvana].
>
> We request to have success in obtaining all of our needs and wishes with the power of the good merit [from the making of the Buddha sculpture] and therefore request to dedicate [the good deed] to our father, Lord of Life [the king] who has died and gone to heaven above in order to increase the merit that he accumulated already. We request that the field of merit increase the happiness [of the father, Lord of Life] in heaven above even more than before.

This inscription reflects the intertwining of past, present, and future that characterizes many donor inscriptions. Peter Skilling has observed that inscriptions position the present existences of donors within the five-thousand-year Buddhist era, with donors looking back in time to the Buddha Gotama and to their ancestors, and forward in time to rebirths in which they may encounter the next Buddha, Maitreya, and attain *nibbāna*.[17] Although Skilling was referring to central Thai inscriptions of the Ratanakosin era, the description is also applicable to the Lanna inscriptions of the Penth data set. Each Buddha image materializes a kind of meritorious knot in time in which strands extending through present, past, and future lives of Buddha, patrons, craftsmen, and monks are twisted and bound together to form a single, unique node in the texture of the Buddhist era.

This inscription also provides an example of the tradition of transferring merit to deceased persons to increase their store of merit for an improved rebirth. Donors mentioned such wishes in ten out of the 312 inscriptions, all from the eighteenth century and later.[18] The merit is believed to bring joy to the deceased, as well as a series of improvements in mental state that bode well for the deceased's next rebirth. In receiving such donations, monks position themselves as intermediaries between the living donors and the deceased relatives they wish to sustain. Donors may have been encouraged by sermons that drew on a canonical text, the *Petavatthu*, a volume of stories of deceased persons living miserably as ghosts who are relieved only after living people donate to the monkhood in their names.[19]

A common wish declared on the above inscription, and on nineteen others, is to achieve *nibbāna*. The wish is expressed as an aspiration for either the donor's own *nibbāna* or for all beings' *nibbāna*. Often the wish takes the form of the Pali phrase *nibbāna paccayo hotu*, "may this be a condition for me (or us) to reach *nibbāna*." As donors looked ahead to *nibbāna*, they assumed that it could be reached only after many lifetimes; some therefore also communicated the hope to experience happiness in their next rebirths until the ultimate goal of *nibbāna* was achieved. For example, the inscription of Image No. 50, a 56-centimeter-high standing Buddha carved from sandalwood at Wat Dok Kham, reads,

> Chulasakarat 1176 [1814 CE], year of the dog [according to the] calculation method of Cambodia; in Thai language, year *kap set*, month *kattika*, full moon night; [according to the calculation method of the] Mon, Friday; [according to the calculation method of the] Thai, day *ka mao*, the person of faith Saen Mueang Ma was the one who originated the thought to build this Buddha image made with sandalwood that is very fragrant, together with his beloved wife, son, daughter, father, mother, and siblings, all of them, in order for it to be an object of worship and homage for humans and gods.
>
> Through the power of this merit the servant [i.e., the donor] would like to obtain whatever he thinks of and requests successful results according to his needs and wishes in all types of things. The servant requests the 3 levels of happiness, with *nibbāna* as the highest. *Nibbāna*

paccayo hotu. [The donor wishes that the future] will be like this. Do not allow this to fail.

Wishes for one's future rebirths could also be more detailed. Image No. 254 is one of Chiang Mai's most famous Buddha images, the Phra Sila, a high-relief sculpture 58 centimeters in height depicting the Buddha, accompanied by his disciple Ānanda, subduing the fierce Nālāgiri elephant sent to attack him (fig. 6.4). The image is presently enshrined at Wat Chiang Man. The style of the sculpture resembles that of images from Pāla India in about the tenth century.[20] Around the Buddha is inscribed in tenth-century north Indian script the restatement of the Four Noble Truths beginning *ye dhammā,* known as the "Buddhist credo."[21] As mentioned in chapter 2, a *tamnan* bearing a date of 1785 recounts Phra Sila's history, beginning with its production by King Ajātasattu in Magadha in ancient India and going on to describe its subsequent journey to Lanka and then to

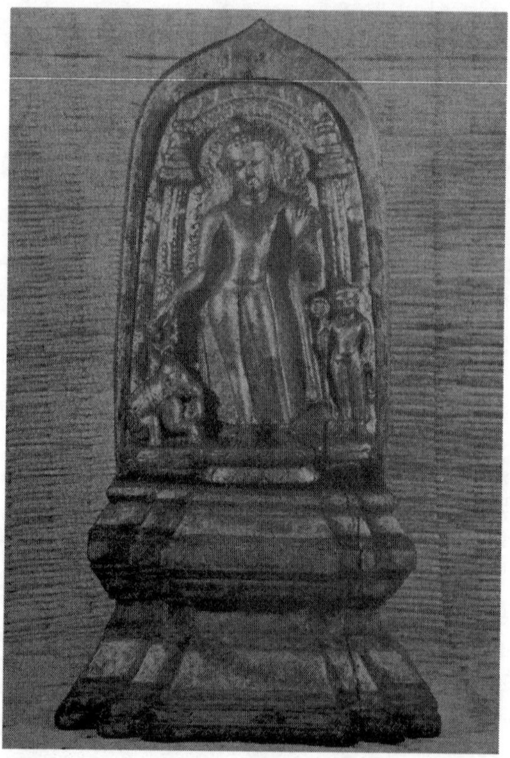

Fig. 6.4. Phra Sila image (Penth Image No. 254).

various towns in northern Thailand, where it came to be established in the royal palace in Chiang Mai in the reign of King Tilok in the late fifteenth century.[22] Aside from this chronicle, no other evidence about how the statue came to Thailand is known. Its fame seems to have surged in the late eighteenth century. Five years after the *tamnan*'s composition, King Kawila, at the head of his family, nobles, and the populace, sponsored a new base and backing for the statue and the application of a golden coating "in order to establish it as a site of worship, worthy of homage for gods and humans." In his inscription, Kawila and his family begin their wishes with the hope that the good deed will bring them the three levels of happiness, with *nibbāna* as the highest level, and then they describe the lifestyles they would like to experience before they attain *nibbāna:*

> [M]ay we be born in a fortunate family of rulers, conquering the whole of Jambudvīpa, and the 4 continents having 2,000 smaller continents surrounding them, and be endowed with all divine aspects, and may we have an outstanding father and mother, entourage, prestige, and wealth. And [we request] fulfillment for all of our wishes, in every birth, indeed.
>
> May the good merit go to paternal grandparents and to Khruba Chao Chuan, paternal grandfather called Surarachai, paternal grandmother called Nang Phimpha, maternal grandfather [called] Noi Wannarot, maternal grandmother called Nang Kon, wife [or wives] called Nang Yot Ruean, Nang Sing, Nang Sutham, 2 children, [and to] relatives on father's and mother's sides, including Ao [Uncle] Khampha, Ao Pho Ruean, Nang Sang, Nang Kham, Nang Kom, Lung [Uncle] Ay, Lung Toe Khwan Moi, Noi Ten, and wives [and] sons [?], indeed.
>
> Furthermore, [we request this merit] to be spread to all animals . . . which [we] have killed, hit, or worked, such as elephants, horses, cows, and water buffalo, for example, and [whom] should receive this royal good deed in order to remove their bad deeds. From this day going forward, all beings should enjoin each other to rejoice, indeed.[23]

Kawila's ambitions for future existences as a powerful and wealthy ruler were befitting a person of his position. The extensive list of those to whom merit should be transferred also reflects the large circle of relations and wealth of assets within the king's purview. Such wishes also contradict popular modern-day visions, particularly in the West, of Buddhism as an antimaterialistic, ascetic, and power-eschewing tradition. Kawila's aspirations to power and wealth resonate with the worldly supremacy of Asoka, the model Buddhist wheel-turning monarch of Jambudvīpa, not to mention the sovereigns and fabulously wealthy persons who patronized the Buddha during his lifetime. Kawila was at this time also establishing himself as the rightful heir to the prestige and power of the old Mangrai dynasty. He restored the Mangrai capital of Chiang Mai, rebuilding its sacred monasteries, monuments, moats, and walls, and established his royal palace in the center of city. He commanded that his coronation be conducted according to Mangrai era rites and claimed the right to wield the regalia of the Mangrai kings.[24] By linking himself to Phra Sila, a powerful Buddha statue, Kawila also followed in the footsteps of the Mangrai kings who had associated themselves with the Emerald Buddha, the Sihing Buddha, and other prestigious images.

Devotees were also mindful that after the end of Gotama's *sāsana* there would follow the next Buddha, Maitreya (Pali: Metteyya), whose enlightenment would inaugurate another Buddhist era. Because of the belief that one could make progress towards *nibbāna* only during a period when a Buddha is living in the world, devotees made preparations to ensure their spiritual advancement during Maitreya's dispensation. If one were to become a member of the entourage of the future Buddha, then one would be assured of receiving guidance towards spiritual progress and attaining *nibbāna.* The wish to be reborn as a disciple of the future Buddha Maitreya is mentioned in four inscriptions, No. 6 (1482–1483), No. 22 (1566), No. 23 (1590), and No. 253 (undated). The inscription on the base of Image No. 253, a 63-centimeter-high bronze seated Buddha image produced by a pair of unnamed donors, notes their wishes to become principal disciples (of Maitreya) as Sāriputta and Moggallāna were for the Buddha Gotama. Similarly, Image No. 23 (1590), a bronze seated Buddha image 114 centimeters high and sponsored by a high-ranking nobleman, Phraya Luang Chao Saen Kham (or Saeng Kham), notes his wishes that in a future life he "be ordained in the order of Phra Arya Metteyya [and] be an *arahant* like Phra Mahāsāriputta and Phra Mahāmoggallāna, whichever of these."

In their inscriptions, some donors noted that they were inspired by various events to create Buddha images. The sponsor of Image No. 89 (1856), a 30-centimeter-long wooden reclining figure, remarks in the inscription that the image is a Phra Chao Chata, a type of Buddha made to commemorate a certain occasion, such as a birthday, or to extend one's life or fulfill a vow.[25] Other donors created sets of small Buddha images or votive sealings to mark birthdays. For example, Image No. 236 (1936) consists of forty-nine small images set in a frame at Wat Thung Yu. An inscription declares,

> Chao Noi Thepwongphok made the silver Buddha images [in a quantity] matching his age [i.e., fifty-nine] and one more image to total 60 images. Phra Aphaisaratha of Wat Thung Yu together with disciples supported and helped to arrange the casting as well as prepared the place [in which the Buddha images were to be installed] in order to support the Buddha *sāsana* and in order [for the images] to be a site of homage and worship for people and gods.

The inscription is unusual in referring to the measures undertaken by monks, whose roles in support of a donation are usually not described in the typically donor-focused inscriptions.

A fascinating example of an image made on the occasion of a life event is Image No. 21, a 126-centimeter-high standing Buddha in bronze dedicated in 1563 and discovered by Penth at Wat Muen Tum. The donor inscribed his last will and testament on the base. Nalang Suthon Khawin, an official or nobleman, offered his three-roomed house to the Buddha statue and ordered that

> when I die, my wife should live in the house in my place and offer rice to the Buddha image every seven days and offer food to the abbot every fifteen days. When my wife has died, have my younger brother named Khamson and my nephew [or grandson] Sunthon take care of [the Buddha image and] the abbot just as my wife did. Do not allow my sons to get mixed up with my house at all. [If] they do not listen [and] come [to live] in my house again, have them ruined.

Perhaps, by inscribing his will onto the base of the image, Nalang Suthon Khawin aimed to reinforce the authority of his words by linking them to a Buddha image that would be enshrined at the monastery. If only we could ask his sons if this acted as a deterrent to contravention of the will.

Devotees also donated Buddha images to monasteries to inaugurate newly built halls. For example, Image No. 209, a 130-centimeter-high bronze statue of the Buddha holding his alms bowl, was dedicated as part of a merit-making occasion to commemorate the ordination hall (Pali: *uposatha;* Thai: *ubosot*), library, bell chamber, and other structures of Wat Sri Koet in 1925. Image No. 237 is a bronze sculpture with an oblong base, on which is seated the Buddha, and arrayed in a horseshoe pattern before him, five disciples, their legs tucked beneath them and hands raised in reverence. The inscription reports that the image was made in 1937 at the time of a festival celebrating the monastic assembly hall (Pali: *vihāra;* Thai: *wihan*) at Wat Sai Mun Mueang.

Buddha images fill, enliven, and define spaces. They are most often placed inside of a *vihāra, uposatha,* or *maṇḍapa* (a hall for images), but they also occupy other spaces such as cloisters or niches built into the sides of *stūpas.* An image's presence highlights the sacredness of a space and directs the attitude, stance, and movements of devotees within it. The image enjoins devotees to make merit. A Buddha image is a most appropriate donation for a new monastic hall, as such a space could not really be complete without an image.

The production of a Buddha image may also have been a means for the agency of the donor, empowered by the authority of the *saṅgha* and the skill of the craftsmen, to establish a presence in the sacred precincts of the monastery. Providing a site for the establishment of names, occasions, and wishes, the Buddha image brings the personal into the domain of the sacred.

Donor Types: Gender, Status, and Sociokarmic Groupings

In his catalogue, Penth provides a listing of all of the proper names appearing in the 312 inscriptions. The list totals 452 names, including those of donors and craftsmen, as well as the names of those deceased persons to whom the donors transferred the merit from sponsoring the Buddha image.[26] As there are only ten evident examples of merit transfer and few craftsmen are identified, the vast majority of the names on the list are those of donors.

Penth's list includes honorifics, which can provide some indication of the social class of the donors. Nine images bear donors' names adorned with royal titles such as *phra chao chiwit* (king), *rachathewi* (queen), or *rachabut* (prince). Nobles or government officials probably constituted the largest social class of donors in Penth's data set. Based on honorifics, they donated about 28 percent of the images, but the actual number may be higher. Nobles carried titles such as *chao, khun, muen,* and *saen.* Titles such as *chao* and *thao* were used at different times to refer to either royal family members or to nobles. Many names in the data set are prefaced by familial terms such as *mae* (mother), *lung* (older brother of father or mother), and *ya* (paternal grandmother); most were probably commoners, but some may have been more elite. Nobles or officials were likely to have represented a good proportion of the devotees of the monasteries in central Chiang Mai. When Kawila rebuilt Chiang Mai in 1796, he settled nobles and their entourages in homes within the city walls, which are within today's *tambon* of Phra Sing and Si Phum, the area covered by Penth's survey. It was not until the early decades of the twentieth century that the residences of rulers and nobles were shifted out of the city center as the old system of nobility was replaced by the government of the modern Thai state.[27] Each monastery's historic constituency of patrons no doubt is one factor affecting the quantity and state of Buddha images that we find in it today.

Among donations in the data set, gifts involving monks total thirty-nine images, a strong figure that reflects how monks not only legitimized donations but themselves acted as sponsors of donations. Possibly, the solid percentage of monks in the data set is because monks were more likely than other kinds of donors to add inscriptions to their donations. In any case, the participation of monks as sponsors seems to be consistent with Daniel Veidlinger's finding in his study of Lanna manuscripts that half were copied through the patronage of monks.[28]

Craftsmen (Thai: *chang, changlo,* or *sala*) are named in only three instances out of the eighty-five inscriptions, all among the more recent images in the set: No. 221 (1928), No. 231 (1932 or 1933), and No. 246 (1971). For Image No. 142 (1891), the donors are a husband and wife, Nan Photha and Nang Khamdip. Nan Photha highlighted that he sculpted (Thai: *salak kae*) the image himself out of *mai kum* (garlic pear tree) wood. Judging from the delicacy of the sculpture (fig. 6.5), he may well have been a craftsman. Nan Photha signalled his desire to support the *sāsana* throughout five thousand years, while Nang Khamdip requested to be a *sāvaka* (disciple) in a future life. Both donors also mention their wish that the merit obtained from the making of the image contribute to their future attainment of *nibbāna*. These wishes being apparently conventional for a donation, it is an open question as to whether Nan Photha was thought to accrue any additional merit for making the image with his own hands.

Craftsmen are rarely named in northern Thai chronicles, even as some chronicles describe in detail the materials and processes of making certain images. The relative anonymity of craftsmen does not mean that their role was unimportant; after all, the monks who consecrated

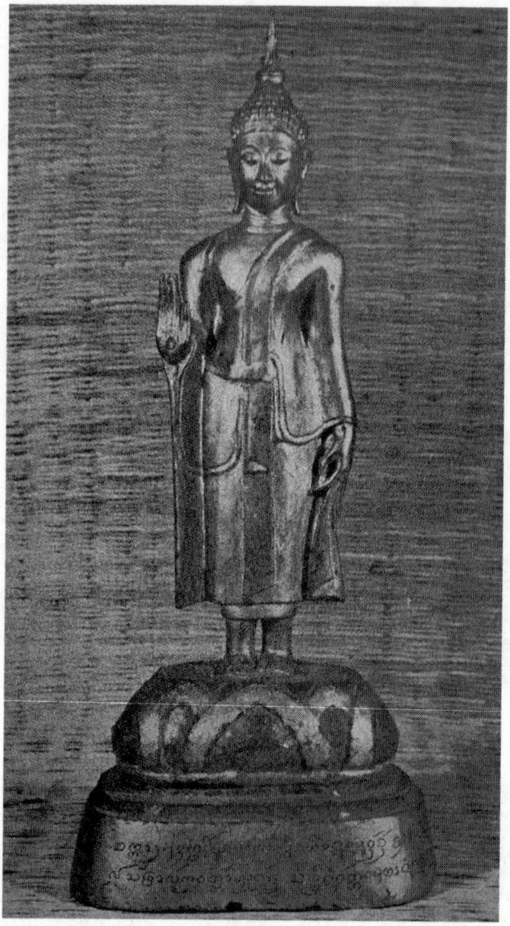

Fig. 6.5. Penth Image No. 142.

an image are not usually named in the texts, either. The focus of these inscriptions and chronicles tends to be on donors' intention and contribution, prioritizing their agency over that of other participants in the image-making process.

Among the names appearing in the inscriptions, 278 (62 percent) are of men and 168 (37 percent) are of women. There were also two examples in which the donors are collectively "people" (Thai: *chao*) and four for which I am unsure of the gender of the name. The larger proportion of men probably attests to their greater political and economic power, particularly as a number were members of the nobility.

The donation of a Buddha image often entailed collaboration between multiple sponsors. For instance, among the eighty-five images for which Penth gives inscriptions in full, thirteen have inscriptions that note joint sponsorship among patrons who include both lay devotees and monks.[29] A further thirty-two inscriptions testify to collaborations between different lay patrons,[30] who are typically members of the same family or household. Such joint making of merit reflects the social dimension of karma, a phenomenon that has been expounded by Jonathan S. Walters,[31] who has observed that, aside from individual acts of karma such as private meditation, all karma has a social context and therefore social relevance. Karma may be shared between individuals who are of the same family or community, such that their existences may be affected by each others' karma, and even such that they may reencounter each other again in shared experiences over many lifetimes. In the inscriptions, this understanding of karma may be seen in donors' allocating merit to deceased family members and requesting to be reborn alongside existing relatives. The chronicles also reflect sociokarma—for instance, in the accounts of ogres, people, relics, and treasures being continually drawn over multiple rebirths to the same places. By means of this repeating cycle of "resociety" centered in one place, the Lanna accounts emphasize the significance of specific sites over a huge time span. Another example is the travelling image chronicles' recounting of kings giving offerings to powerful Buddha images to share merit and thereby bolster the prosperity of themselves and their people. Patronage of Buddha images could be occasions to reaffirm and extend karmic networks. The image in this way objectified these networks.

Materials: Economic and Social Values and Merit

Penth's catalogue provides a valuable listing of the material of all 312 images.[32] The donors' choice of materials attests to the availability of natural resources, as well as to other influences: beliefs about the suitability of different materials to be formed into Buddha images, the economic cost of materials, the wealth of the donors, and the skills of local craftsmen. By my count, of the 312 images, 198 (63 percent) are made of wood; seventy-three (23 percent) of metal; twenty-four (8 percent) of *muk,* a pulverized substance; five (2 percent) of hollow silver filled with *muk,* and twelve (4 percent) of other materials.

The materials of these images also reflect their durability against climate, age, insects, and other forces of destruction. The twenty images that have come down to us from the period before the Burmese takeover to the present are those of a sturdy material, bronze (Thai: *thong samrit*). The four images created in the late sixteenth century during the early phase of Burmese suzerainty are also made of this material. The range of materials is greater for images created since the late 1700s, reflecting the greater survival of materials as well as the use of new materials such as cement.

The wooden images are made from different kinds of trees identified in the inscriptions as bodhi, or sacred fig; jackfruit; garlic pear (*mai kum*); jujube (*mai thanphuthra*); and sandalwood, but most images (186) are generically identified by Penth as "wood" (*mai*). Wood is a readily available material in well-forested northern Thailand and may be enhanced with a lacquer and gold coating to increase the value of the donation, help protect it from insects and moisture, and evoke the luminous appearance attributed to the Buddha. Scarcity of more precious materials at different periods may also have contributed to the popularity of wood as a material for images.[33] The prevalence of wood in the data set casts the travelling images in sharp relief as they tend to be made from expensive or scarce materials: the bronze of the Sihing Buddha, the green stone of the Emerald Buddha, and the crystalline stone of the Setangkhamani.

Nonetheless, for donors, specific types of wood were seen to be auspicious or had special associations.[34] For instance, sandalwood was scarce and perceived as being extraordinary; thus donors tended to highlight its use. In the inscription of Image No. 50 (1814), quoted earlier, the donor announced that he made the image "with sandalwood that is very fragrant." The famous scent of this wood also featured in the Lanna *tamnan* of the Sandalwood Buddha image, which related that the image's fame was spread after the distinctive scent wafted to senior monks from a novice who had used his robe to cushion the image's base.[35]

Of the images crafted from metal, seventy are made of bronze, two of silver, and one of gold. The bronze images tend to be larger than other images in the data set. The average height of all sculptures in the data set, including their bases, is 38 centimeters. Twenty-six images in the set are one meter or taller in height; of these, twenty-two are made from bronze. The largest image in the data set is the 241-centimeter-high

Image No. 22, Phra Chao Mueangrai, the bronze image made at the instigation of a Burmese general in 1566.

Image No. 4 (1477) is a 58-centimeter-high seated bronze image popularly called Phra Chao Thong Thip, the Lord of Divine Metal. On the statue's robe under the right arm there is a round point of blue color about six millimeters wide. According to Penth, the northern Thai called this point *thong thip* and saw it as evidence that during the mixing of alloy to cast the image, a deity carried metal down from heaven and secretly deposited it into the crucible.[36] The trope of a divine contribution to the material of a Buddha image is also found in the stories of the creation of the Emerald, Setangkhamani, and Sihing images. For devotees, the creation of a Buddha image is a collaborative production that may involve not only humans but also other divine beings who likewise reverence the Buddha. Metal casting is a difficult process and subject to occurrences that can appear to be beyond the control of human beings.

Given the claim of celestial endowment for the Lord of Divine Metal, it is unsurprising that the image is also associated with one of Lanna's most highly revered kings: the *Chiang Mai Chronicle* recounts that in 1805, Sri Mahanāma and Paña, two monks from Ban So in the area of Chiang Khang, presented the image to King Kawila. The monks reported to the king,

> In the generation before ours, it was said that in the future, there will be a ruler of great majesty and power who will come from Chiang Mai in the south and bring up a great army and defeat the forces of evil, the enemies in all directions in all localities, great and small, [all across] the Lan Na region . . . and he will take charge of the domains and make them right and make Buddhism prosper and flourish, as they were in the time of King Mangrai. At that time, we were to bring forth the Thòng Thip Buddha image and present him to you. So we were instructed by the Teacher who died. . . . This Buddha image is the image of the ruler of Chiang Mai.[37]

As of 1990, the Lord of Divine Metal was kept in the cell of Wat Phra Sing's abbot, Phra Rachasitthachan, who stated that King Kawila had venerated it as a personal image.[38]

Donors were also partial to creating images formed with *muk*, which in Tai Yuan means "detail, dust, powder, or particle."[39] *Muk*

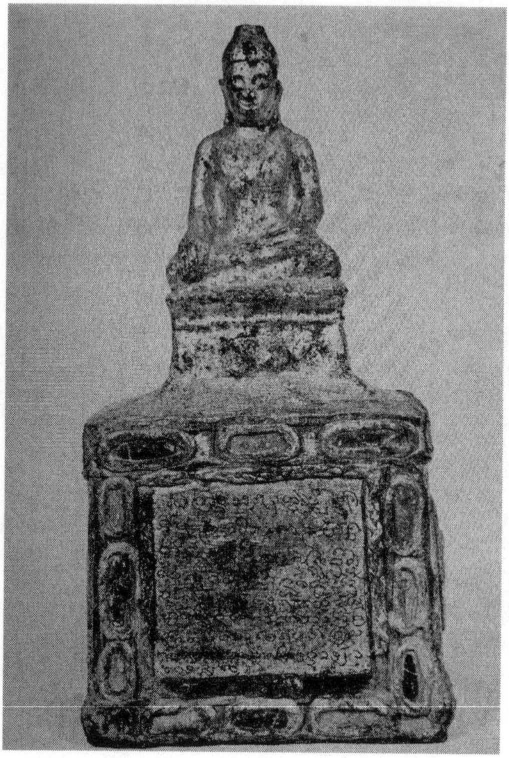

Fig. 6.6. Penth Image No. 34.

dokmai consists of dried flowers pulverized and mixed with lacquer (fig. 6.6); *muk keson* is made with flower pollen, and *muk nga chang* with crushed ivory. *Muk khao chiwit* is the ash from burning the amount of rice one has foregone for one day by fasting.[40] The ash was molded into a Buddha image, as in the case of Image No. 143 (1893). Sometimes the *muk* was encased in a silver shell. Twenty-three of the images made of different types of *muk* date between 1811 or 1812 and 1921; six *muk* images are undated. *Muk* images tend to be small: only four are more than 20 centimeters high. No. 53 (1817) and No. 98 (1867–1868), made of pollen *muk,* are comparatively large, at 49 centimeters and 56 centimeters high, respectively. No. 54 (1821), No. 56 (1821), No. 58 (1821), and No. 280 (undated) are all sets of *phra phim* (votive sealings) of *muk* mounted in wooden frames. The inscriptions do not reveal if there was any specific reason why the donors chose to make the images with *muk*. Of the nine *muk* images for which Penth gives the full inscription, the use of *muk* was noted in five of the inscriptions: No. 34 (1811–1812), No. 53 (1817), No. 98 (1867–1868), No. 143 (1893), and No. 168 (1904). *Muk* may have been considered a special material worthy of notice.

An interesting example of the use of *muk* is given in the *Chronicle of the King of the Dhamma* (*Tamnan Phraya Thammikarat*), a Lanna *tamnan* that may date to the nineteenth century. The chronicle predicts the coming of a king devoted to the *dhamma,* and explains that the king will correct various ills of the world. For example, he will gather manuscripts of erroneous teachings and deposit them in a golden box; the box will be burned and the ashes mixed with lacquer to make *muk rak* to paint on Buddha images.[41]

There are twelve images made from miscellaneous materials: cement, clay, crystal, horn, ivory, marble, and stone. One example is Image No. 252, the two elephant tusks of the royal elephant, the Conqueror of Mueang Ma, carved with Buddha images and donated by royal family members. At Wat Khuan Kha Ma, Penth discovered three Buddha images made from cement in 1937–1938, Nos. 238, 239, and 240, from three different donors, all bearing identical features and inscribed with the same statement that the cement image was made to support the *sāsana* for five thousand years.

Donors also considered aspects of the production of the image worthy of remark in inscriptions. The donor of Image No. 142, Nan Photha, highlighted that he sculpted the image of *mai kum* himself. The sponsor of Image No. 89 (1856), a reclining Buddha 30 centimeters long, declared, "The making and the performance of the consecration ritual [Pali: *buddhābhiseka;* Thai: *phuttaphisek*] in all aspects was completed within one day." As we have seen, the process of how a Buddha image came to be created is also a common topic of attention in chronicles.

The statue of the Buddha, though it channelled the Buddha himself, was still appreciated for its quality as a physical object resulting from various materials shaped by the physical and mental efforts of devotees. The choice of material was significant because it affected the merit-making value of the donation: generally, the more expensive the material, the more merit the donor could potentially generate. The matter of the selection of materials is highlighted in a Lanna palm leaf manuscript titled *Meritorious Blessing for Making Buddha Images* (*Anisong Kankosang Phra Phuttha Rup*). This text seems to have been meant for recitation during the image consecration ceremony.[42] It recounts that the Buddha in his lifetime visited a village of wealthy potters, who honored him by using clay to make millions of small Buddha images. The Buddha then preached a sermon about the meritorious blessings of making Buddha images, explaining,

> Those who have had a Buddha image made in order to promote the religion of the *tathāgata* [the Buddha] and for the benefit of human and celestial beings will receive great rewards. They will be reborn for several lifetimes as a king of kings (*cakavatti-rāja*), a conqueror of the four continents, as rulers of both large and small cities, as persons of great wealth (*mahāseṭṭhī*), as Brahmans who have mastered the three Vedas, as Indra, as the head of all female celestial beings (*devakañña*), and also as Brahmā, the highest of all the Brahmās.
>
> O *bhikkhus* [monks]! In addition, the laity who build an image of the *tathāgata* will not experience any suffering, nor will they be reborn in any family of low class such as a hunter of birds or animals. Rather, they will be reborn into a wealthy and noble family with male and female servants, elephants, horses, cows, water buffalo, and workers, as a consequence of making an image of the *tathāgata*.[43]

The Buddha also cited a long list of materials and enumerated the number of eons of meritorious blessings that would be accrued by a person making a Buddha image out of each material: "Whoever is full of faith and makes an image of the *tathāgata* from a leaf will receive meritorious blessings for five eons; those full of faith in the Triple Gem who make an image of the *tathāgata* by painting it on cloth, will receive meritorious blessings for ten eons," and so on. The materials and the blessings to be earned by image donors are summarized in table 6.1.

An aspiring donor could still accrue no fewer than five eons of blessings as well as look forward to a more favorable rebirth by shaping an image out of a modest leaf. By highlighting the breadth of types of materials, the Buddha encouraged potential donors at all levels of wealth to fashion Buddha images. The hierarchy of materials apparently provides a very clear rationale for patrons' selection of materials that generate long-lasting blessings, such as flower pollen *muk*, sandalwood, and bodhi tree wood. The costliness or scarcity of a material and its symbolic associations directly relate to its merit-making potential. Notably, a cloth painting of the Buddha generates one of the lowest rewards, drawing into question the value placed on painters' skill. One wonders how much, if at all, the difficulty of engaging skillful

Table 6.1. Materials of Buddha images and rewards. Based on *Anisong Kankosang Phra Phuttha Rup.*

Material	Eons of Meritorious Blessings
Leaf	5
Cloth (painting)	10
Clay	15
Wood	20
Horn/tusk	25
Bricks	30
Stone	35
Lead/tin	40
Brass/copper/iron	45
Silver	50
Flower pollen	55
Gold	60
Precious gems	65
Sandalwood/Bodhi tree wood	70 or forever

craftsmen and the renumeration paid to them factors in this hierarchy. The Buddha image is the product of a transformation of the nonsacred into the sacred. In this process the nonsacred nature of the material is not subsumed or dissipated but persists in defining the identity of the object even after it is physically and ideologically sculpted. Despite its visual appearance and enshrinement in a sacred precinct, the Buddha image arose from and was part of the economic and social world of its makers and worshippers. We will further consider the significance of materials and economies to the production of Buddha images in chapter 7.

The Postures of the Images: The Images and Their Description

To anyone who has ever visited a Thai temple or even just skimmed a few books on Thai art, it would be no surprise to discover that a large proportion of Buddha statues in the Penth data set—207 images (67 percent)—are seated and making the gesture of touching the earth or victory over the demon Māra (Pali: *māravijaya;* Thai: *marawichai*). The next most common posture is meditating (Pali: *samādhi;* Thai: *khat samathi*), found among thirty-seven (12 percent) of the images. The rest of the Buddha images are distributed among nine other postures, each of which makes up 6 percent or less of the total.[44]

The *māravijaya* attitude or posture (Pali: *iriyāpatha;* Thai: *iriyabot; pang*) is considered to represent the Buddha's triumph over the demon Māra, who tried to prevent the Buddha from reaching enlightenment under the bodhi tree. The position is believed to have originated with Buddha image making in northern India and to have become popular in Tai territories in the thirteenth century, when it may have been closely associated with the Mahābodhi Temple at Bodh Gaya.[45]

The *māravijaya* posture commemorates a significant event and recalls a famous place of pilgrimage, but it is interesting that wherever Buddha images are mentioned in Lanna chronicles, their postures are seldom noted. This is true even in the most elaborated accounts of images, the travelling image chronicles. The absence is not readily explainable. It cannot be assumed that those who copied, recited, or heard these chronicles were familiar with the appearance of the images. Possibly, as in Burma, *māravijaya* was considered the "default" posture for a Buddha image and was simply presumed unless otherwise specified.[46] The only travelling image chronicle that mentions posture is the *Chronicle of the Sihing Buddha Image,* which notes that the image is in the attitude of meditating.[47] Because that posture is more common among Lankan images, it seems to support a Lankan origin or inspiration for the Sihing Buddha. With regard to the other travelling images, it is interesting that while some chronicles proclaim a connection of the image to the Buddha through, for instance, the insertion of his relics into the image, the image's posture is not highlighted for its function in connecting the image to the person or biography of the Buddha.

Among the eighty-five full-text inscriptions, there are six that mention the posture of the image. These include Image No. 2 (1470), "sitting" (Thai: *prathap nang*); Image No. 21 (1563) and Image No. 91 (1857–1858), both "standing" (*yuen*); and Image No. 117 (1879), two wooden images on the same base, in the attitudes of "holding bowl" (*rap bat*) and "forbidding Māra" (*ham man,* a posture also called "forbidding relatives," *ham yat*). Additionally, there are two images, No. 114 (1877) and No. 216 (1926), whose inscriptions refer to images being donated in each of the "four *iriyabot* [postures],"—that is, reclining, sitting, standing, and walking. There is no obvious relationship between the content of the inscriptions and the postures of the statues; why donors selected these postures is not indicated. Statues in certain postures may have had particular associations at different times and places, as in the examples of the storied Buddha Image Lying on a Mango-Tree Log and Buddha Image of the Honey Inlet discussed in chapter 4.

Among the eighty-five inscriptions in the data set, by far the most evocative descriptive language about a Buddha image is that written in two languages for Image No. 2 (1470), a 134-centimeter-high bronze seated image at Wat Phra Chao Mangrai The first inscription is in Pali:

> Sri Saddhamma Mahāsaṅgharāja had this Sahing [Sihing] image made sitting on an excellent throne; it is like the sun appearing above Mount Yugandhara [a mountain range around Mount Sumeru] and like the moon shining brilliant in the heavens.

The second inscription is in Tai Yuan:

> Sri Saddhama Trilokratanacūḷāmahāsaṅgharāja . . . had this Buddha image Sahing cast in order to be a torch for the world, [which] people can venerate and to provide merit in order [that they may] be born in heaven and [reach] *nibbāna* where old age and death are unknown . . . the base [of this Buddha image] has a weight of 24,000.

The comparison of the statue's radiance to that of the sun, the moon, and a torch echoes common textual descriptions of the glowing appearance of the Buddha himself resulting from his enlightenment. The designation "this Sahing" has no clear meaning, but Penth suggests it is a rendering of the Sihing Buddha.[48] Perhaps the term refers to the image as an imitation of the famous Sihing image. In any case, the fact that the image was referred to with its own name is noteworthy; while the inscription writers, through their description of the statue's luminosity, alluded to its role as a sign of the Buddha, the fact that they refer to it by a separate appellation suggests they understood the statue as not only being the Buddha or representing him, but as having its own significance as an object.

Among the eighty-five inscriptions, as far as features of the images are concerned, the most typically referred to are materials (twenty-three inscriptions[49]) and weight (thirteen inscriptions[50]). This contrasts with the mentions of posture, totalling six. Perhaps the small number reflects Penth's selection of inscriptions. At the same time, chronicles also seem to refer less frequently to posture than to other characteristics of images. The *Jinakālamālīpakaraṇaṁ* (*JKM*), the *tamnan* of Buddhist history, contains eighteen mentions of the making of Buddha images in Lanna; among these, the material is noted in fifteen cases, the weight or height in eight cases, and the posture in three cases.[51]

Perhaps the reason why the material and weight were stated is because they are features that may not always be apparent to the beholder of the image, while posture is not mentioned because it is visually obvious. By highlighting materials, donors also invoked their auspicious or divine associations, as well as alluded to the economic and potential merit-making value of the donation.

Another way for donors to make expensive gifts was contributing materials in the amount of one's own weight or having an image built to match one's own height. Image No. 209 (1925) is a standing, 130-centimeter-high image made of bronze at Wat Sri Koet. Although it is not inscribed as such, the abbot of the monastery told Penth that Nang Khamsai of Yong Huat was the donor of the image and that its weight was the same as hers.[52] Another example of this kind of gift is recorded in the *JKM:* in 1510, King Kaeo of Chiang Mai donated pure gold sheets of a weight equivalent to that of his own body; the gold was measured out on the royal scales, with monks in witness, and the total value was about sixty-thousand pieces of gold. A sitting Buddha image was then created that had the same height as the standing height of the king.[53] In northern Thai tradition, Buddha statues made according to the height or weight of the donor are called Phra Chao Kha Khing.[54] Images of this kind are also recorded in texts of other Buddhist cultures. In ancient India, Xuanzang observed that a great king, Śîlâditya-râja of Kanauj, constructed a monastery in which he established "a golden statue of Buddha, of the same height as the king himself."[55] Inscriptions found in Burma and dated between the eleventh and fourteenth centuries applied special terms to this kind of statue: *ryap tuiṅ purhā* (image made to the donor's height) and *kuiw ryap tuiṅ purhā* (image made to the donor's measurements).[56] The nineteenth-century Burmese *Glass Palace Chronicle* and *Sāsanavaṃsa* also record donors undertaking this type of gift.[57]

The building of a statue corresponding to the physical dimensions of the donor enabled the agency of the patron to be literally embodied by the Buddha image. Devotees recognized the image as a form that represented the Buddha while relating to a specific sponsor. The image's face might also have incorporated a devotee's personal aspects. Image No. 105 (1872) is a wooden image that King Intrawichayanon

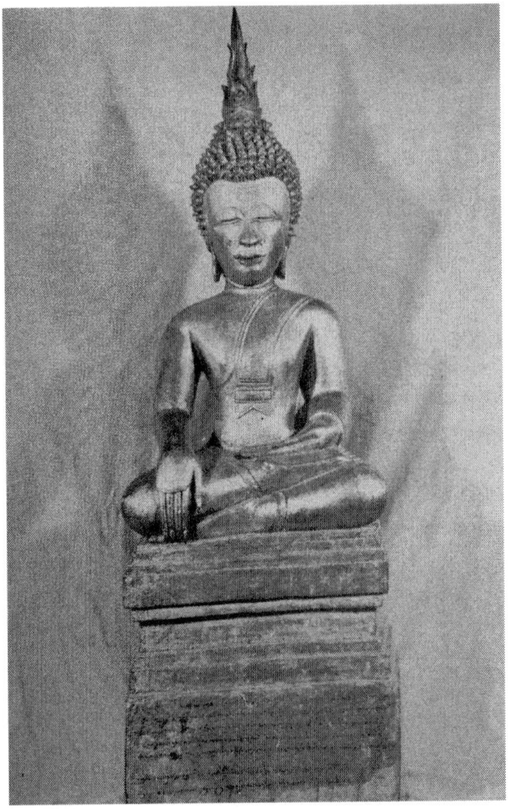

Fig. 6.7. Penth Image No. 105.

(r. 1871–1897) donated, together with his family, in order to generate merit to transfer to his deceased father, King Kawilarot Suriyawong (r. 1856–1870). Penth observed that the facial features of the image have some resemblance to photographs of Kawilarot Suriyawong (fig. 6.7).[58]

Refurbishment of Existing Images: Never-Finished Sites of Merit Creation

Most of the inscriptions document donations of new Buddha images, but a few record instances of alteration or addition to existing images. For instance, Image No. 236 (1936) consists of many small silver images set in a frame, of which forty-eight are 2.6 centimeters high and one is 3.5 centimeters high. Two inscriptions are discernible on the frame. One is dated 1905 and recounts that two monks, Phra Aphiwong and Phra Siwichai, applied lacquer and gold to twenty-eight Buddha images "built in a previous age" and held a new consecration for them. The other inscription, described previously, is dated 1936 and reports that Chao Noi Thepwongphok made sixty images to commemorate his age. The 3.5-centimeter-high single image bears traces of lacquer and gold and is probably one of the set that the two monks redecorated in 1905. The frame was recycled in 1936 to house Chao Noi Thepwongphok's images, of which forty-eight apparently remain. The current assemblage of objects represents donations from three different occasions.

Earlier I noted Image No. 21, the bronze standing image inscribed with Nalang Suthon Khawin's last will and testament. In his inscription he describes the image as "newly made." Penth observed that the letters of the inscription were incised onto the metal base in many short strokes; had the letters been inscribed on the mold before the casting, they would have been written with a flowing line.[59] Thus the inscription was added to a preexisting image. Perhaps the Nalang wrote the will on the base as an afterthought, or maybe he was prompted to do so by some urgency that precluded casting a new image. In any case, he was drawn to a Buddha statue as a suitable site to lend authority and perhaps even a sacred character to his words.

Indeed, Buddha images often seem to draw donors into their orbits. In 1791 King Kawila added a base and backing of wood to Phra Sila, Image No. 254, creating a connection between the well-known image and himself. Another example of royal refurbishment is provided by Image No. 255, the Setangkhamani, which like Phra Sila is enshrined today at Wat Chiang Man. The inscription relates that in 1873, the king and queen, together with family members, donated a gold-plate-covered sandalwood base; a couple of other family members also contributed gilding for the umbrella over the image's head. The donors expressed the desire to support the *sāsana* at Wat Chiang Man for five thousand years and the hope that the merit would lead them to *nibbāna*.

Where a statue is seen as one that is especially powerful, the potential to access its special potency draws donors to not only make offerings but seek to make more lasting their association with the image by making a renovation and adding an inscription to it. The donors appended themselves to the image's historic lineage of patrons. Perhaps the donors also believed that the powerful image on which they inscribed their wishes and aspirations would help ensure the efficacy of the truth statement and make the fulfillment of their wishes more likely.

The examples of refurbishments of Buddha images also remind us that the endurance of Buddha images over time has a "survival of the fittest" aspect. Those images that attract the attention of devotees are the ones that will receive maintenance, repairs, and additions and thereby continue to "live" as enduring presences, while those that fail to do so will be left to chance and the risk of deterioration.

Renovations are also reminders that the appearance of an image at any particular moment is a function of the efforts of not only the image's original craftsmen and donors but also of subsequent ones. As Skilling has observed, a Buddha image is "never finished," but is constantly subject to renovation "in the insatiable quest for merit and perfection."[60] The statue seen today in a monastery is a palimpsest of the intentions and actions of devotees. The image is the result of a process of production that is not terminated with the conclusion of the consecration ceremony. The statue continues to be understood by devotees as a material object, with all of the physical strengths and weaknesses of its form; it is seen as openly vulnerable to, or even deserving of, manipulation by human agency. The Buddha image has the power to attract devotees to it. These devotees add the visible, substantial marks of their agency, and confirm the image's potency, by mounting it on a new base, spreading on a new layer of lacquer, or applying a square of gold leaf to its face. Although an image may be considered to resemble Gotama Buddha, its appearance is not necessarily sacrosanct. The image is recognized as a site of constant, ongoing exchange of agency between image and devotees, as well as between devotees across different eras.

The inscriptions indicate how even as Buddha statues are shaped following a standardized, restricted repertory of iconographic forms, and are produced and employed according to ritual traditions, each image is an individual production undertaken in specific circumstances. As Skilling has noted, inscriptions are "expressions of contemporaneous mentalities" of the image's donors, and an image found on an altar needs to be recognized as arising from a "social moment of production."[61] Viewing the innumerable statues of the Buddha that today fill the altars of Tai temples, and the plethora of photos of Buddha images in volumes of art history, we should not lose sight of the fact that each statue was the outcome of the efforts of a specific set of donors, monks, and craftsmen acting in a particular context.

Chapter Seven

Buddha Images as Objects of Transferrable Power

The Physical and Social Processes of Copying Images

For the present-day reader, one of the interesting aspects of Buddhist *tamnan* (chronicles) and inscriptions is their authors' apparent lack of interest in describing what the Buddha images look like. Even where the process of production of a statue was related enthusiastically and in detail, the visual appearance of the statue itself was usually not. The *tamnan* and inscriptions drew attention to social values and political aspects of Buddha images that are not physically apparent. Certainly, the features of Buddha statues were carefully formed according to a tradition of iconography. How did the abstract concepts relate to the visual aspects of the statues?

Thus far, modern art historians have made limited use of *tamnan* aside from delving into them to extract chronologies and other kinds of factual information as evidence for the spread of artistic styles.[1] This restricted use of *tamnan* is owing to Thai art historians' tight focus on the study of three subjects: iconography, style, and dating. This scholarly orientation is exemplified by numerous texts about Thai Buddha images, including such well-known works by prominent art historians as Prince Damrong Rajanuphap's *Tamnan Phra Phuttha Chedi nai Sayam* (*A History of Buddhist Monuments in Siam,* 1926); M. C. Subhadradis Diskul's *Sinlapa nai Prathet Thai* [Art in Thailand] (1963); No Na Paknam's *Phuttha Pratimakam nai Prathet Thai* (*Buddha Statues in Thailand,* 1990); Santi Leksukhum's *Sinlapa Phak Nuea [Art of the North]: Hariphunchai-Lanna* (1995); Hiram W. Woodward Jr.'s *The Sacred Sculpture of Thailand* (1997); Carol Stratton's *Buddhist Sculpture of Northern Thailand* (2004); and Piriya

Krairiksh's *Rakngao Haeng Sinlapa Thai* [*The Roots of Thai Art*] (2010), to name just a few.

These works have made very substantial and often groundbreaking contributions to our understanding of Thai art history. Their methodology, which is conventional for the study of Thai art history, depicts the historical development of Thai art as a series of "influences" of styles and iconographies from one place or people to another, based on the assumption that in creating Buddha images (and other Buddhist artworks), people of the past practiced deliberate, ongoing copying in all periods and places. Following tradition, devotees purposefully selected revered models to copy in order to transmit sacredness and to ensure the creation of merit. Tradition explains the *why* of copying, but we are still faced with the question of *how* copying was conducted in practice. What was the nature of the reasoning, methodology, and process undertaken by people in the past that led them to select particular objects, as opposed to others, as the preferred models to be copied?

One exceptional example of scholarly investigation of Buddhist copying in Southeast Asia is in the field of architecture: the Mahābodhi Temple complex, at the site of the Buddha's enlightenment in Bodh Gaya, India, and the copies built of it in China, Myanmar, and Thailand, which have been the subject of at least four studies.[2] Certainly, amidst the examples of Thailand's extant art and architectural heritage, there are numerous instances of copying that are difficult or even impossible to study because of the limited availability of data, especially in the earlier time periods. Still, because the operation of copying as an institutional and cultural practice has been widely recognized as a fundamental factor in the development of Buddhist art in Thailand, it is surprising that only a handful of scholars have dedicated attention to it.

The Lanna *tamnan* and inscriptions provide historical evidence for ways of thinking that underlie how people of the past selected Buddha images as models for copying. This textual evidence is valuable for understanding particular Lanna examples and also worth considering for its implications for the wider sphere of the study of Buddhist art production.

In this chapter I will first review the writings of four scholars on the copying of Buddhist art in Thailand. Then these will be considered in light of the ways in which Buddha images and their creation and copying were described in Lanna chronicles and inscriptions. As we shall see, such descriptions highlight the social and economic aspects of the Buddha image. Iconography referred to the divine nature of the statue, but it also played a role in the commoditization of the image. The lack of visual distinctiveness of Buddha statues, even the most famous images, was considered necessary, even desirable, to allow the proliferation of copies as well as to facilitate the assessment of each statue's financial and merit-making value.

Copying "Unusual Magical Power"

One of the earliest scholars of Thai art—in fact perhaps the earliest—to write at length about the process of copying was the art historian and epigraphist Alexander B. Griswold. In his pioneering volume *Dated Buddha Images of Northern Siam* (1957) Griswold observed that, historically, the range of types of anatomy, dress, and posture of Buddha images found in Thailand has been quite narrow, especially in comparison to the "rich iconography" of images produced in other places where Mahāyāna and Brahmanic traditions have flourished. In Griswold's view, a confined evolution of Thai Buddha images was the result of the nature of craftsmen and donors and their roles in the process of production of a Buddha image. Of the typical Thai craftsman, Griswold wrote,

> Unlike European artists, he has no desire to be original. On the contrary, he prides himself on being a copyist.
>
> There are good reasons for this. The patron who commissions an image is usually not a connoisseur: he is either a prince offering a handsome gift to religion, or else merely a citizen wishing to "make merit"—perhaps in connection with his sixtieth birthday or some other occasion. So when the sculptor asks him what he wants the image to look like, the line of least resistance is for him to say: "Oh, make it look like such-and-such," naming one of the best-known statues in the community. In any case, unless the patron is a severe rationalist (and rationalists must have been in the minority in medieval times), he hopes to produce a miraculous device. In order to inherit some fraction of the infinite power the Buddha himself possessed, an image must trace its lineage back to one of the legendary "authentic" likenesses, such as the sandalwood figure carved at Kosala by artists who knew him personally. But how can the patron be certain that the statue he chooses as a model is really in the true succession? The safest course is to choose one that has proved itself by displaying unusual magic power. Since by that very fact it will have already become illustrious, there is every reason to copy a famous

model, none at all to copy an obscure one. In this way a few models would each inspire an endless series of imitations.[3]

But the features of the imitations, Griswold further observed, were not exact facsimiles of their originals. The model's iconography would be duplicated. The style would depend far more on the training and experience of the craftsman than on the model, and he could make variations on the original. In most cases, "the innovations he makes in repeating the old formulas will be very discreet." However, a more involved sponsor also affected the copy's style; new styles of art could be developed through more active participation by the patron, such as the introduction of foreign models, the hiring of craftsmen from other regions, or the commissioning of lavish projects.[4]

Griswold read the *tamnan* about famous travelling Buddha images such as the Sihing image as records of the places in which copies of Buddha images were made, or at least where the technologies and iconography of image making were introduced.[5] Indeed, occasions in which copies of images were made were noted in the Lanna chronicles; the Sihing and Sandalwood Buddha images, for instance, were said to have been copied by specific patrons at different points in their chronicles. Nonetheless, Griswold lamented that Lanna *tamnan* such as the *Chronicle of the Sihing Buddha Image* "offer tempting but enigmatic clues to chronology."[6] Like other modern art historians, he found *tamnan* contained insufficient evidence for the construction of an art historical chronology of style and iconography. Of course, manuscripts and images were not typically inscribed with the intent in mind to record styles or iconographies.[7]

Griswold's conception of copying shares commonalities with the views of two other trailblazing scholars of Thai art who were also active in the mid-twentieth century, Luang Boribal Buribhand and Jean Boisselier; Griswold was a collaborator with and friend of both men. Like Griswold, Luang Boribal pointed out that the craftsmen who made Buddha images prided themselves on being copyists. He noted that the models chosen for copying were those images that were "famous and venerated among a certain group of people" but did not go into the reasons behind the images' fame,[8] which Griswold attributed to the perception of the images' magical abilities. Jean Boisselier also held that certain Buddha images were seen to have special powers that devotees sought to access by copying. He observed that the models chosen to be copied were usually either images that were situated in highly venerated sites or those images seen to have protective powers over the towns or monasteries where they were installed. Copies of such images were made "with a view to extending their presence and their beneficent power." Like Griswold, Boisselier noted that the model's iconography was always copied while the style depended upon the craftsman. The style, he believed, was a result of the craftsman's sitting in meditation upon the model: the copy conveyed the craftsman's vision of the "essence" of the model. Whether or not craftsmen actually did this is open to question, however, and Boisselier offered no evidence to support his claim.[9]

Griswold's explanation of image production inspires further questions. How exactly are the "unusual magical powers" manifested by or recognized in an image? Why was it believed that the style was not necessary to imitate? What about the role of the *saṅgha* (the community of monks), without whose ritual sanction a sculpture could not become a Buddha image?

Copying and "Galactic" Polities

Responses to some of these questions were suggested by the anthropologist Stanley J. Tambiah. As part of two works, "Famous Buddha Images and the Legitimation of Kings" (1982) and *The Buddhist Saints of the Forest and the Cult of Amulets* (1984), Tambiah drew attention to the wider objectives and impacts of donor and donation. He noted that the lineage of copying and its perpetuation, far from reflecting a lack of initiative or creativity as Griswold suggested, evidenced a broader social and historical interest of donors who sought "the continued maintenance of Buddhist religion and civilization, with the continuity achieved through the replication and renewal of earlier forms."[10]

In Tambiah's view, the "unusual magical power" of Buddha images was part of the culture of belief and social power of the societies that made them. The belief in the supernatural abilities of any particular image, he suggested, was rooted in devotees and their interactions with each other: "The *sacra* themselves are seen to derive their powers to affect and transform the world from their authenticity, their likeness to the original, and their pedigree—all of which, in the last resort, are values generated and conferred upon the objects by humans."[11] In essence, the power of an image depended on whether devotees accepted the image as having power.

The belief that a particular statue was especially powerful, Tambiah claimed, had substantial value in the past political structure of Thai territories and elsewhere in mainland Southeast Asia. This was because legitimacy to rule was endowed not merely by blood ties. Instead, a king had to demonstrate his right to the throne, and one way to do so was to flaunt a famous image as palladium.[12] According to Tambiah, political organization in early Southeast Asia was "galactic": polities were arrayed in unstable suzerain-vassal relationships that constantly shifted over time as different rulers in the region endeavored to assert superior claims to power. Tambiah thus read the *Chronicle of the Sihing Buddha Image* as accounting for the locations where Sihing copies were made and displayed for the purpose of buttressing a local ruler's claim to political superiority.[13]

Even if critical skepticism remains about the galactic theory, Tambiah's analysis of the Sihing chronicle suggests how competition for political power and practices of devotion to the *sāsana* could have been interlinked. This conception, in my view, finds support from the evidence in *tamnan*. As we have seen, one purpose of the composition and dissemination of the travelling image *tamnan* was to spread beliefs about the power of certain images and the benefits to devotees—especially monarchs—to venerating them. Models considered suitable for copying were those around which claims of magical power, which we could describe as the ability to exert an extraordinary agency upon devotees, were successfully asserted and believed.[14]

Copying as a Practice of the Buddha *Sāsana*

In contrast to Tambiah's attention to the political aspects of Buddhist art production, the eminent art historian Piriya Krairiksh has emphasized that the copying of Buddhist art is a practice whose main purpose was to serve the *sāsana* and no other (nonreligious) concern. Through various thought-provoking works published since 1980,[15] Piriya has argued that the method of periodization of Buddhist art history in Thailand currently in use by most art historians has wrongfully aligned art history with political development. The conventional Thai chronology, which was initially sketched out by Prince Damrong and George Cœdès in the 1920s and adjusted by subsequent generations of art historians, categorizes art according to periods named after polities: Dvāravatī, Śrīvijaya, Lopburi, Chiang Saen, Sukhothai, and so on. Piriya points out that this periodization linked the development of Buddhist art with "empires" whose existence and influence is in many cases incompletely understood today. The difficulty is that "once art objects are used to reinforce an idea of empire, they become evidence for the expansion of political power and artistic influence of a particular empire." He posits that the depiction of art history within an imperial history was motivated by scholars' desire in the early twentieth century to construct a history for Thailand on a par with that of the European powers.[16] He perceptively points out that domestic and global politics were factors in the early development of Thai art historical scholarship.

In Piriya's view, political influences have obscured the actual nature of Buddhist art objects, which were created first and foremost for the purpose of supporting the requirements and objectives of religious doctrine. Buddhist art "is evidence relating to *sāsana* and beliefs only. It does not provide a picture of the characteristics of daily life either at the level of the common people or of the royal household." Moreover, the making of Buddhist art in Thailand in the past "placed importance on beliefs in the next life more than existence in daily life."[17] According to Piriya's view, Buddha images were symbols of particular beliefs and testimony of a practice with a specific, limited purpose, the making of merit for the next life. "Indeed, beliefs are important in influencing similarities in style. This is particularly true of religious art where images of the Buddha or deities have certain identifying features." Moreover, "Changes in iconography arise from developments in the belief systems, which underlie and inspire the creation of works of art."[18] In the periodization set out in his recent book, *The Roots of Thai Art* (2012; originally published in Thai as *Rakngao Haeng Sinlapa Thai* in 2010), Piriya proposes replacing the traditional Sukhothai, Chiang Saen, and Ayutthaya eras with periods named for religious schools of thought: "Theravāda Nikāya" (mid-ninth to mid-fourteenth centuries), "Mahāvihāra order of the Theravāda Nikāya" (mid-fourteenth to mid-fifteenth centuries) and the "Sayamnikāya" (early sixteenth to mid-nineteenth centuries).[19]

Piriya's approach to chronology remains controversial among art historians and has not yet displaced the conventional periodization in common usage. Among others, the art historian Nandana Chutiwongs pointed out in a commentary in the year 2000 that while the conventional chronology has its weaknesses, there are a number of challenges to implementing Piriya's approach. Among other points, Nandana observed that detailed information about past beliefs, and how they relate to specific artworks, is often unavailable to us in the present. In addition, the same iconographical forms were at various times in history venerated by multiple sects simultaneously, so that associating a specific statue with a particular order is not an easily practicable endeavor. Indeed, even determining whether the characteristics of an artwork signify that it was a product of "Theravāda" or "Mahāyāna" veneration may be a challenging enterprise given the current state of evidence.[20] Moreover, as Nicolas Revire has observed more recently, labels assigned by Piriya such as "Theravāda," "Mahāyāna," or "Tantrayāna" have not been found in inscriptions in Southeast Asia. Furthermore, these labels cannot describe the complexity of religious practices through many hundreds of years.[21] The chronological categories in *The Roots of Thai Art* also reflect a central Thai bias and obscure the diversity of practices and arts in the different regions of Thailand. For instance, under this system, Lanna art of the early sixteenth to mid-nineteenth centuries would fall within the "Sayamnikāya," the Siamese order, a category that Lanna devotees of the time did not apply to themselves and that would be historically inaccurate in describing the religious lineages of Lanna.

Piriya is one of the few art historians to consider the methodology of copying in Thai Buddhist art. In *The Roots of Thai Art* he seems to nod to criticism of his earlier writings while still hewing to a restricted view of the nature of artistic production:

> works of art in Thailand in the early 14th–mid-19th centuries were created to serve Buddhism by anonymous artists. Their aim was to create Buddha images as close to their original prototypes as possible in order to preserve the appearance of sacred images which had served as the models. The word *patima* (Thai for sculpture) in Pali means replication, and referred to Buddha images made to commission. Certain images that were particularly popular were replicated frequently down the years. For this reason, it is unrealistic to assign Buddha images to periods based on their characteristics. In fact Buddha images in different styles were created in the same period, and simply reflected the various images that Buddhists revered at that time.[22]

While Griswold saw the craftsman's agency as an influence on an image's style, but not its iconography, Piriya views the craftsman as one whose task was to duplicate, and he discounts the independent expression of craftsmen in both style and iconography. This understanding of style is often difficult to reconcile with the evidence of existing Buddha images themselves, which typically display differences from other images: even where a certain image is stated to be the product of copying, it has obvious differences from the original.[23] What of the influence of donors? In *The Roots of Thai Art,* Piriya notes that the archaeological remnants of ancient sites "show us that the people who lived in these ancient sites combined their wealth and most advanced technology to bring the gods in palpable form into their midst to ensure their own protection and their future efflorescence in this world and the next."[24] He thus highlights the important contribution of donors to the production of Buddhist art. But he views the influence of donors on the development of artistic forms as being limited: as his writings have emphasized, Buddha images are materializations of Buddhist philosophical concepts and could not transmit those abstract ideas if they were made according to the whims of the makers.[25] However, Piriya's proposed chronology based upon religious orders would actually seem to imply that donors' agency may not have been all that unimportant: monastic orders or changes in beliefs could only achieve influence with the support of lay devotees—particularly those with political power who were able to allocate resources to the maintenance of monks, monasteries, and ritual equipment. The rise and fall of different monastic orders was related to, if not directly caused by, the support or rejection of lay devotees. Piriya's approach raises useful questions about the *process* of adoption of changes in artistic forms over time. How did particular beliefs drive changes in style and iconography? Who determined which form best conveyed a specific belief? How did some forms become popular to more than one sect?

"Actual" Copying and "Conceptual" Copying

The art historian M. L. Pattaratorn Chirapravati has highlighted the fact that for Buddhists, it is not always the physical form of the original that the copyist aims to replicate. Instead what is sought are the abstract values expressed by the original. Visually, then, the copy may actually not resemble the original at all. In Pattaratorn's article, "From Text to Image: Copying as Buddhist Practice in Late Fourteenth Century Sukhothai" (2009), she discusses artistic exchange between Lanka, Martaban (the city now known as Mottama, in Lower Myanmar), and Sukhothai. She begins by noting that copying was believed to be *ānisaṃsa* (Thai: *anisong*), meritorious; the desire for merit and favorable future rebirths was the main factor motivating patrons to sponsor copying of a Buddha image: this explained the reason why powerful images such as the Sihing Buddha were copied in many places. Piriya also emphasized copying as a merit-making practice and noted the popularity of particular images such as the Sihing, but here the similarity with Pattaratorn's view ends. In contrast to Piriya's depiction of the development of Thai Buddhist art objects as independent of political concerns, Pattaratorn points out how considerations of "power and prestige" drove the copying of selected aspects of a model's appearance.[26]

Pattaratorn distinguishes two types of copying for *ānisaṃsa:* " 'actual copying' of the likeness of a revered original object and 'conceptual copying' of a revered object from an available example."[27]

As an example of "actual copying," she cites the numerous copies across Asia, in the form of sculpture, paintings, and votive sealings, of what was thought to be the appearance of the main Buddha image presiding at the Mahābodhi Temple at Bodh Gaya in India: an "image of the Buddha seated with hands performing *bhūmisparśamudra* [the earth-touching gesture] and the legs crossed in either *vīrāsana* or *vājrāsana* [laid one upon the other, or crossed "lotus-style"], under a large tower structure with *bodhi* branches spraying out on the sides."[28] This view that copying entailed depicting specific features suggests that the iconography of the original model was very important to copy and as such recalls Griswold's hypothesis.

Pattaratorn recognizes a further nuance to the matter of patrons' choice of what to copy. She observes that while Lanka's *saṅgha* had claimed a long and close relationship to the Mahābodhi Temple (as the *Mahāvaṃsa* asserts), the production of Buddha images in earth-touching gesture was rare in Lanka compared to Buddha images in meditation posture. Pattaratorn suggests that this inclination of Lankans to lean away from copying the image so linked to Bodh Gaya may have been related to the island's self-portrayal as the predominant world center of Buddhism, particularly after the Muslim takeover of Buddhist centers in northern India in the late twelfth century. She observes that Lanka apparently had developed its own preferred hallmarks of iconography and style by the time it became the leading center of Theravāda Buddhism in the thirteenth to fifteenth centuries.[29]

Thus, Pattaratorn's presentation suggests that examples of copying could have been the outcome of a selective process taking into consideration not only miraculous powers or sacredness being attributed to a well-known image but also how association with the image would reflect upon the image's patrons in turn. The Buddha image, in its capacity as both a production of merit and a source of supernatural power, was understood by its makers as a product of their agency and as an agent that would act upon the patrons themselves; this potential was also recognized by Griswold and Tambiah. This suggests a question about Piriya's depiction of images: How did particular beliefs come to be selected as the visual trademarks of specific sects? As Pattaratorn's example suggests, the adoption of particular symbols by orders of monks, and their dissemination by their lay supporters, would seem to have been motivated in at least some cases by notions of power and prestige which were very much of the "present life."

Pattaratorn also insightfully observes that in some cases in Buddhist art history, it seems the model that patrons claimed they were copying was not actually the model used to make the copy. This practice is what Pattaratorn terms "conceptual copying." As an example, she refers to Sukhothai Inscription III, dated to about 1357, which notes that copies in sculpture of the Buddha footprint at Sumanakūṭa in Sri Lanka were made at the behest of Phraya Dhammikarat (Mahādhammarāja I, or Lithai) of Sukhothai. Four copies were each installed at different locations within the Thai kingdom. Pattaratorn notes that although the model for the Thai footprints was said to be in Lanka, they had symbols carved on them in a configuration resembling Burmese footprint sculptures. She therefore suggests that the copying referred to in Inscription III was done "symbolically": the Sukhothai craftsmen who made the four footprints used a contemporary Burmese model because that was what was available to them. The inscription's reference to Lanka hints at how the copying of honored forms "was used as a political tool for legitimating the power of the king and the prosperity of his kingdom."[30] It is also important to note that in explaining her definition of conceptual copying, Pattaratorn observes, "Once the object was made and blessed in association with the revered original (e.g., Mount Sumanakūṭa), it would be considered sacred." In other words, the copy is recognized as valid once it has been consecrated as such. Thus conceptual copying could not have been validated as successful copying of an original without the sanction of the monkhood. Conceptual copying highlighted the meanings and associations of a certain artwork apart from its specific visual features. It was achieved through collaboration between the laity and the monkhood in the donation.

Pattaratorn indicates that copying can entail the replication of material and abstract features that do not necessarily come from the same model. Presumably the Lankan footprint was identified as the model because of its fame, which made it more prestigious and meritorious to copy than a Burmese footprint. It is certainly possible that the Burmese footprint was thought to be a copy of the Lankan footprint or that the Burmese model was chosen because the Lankan iconography was unknown. Yet because the Sukhothai inscription only mentions the Lankan footprint, it may be inferred that the Lankan footprint was seen as a more prestigious model than the Burmese one.

As in Tambiah's analysis of copying, Pattaratorn's presentation suggests that making a copy is in the end as much a social process as a work process. Tambiah and Pattaratorn recognized that copying can involve not only the appearance or materiality of artworks but their social agency as well. In the practice of copying, agency may be asserted or subverted. In the example of the Sukhothai footprints, the agency of the Burmese footprint was denied, even as it was the actual model. A copy that does not resemble its original may still be recognized as a copy as long as people accept it as a copy. This might seem to reduce the importance of the visual features of a copy itself, but in the case of the Sukhothai footprints, it was clear that it was still important for them to be copies of some existing consecrated model.

In summary, the four scholars' presentations of copying highlight the potential complexity of the process of making a copy of any particular work of Buddhist art. Piriya privileged the meaning of a Buddha image as a material representation of concepts of the *sāsana* promoted by specific orders of monks and as the product of a sponsor's desire to generate merit. Yet models chosen or rejected, as the analyses by Tambiah and Pattaratorn suggest, may have been more indicative of interests of social prestige than of devotion to specific doctrinal beliefs. Griswold pointed to the magical powers attributed to images; ultimately, as Tambiah observed, the attribution of powers to any image arises from the consensus of devotees: a particular Buddha image was understood as having a powerful agency if devotees so believed. A Buddha image's reputation for magical power—which rendered it suitable to be a model to be copied—arose from the interaction of social agencies around and through it.

Keeping these perspectives on copying in mind, let us examine how Lanna monastic texts, including manuscripts and inscriptions, described Buddha images. These cast light on how devotees perceived and valued images and determined which were worthy of copying.

Some Lanna Texts on Buddha Image Production

Works of modern scholarship on Buddhist art history in Thailand often note that Buddha images were shaped to exhibit the "thirty-two marks of the Great Man" (enumerated in the classical Pali text, the *Lakkhaṇa Sutta* of the *Dīgha Nikāya*), which were said to distinguish the Buddha Gotama's person. These marks, including such features as legs "like an antelope's" and jaws "like a lion's,"[31] tend to provide a rather subjective guideline, flexibly interpreted for the sculpting of Buddha images in Thailand, as can be easily assessed by glancing at different images. Among the descriptions of Buddha images in the *tamnan* that we have examined, only the story of the *Chronicle of the Sihing Buddha Image,* composed as early as the fifteenth century, refers to the marks of the Great Man.[32] There may actually have been only limited interest among devotees in enforcing the presence of the set of marks on any particular image, perhaps because the language used to describe the marks could be construed in many ways. Making the claim that a statue possessed the thirty-two features may have been more important than actually confirming that it indeed possessed them.

Donald K. Swearer has translated three texts found in Lanna that relate to the making of Buddha images. The texts, which may date to the fifteenth and sixteenth centuries, are mostly about the conduct of ritual practices, in particular the chanting of *paritta* (protective chants) and the preparation of tiles inscribed with *gāthā* (verses) or *yantra* (magical formulae) which are to be inserted into the statue. As Swearer notes, these texts emphasize the ritual aspect of making Buddha images, the importance of the protective devices, the correspondence of the image to the *dhamma,* and the essential role of merit.[33] There are a few references in the texts to the physical characteristics of images. For example, one of the manuscripts that Swearer has translated, *Meritorious Blessing for Making Buddha Images* (*Anisong Kankosang Phra Phuttha Rup*), which was discussed in chapter 6, includes a list of various materials and the blessings a devotee would acquire by making a Buddha image with each material. Another manuscript, the *Manual for Making a Buddha Image* (*Tamra Kankosang Phra Phuttha Rup*), provides instructions for determining the proper bodily proportions of a Buddha image:

> If one wants to construct a Buddha image equal in size to the Buddha himself, measure from knee to knee when seated in a cross-legged position; divide this distance into four lengths—one part equals the distance from the base of the spine to the navel, a second from the navel to the chest, a third from the chest to the chin, and a fourth from the chin to the hairline. The upper arm from the armpit to the elbow equals the length of the face; the length from the elbow to the wrist also equals that of the face, as does the distance from the wrist to the end of the fingers; the length of the fingers is half the length of the face; the length of one finger joint equals one-third of the side of the face . . . the pupil of the eye is rounded like the hoof of a bull; the eyeball is made to shine like a clove of garlic; the eyebrow is curved like Indra's bow; the ears are as long as the face; the top of the ear is level with the eyebrow. The image reflects three different faces: Thai, Khom [Khmer], and a robber [king]. The Thai face is similar to that of the king of kings. The blend of these three, which characterizes the Buddha image, is called the *rājasiṅha* (the Lion Lord).[34]

The proportions of a Buddha image are also the subject of another text that has been found in Lampang and described by the art historian Hiram W. Woodward Jr. The text defines three models of images with different ratios of measurements. The most squat type of model is called the *nigrodhalakkhaṇa* ("banyan characteristics"); then there are the *gajalakkhaṇa* ("elephant characteristics") and the *sīhalakkhaṇa* ("lion characteristics" or perhaps "Lankan characteristics").[35]

Did monks or lay devotees actually apply these or other standards of measure to deciding the validity of any Buddha image? Woodward observes that, as yet, there are no specific statues definitively identified as belonging to any of the three types, so there is no evidence for how the Lampang text influenced the creation of images. He suggests that the names presented "ideal types" rather than detailed prototypes for craftsmen, and that while craftsmen were likely aware of such instructions, the extent to which they adhered to them is not apparent.[36] In Swearer's detailed description of contemporary Buddha image production in the Chiang Mai region, it is noteworthy that he does not mention actually observing the craftsmen or anyone else taking proportional formulae into account.[37] If one of the proportions of an image was off the mark, was the image then deemed invalid as a representation of the Buddha? Even if texts such as these were well known to devotees, the extent of practical application of these standards is an open question. Moreover, it is interesting, in view of modern art historians' fixation on iconography, that not one among the mentioned texts seems to refer to the gestures of the statues.

Rather than providing technical instructions for the making of Buddha images, these manuals were probably meant to present ideals. They may have provided support to the authority of the *saṅgha* in its role as the guarder and regulator of the forms and qualities of representations of the Buddha. Because a Buddha image was not recognized as such until it was consecrated by the *saṅgha*, monks had to determine whether any specific sculpture presented to them was worthy of consecration as an appropriate representation of the Blessed One. No image is recognized as a Buddha image without undergoing ritual consecration. The northern Thai consecration ceremony for Buddha images as it is practiced in contemporary times has been powerfully described and analyzed by Swearer in *Becoming the Buddha* (2004). To briefly summarize his description, the ceremony is held in the compound of the monastery and includes participation by monks and lay devotees. It usually takes place between sunset and sunrise, with the duration of the ceremony depending on the texts recited, the number of objects being consecrated, the number of monks, and the rank of the image's patrons. The main activities include chants, sermons, meditation, and presentation of gifts to the *saṅgha*. Although individual rituals might differ from one another, the northern Thai ceremony essentially is "a mimetic reenactment of the night of the Buddha's enlightenment."[38] Consecration is a ritual of "performative power to create a living representation of the *tathāgata*" and "fuse[s] the person and story of the Buddha with the image of the Blessed One."[39] The undertaking of the consecration of Buddha images is noted, though usually not recounted in detail, in chronicles dating from the fifteenth to twentieth centuries of the Emerald, Grand Lord, Setangkhamani, Sihing, and Sila images as well as the Buddha Image Lying on a Mango-Tree Log and the Emerald Buddha of Don Tao.[40] The noting of the consecration highlights the importance of the ceremony and the key role of monks in the creation of Buddha statues.

Descriptions of Buddha Images in Lanna Chronicles and Inscriptions

There are consistencies in the ways in which images are described in *tamnan* and inscriptions dating from the fifteenth through twentieth centuries.

In chapter 2, we noted that travelling image chronicles typically include a description of the process of the image's crafting. For example, according to the chronicle of the Sihing Buddha image, whose casting was sponsored by the kings of Lanka,

> At that time, the kings called for metal craftsmen who had great skill to form in beeswax a Buddha image with the characteristics as the kings remembered them. When the model was finished, a large crucible was arranged in the middle of the charcoal-fired kiln for the smelting. Then groups of [various kinds of deities, including] *sura, asura, garuḍa, manusaya, bhujaṅga, gandharva, vijāḍara, kinara, suparṇa, kuṁbhaṇḍa, devatā, nāga, yakṣa,* and *mahābrahma* helped to contribute metal such as gold, silver, copper, and brass: 16 crucibles of metal to be mixed together and then put into the crucible in the middle of the kiln. When the metal was fluid and all the impurities removed, a large pair of tongs was used to grip the crucible and pour the metal into the mould.[41]

Those who read this text or heard it preached were probably familiar with the method by which a Buddha statue is cast. The author probably aimed to impress them with the long listing of various kinds of deities who donated metal. Given the divine origins of the alloy of the statue, it is interesting that the later history of the Sihing turns on its rather unremarkable appearance. The chronicle recounts that when the Sihing Buddha image was brought to Ayutthaya, it was placed in a hall together with other bronze Buddha images, and people could not see why it was distinctive from the others. Later, when Mae Luang, the Queen Mother of Kamphaeng Phet, went to the hall in order to lift away the Sihing, she did not know which statue it was and had to bribe the curator to identify it.[42] Upon obtaining the statue, Mae Luang loaded it onto a boat and sent it off to her son, the ruler of Kamphaeng Phet. When the statue's disappearance was discovered, the King of Ayutthaya angrily confronted Mae Luang. To appease him, she promised to make a copy of the Sihing in Kamphaeng Phet and then return the original to Ayutthaya; naturally, in the end the people of

Kamphaeng Phet kept the original and shipped a copy to Ayutthaya.[43] Even though the statue was produced by divine donors and had an illustrious origin with the kings of Lanka, the Sihing did not have a particularly notable appearance.

A similar story was told about the Emerald Buddha, which was made from the Amaragaṭa, a divine jewel so powerful that before it was donated by the gods to be sculpted into an image it was ensconced on Vipulla Mountain, surrounded by an assemblage of 750 jewels. During the sixteenth century, Chiang Mai was ruled for a brief period by a Lao prince of Lan Chang, Jethādhirāja (Thai: Sethathirat). When his father died in Lan Chang, Jethādhirāja decided to return there, taking the Emerald Buddha with him. According to one version of the story, the prince did not know which Buddha image was the Emerald Buddha, "as there are so many statues of Buddha made of precious stones." He therefore bribed the curator of the image hall, who placed a red flower on the Emerald Buddha's hand to identify it.[44] These similar vignettes of the Sihing and Emerald Buddhas indicate that people of the past understood that very powerful Buddha images were not necessarily visually striking.

The *tamnan* of the Sandalwood Buddha image refers to the making of copies. According to the chronicle, which may have been composed in the fifteenth or sixteenth century, the Sandalwood image was transported out of India and into the northern Thai territories through a deception involving copying. The *tamnan* recounts that after Pasenadi died, his son Viḍūḍabha succeeded him as king of Kosala and keeper of the Sandalwood image. One day the Tai ruler Phraya Suvaṇṇabhūmi sent Viḍūḍabha a letter requesting the statue. Viḍūḍabha, wishing to avoid friction with Phraya Suvaṇṇabhūmi, consented to the request but did not hand over the statue directly. Instead he had craftsmen sculpt two images in sandalwood, "large and tall, of the same weight" as the Sandalwood image and of which "the body and facial features were the same in all respects." The two copies were lined up in a hall on the same platform as the Sandalwood image, one to the right and one to the left of the original statue. Phraya Suvaṇṇabhūmi's servants were then led to the hall and informed that all three statues were the Sandalwood image, and they were welcome to take any one of them. The servants wanted only the image "built by Phraya Pasenadi of Kosala" but did not know which of the three it was. They spotted a neighborhood child outside the hall. With a string of pearls they enticed the child to identify the Sandalwood image "from ancient times." The child discreetly marked the base of the original image with a piece of lime. Phraya Suvaṇṇabhūmi's servants then hauled that image away and seated it on a boat heading back to their native land.[45] The statue was later moved by various people, including monks, noblemen, and a hunter, from place to place in Lanna.

This account of the Sandalwood Buddha again illustrates how a Buddha image could be duplicated to perfection, with apparent ease. As in the story of the Sihing Buddha, copying of the Sandalwood image enabled its distribution to devotees in various places; it was the progenitor of a lineage of images and contributed to the prosperity of Buddhism. Copying is an activity undertaken by the devout. At the same time, the colorful stories of deception in the Emerald, Sandalwood, and Sihing chronicles point to the great value that devotees placed on possessing powerful statues and the ploys they needed to undertake to obtain them. The involvement of rulers in the three images' stories reflects the particular importance, observed by Tambiah, of famous images for kings.

In the accounts of Lanna Buddha statues, the images' physical characteristics, when they are described, usually include material, weight, and size. Some texts highlighted the material's expense, scarcity, and special qualities such as scent (for example, of sandalwood) or mode of production (as for the pulverized substance *muk*). In the chronicle of the Emerald Buddha, the physical aspects of the statue noted are its material, the divine Amaragaṭa jewel, and its height, one *sok*, seven *niu* (about fifty-three to fifty-nine centimeters).[46] The *tamnan* of the Sandalwood image provides a more detailed description of its subject:

> At that time, Phraya Pasenadi of Kosala thus had a royal envoy go to get red sandalwood from a Phraya of Suvaṇṇa. The base was 6 *ongkhuli* [about eleven centimeters] in height. The width and height of the Lord Buddha was 22 *ongkhuli* [about thirty-nine centimeters] and the width between the two shoulders measured 23.5 *ongkhuli* [about forty-one centimeters]. And the Phraya then incised beautiful hair and had the cloth of the *saṅghāṭī* put on one thumb. And the Sandalwood image when it was created, it weighed 8,000 [about eight kilograms]. When it was decorated beautifully and completed, Phraya Pasenadi of Kosala went to invite the Lord Buddha to come in order that he could see the Buddha image.[47]

The *Chronicle of the Grand Lord* (*Tamnan Phra Chao Ton Luang*) describes the creation of the giant Grand Lord statue of Phayao. The author lists the measurements of the statue in detail. For instance, "The neck was 2 *wa* and 1 *khuep* long [about 3.7 meters] and 3 *wa* [about 5.3 meters] around. The shoulder was 3 *sok* [about 1.3 meters] long. The collarbone was 4 *wa* [about 7 meters] long. From the chest to the chin was 2 *wa* [about 3.5 meters]."[48] This list recalls the style of enumerating dimensional specifications found in the manual of Buddha image proportion discussed earlier. It is interesting that other versions of the same story of the Grand Lord have different figures for the same measurements.[49] This may indicate that what was important was not so much presenting an accurate recording of measurements as emphasizing the immensity of the image. The chronicle also provides a detailed accounting of materials and costs used to make the image—for example, "people were hired for 2,000 gold; to buy lacquer, 500 gold was spent; to buy lime, 2 million [units of money] was spent," and so on.[50] These amounts also served to highlight the huge scale of the Grand Lord. As in the case of the size measurements, other versions of the same story have different figures for the expenses.[51]

In various texts, size and weight are also presented as measures evidencing the equivalency of model and copy. For instance, the Grand Lord statue is said to be the same size as the previous Buddha Konāgamana,[52] reflecting the traditional belief that Buddhas of the distant past were enormous, though they became successively smaller, with each shorter than his predecessor. The *Chronicle of the Buddha Image Seated on the Earth* (*Tamnan Phra Phuttha Rup Chao Nang Din*), a nineteenth-century chronicle about a statue still revered today in Phayao Province, recounts that a lay devotee made a Buddha image at the Buddha's request. However, the Buddha found the image to be too small and had the devotee remake it to be the same size as the Buddha.[53] Size and weight in these examples are key features of the Buddhas that had to be replicated in their images.

Tai texts also record examples of the making of Buddha images according to the height and/or weight of their sponsors. As was mentioned in chapter 6, the early sixteenth-century *Jinakālamālīpakaraṇaṁ* (*JKM*), the *tamnan* of Buddhist history, records that in 1510, King Kaeo of Chiang Mai donated about 60,000 pieces of gold, an amount equal to his own body weight, to cast a seated Buddha image with a height equivalent to his standing height.

The custom of describing Buddha images according to size and material was not unique to Lanna, but seems to have been a Buddhist practice dating back many centuries. This is suggested by evidence from early Chinese and Lankan texts. For example, Robert L. Brown studied the descriptions of images in the seventh-century travel account of ancient India written by Xuanzang and observes, "Xuanzang basically records only four characteristics about the images he mentions: their size, the material they are made of, their location, and their miraculous nature." He adds, "Xuanzang was interested in mostly large images and in images made of precious materials."[54] For medieval Lanka, Wilhelm Geiger has noted that in the *Mahāvaṃsa* and *Culavaṃsa,* Buddha images were described according to their materials and postures (standing, sitting, or reclining.) He also observes that there are no mentions of *mudrā,* symbolic gestures of the statues, anywhere in the chronicles.[55]

Likewise, the writers of Lanna *tamnan* and inscriptions devoted little attention to the postures and gestures of images. As discussed in chapter 6, only one of the travelling image chronicles, that of the Sihing Buddha, and six of the eighty-five full-length inscriptions catalogued by Hans Penth mention the posture of the statue. Only three out of eighteen mentions of the making of images in the *JKM* cite the image's posture. The Sandalwood image is by its measurements implied to be a seated image, though its posture is not stated in the description of the craftsmen's work; the *mudrā* of Buddha statues are also usually not mentioned in chronicles and inscriptions. One exception is the Phra Sila chronicle, possibly dating to the late eighteenth century, which describes the image as being in the position of "collecting alms."[56] Unexpectedly, it does not refer to the figures of the monk and an elephant next to the Buddha, which indicate that the sculpture illustrates the Buddha subduing the ferocious Nālāgiri elephant. The Sanskrit word *mudrā* (Pali: *muddā*) does not seem to be found in Lanna *tamnan* or inscriptions; as far as I am aware, *mudrā* was not used in Thailand to describe Buddha images until the early twentieth century when the modern study of art history began there. Notably, a paucity of physical description is also found in Japanese medieval stories about statues.[57] In some Chinese medieval stories about statues, the specific Buddha or Bodhisattva that the statue represents is not even mentioned.[58]

This is not to say that people of the past lacked appreciation for the aesthetic qualities of Buddhist art. Style may well have been much appreciated but not perceived as being particularly worthy of remark in Tai monastic writings. There does seem to be some evidence, though scant, in old Lanna texts that people of the past understood, perhaps even categorized, statues at a stylistic level. The inscription for Image No. 2 (1470) in the Penth data set, which was discussed in chapter 6, refers to the statue as "this Sahing." It is possible that "Sahing" was then recognized as the name of a particular style of Buddha image. There are also possible mentions in the *JKM* of artistic or architectural styles. The text relates that in 1483 King Tilok of Chiang Mai had his commander-in-chief Sīhagotta and great minister Āṇākiccādhipati begin casting a large bronze Buddha image "resembling the Lava [Lopburi] image."[59] The reference may suggest that the appearance of the statue was recognized as being of a different style than locally made statues in Chiang Mai. Griswold hypothesized that this "Lava" image was a copy of "some famous Ûtòng statue at Lopburî."[60] Other descriptive terms found in the *JKM* may also refer to specific architectural styles. During the early sixteenth century, King Kaeo of Chiang Mai had an ordination hall built with *usabha* (taurine) features.[61] He also constructed a new courtyard (*parivena*) with *gaja* (elephantine) features at the Great Rattavana Monastery (Wat Pa Daeng Luang).[62] It seems possible that the terms *usabha* and *gaja* refer to styles of decoration or architecture.

Material and Merit: Economic Aspects of the Buddha Image

The allusions to material, size, and weight likely reflect the significance of the donation of a statue (or any other donated object) as an exchange of material for merit. Such transactions make up the chief "economic" activity of a monastery. The knowledge of a Buddha image's material, size, and weight enable the image's economic and merit-generating values to be assessed as well as compared with those of other images and donated objects. In the exchange of material for merit, the main counterparties are donors and monks. Craftsmen typically do not seem to have been considered principal parties to the transaction despite their role in the production of the statue. Though their aesthetic and technical skills were appreciated, and perhaps they were seen to obtain merit for their support to the *sāsana,* the craftsmen's role was to enable the material-merit exchanges between donors and monasteries. The craftsman was compensated for his work with money or goods from the donor; the donor's financial outlay was the key material element in the assessment of the merit-generating value of the donation. The limitation of the craftsman's agency seems also to be reflected in Griswold's observation that the craftsman was usually valued for his skills as a copyist and not for his distinctive style. As we have seen, craftsmen were typically not mentioned in Lanna *tamnan* and inscriptions. In the copying of a Buddha image, the emphasis on replicating iconography, and the lesser interest in imitating style, may have further narrowed the perceived contribution of the craftsman. The limited value placed on the craftsman has the effect of preventing his agency as expressed by the image, which is his handiwork, from overwhelming other agencies that the statue represents: that of the Buddha, whose forms of representation are regulated by the monks, and that of the donor, to whom the merit accrues.

The making of a Buddha image thus arises within a framework of cultural values and economic factors; the image is "sacred" but also may be subject to forces of the wider economy through the connection of merit to the value of the donation. The insight that objects can vacillate between sacred and market spheres, and that cultural values influence how and when it shifts between them, has been raised and analyzed by Igor Kopytoff.[63] Adopting Kopytoff's framework, we can see how a Buddha image may be regarded at different moments in its "life" as a site of worship or as an economic asset. As the Buddha image takes up its sacred throne in the hall, it preserves to a certain extent its "singularity" or status as sacred and thereby insulated from market forces, to use the term as developed by Kopytoff. The act of sacralization, as Eric Reinders has observed, enables items of economic value to be removed from circulation and rendered to the domain of the monastery.[64] Nonetheless, even within the monastery, a Buddha image may still be recognized for its "commodity" value within the material-merit exchange system of the monastery. While the merit earned by the donor for the gift may not be precisely quantified, the gift still provides a point of comparison; with the completion of each donation, a new example of financial outlay is manifested to which future donations may be compared. In other words, as Reinders has noted, the material of the image may continue to assert its own agency even following reshaping and consecration into something more than just a piece of wood or metal.[65]

The sculpting of raw materials into a statue of the Buddha is accomplished by following a standardized repertory of iconography.

This standardization provided a means by which monasteries control the way the Buddha is depicted. It also affected the nature of the production of images. Even the most famous images drew on a historical set of iconographical forms familiar to any craftsman. Indeed, as the stories of the Emerald, Sandalwood, and Sihing images show, the lack of distinctive appearance was not presented as a weakness of the form but as a useful feature that could facilitate their copying, which was highlighted as a meritorious act undertaken by devoted worshippers to support Buddhism. The range of standardized image types may reflect the popularity of specific images—those that, as Griswold suggested, were perceived to have magical powers. Notably, standardization also facilitated the valuation of images within the economy of the monastery. The limited range of iconographies in Lanna made it easier to compare statues of different sizes. This standardization of form, combined with the traditional esteem for copying, supported the proliferation of Buddha images, as the craftsmen could repeatedly follow set formulae.

Copying and the Power of Buddha Images

Of course, standardization of form did not prevent specific images from developing their own individualized agencies. In the travelling image chronicles, it was the social interaction between the statues and their devotees that was emphasized and that distinguished the images from others. As mentioned earlier, the Sihing Buddha image, when placed in the hall of images at Ayutthaya, appeared no more interesting or significant to the people there than any other statue. However, those who had been informed of the Sihing's prestigious history understood its importance and determined to possess or copy it. The recounting of the *tamnan* of the image served to confirm and disseminate the knowledge of its illustrious history and power.

The chronicle's important role in revealing the intangible significance of a particular Buddha image was explicitly recognized in some of the texts themselves. For instance, the *Chronicle of the Sandalwood Image* states that the chronicle was originally written by the *mahāthera* Nāgasena in Rājagaha in ancient India. This was said to have been copied by a Lanna monk who brought it to Lanka, where another monk copied it and took it to Lanna to preach it: "He told the people that this Sandalwood image had great supernatural power." The *tamnan* was copied and preached by others as well, so that more people, including the ruler of Chiang Mai and visiting officials from Ayutthaya, knew of the statue, "which Phraya Pasenadi of Kosala created when the Lord Buddha was still alive," and were inspired to go venerate the Sandalwood image or even to obtain it for themselves.[66] Another example of the significance of a *tamnan* for explaining the nonvisible significance of a Buddha image is found in the *Chronicle of the Grand Lord,* which tells us that the Burmese swept up the people of Phayao and forcibly resettled them in Chanthaburi (probably Vientiane). The "temple slaves" who had been the caretakers of the Grand Lord had managed to pack the *tamnan* with them but then lost it. They became worried about the condition of the statue back in Phayao: "There was no one who knew, not one person, it was said. Because of that the people then together wrote a chronicle and had Muen Uttama, a person of Chiang Khong, take it and show it to householders and ordinands in Phayao."[67] Those people of the past who heard the preaching of these and other *tamnan* about Buddha images received lessons in the rewards of pious behavior towards Buddha images. They also obtained useful knowledge about a Buddha statue whose power might benefit them. They were being invited to join the prestigious lineage of devotees of a powerful image and to improve their karmic futures, just as previous donors had.

Copying of a Buddha statue involved not only the replication of a physical object but the extension of a specific social or karmic network to new devotees. By making copies, the new devotees aimed to deploy the agency of the original for their own purposes. Walter Benjamin suggested that religious images were sequestered within the world of ritual until the development of mechanical reproduction, which freed them to assume new roles in other realms—particularly that of politics.[68] Yet as we have seen, Tai Buddha images, long before the advent of mechanical reproduction, were not insulated from political and economic concerns; *tamnan* were authored by monks who were attuned to circumstances in the wider social worlds of their devotees. Sacralization never fully freed the Buddha image from the world of commodities, nor of relations of social power. At the same time, original images continue to exude a powerful "aura" even after their replication, as is most obviously understood in the case of the Sandalwood image, the model upon which all other Buddha images are said to be based. The copy at least initially draws upon the aura of the original, but it is understood as having the potential to develop its own repertoire of powers and its own community of patrons. This potential of the copy for individualization may be related to the fact that so many copies of Tai Buddha images are not utter facsimiles of their supposed models. As the art historian David Freedberg remarked regarding copies of revered Christian statues and paintings at pilgrimage sites in Europe, "The people who produce these images do not set out to ensure that they look like their effective archetypes (although, that in part is what makes them effective); they set out to ensure that they look just a little different. Then, often, the images work better and more distinctively."[69] Perhaps a similar conception influenced the degree of freedom, noted by Griswold, permitted to craftsmen in designing an image's style.

In sum, the patron may have wanted to sponsor a "magical device" to achieve his own ends, but the appearance of an image was also influenced by the materials, craftsmen, and monks. The visual form of a Buddha image is the result of the integration of these different agencies, whose influences may have varying degrees of strength; copying is the result of a process of collaboration, conflict, and compromise. An image that is seen as magically powerful and thereby attracts a large following of devotees is basically an image in which agencies have been integrated and channelled in a way to which devotees have been receptive.

Lanna's chronicles and inscriptions add depth to our understanding of art history in Thailand, revealing some of the historical complexities of the actual production and use of Buddhist art, and suggesting how images of the past were valued before they became commodities of a different sort than described here, as goods of the art market.

Conclusion

Lanna chronicles and inscriptions depict Buddha images as person-like objects that materialized and advanced social values and objectives. Buddha statues were not finished at consecration, as art historical texts often imply, but were constantly shaped by physical and conceptual interaction with their devotees. The narrative structure, motifs, and themes of stories about Buddha images indicate the configurations of social agency acting around and through the images. Presented as bearing characteristics of both persons and commodities, the images were integrated into the social and economic worlds of their makers and worshippers. Buddha images were in fact positioned as the focal points around which history was structured.

In the travelling image chronicles discussed in chapter 2, the history of Lanna was presented as a series of interactions between great Buddhist patrons and Buddha statues. The narratives wove together illustrious personages, places, and motifs in a panregional, politicoreligious lineage. This vision of history is a significant contrast to that presented in ancient manuscripts such as the *Jinakālamālīpakaraṇaṁ*, the *Mahāvaṁsa*, and Burmese/Mon chronicles, as well as in modern-day works which structure history as a chronology of rulers or capital cities. The Buddha images were depicted in the travelling image chronicles as embodying concepts of lineage, place, and monarchy, and by enshrining them, Tai kings of the fifteenth and later centuries could attach themselves to a deeper history and wider landscape of Southeast Asia and the broader Buddhist world.

Monks needed to manage relations with their various patrons in order to ensure the enduring existence of their monasteries and orders even as death and conquest caused disruptions among local political authorities. The travelling image chronicles may be understood as discursive tactics in the political and economic strategies of the monkhood. For monks, Buddha images provided means by which they could influence the agency of lay devotees, especially kings.

Another view of the power relations between royal patrons and monastic beneficiaries was presented in the different versions of the *Mūlasāsanā* discussed in chapter 3. This was revealed by focusing on an important aspect of the *Mūlasāsanā* unexplored by previous studies, the fascinating descriptions of the various tactics deployed by monks in a dispute between two orders. Contradicting Weberian visions of monastics as renunciants who avoid entanglement in the political and economic intrigues of the lay world, the monks deliberately embroiled the laity across the region in their feud. Notably, one of the ways monks drew in lay devotees was by broadcasting claims involving Buddha images. The emphasis on the significance of monks' relation to images contrasts with the link between lay patrons and images underscored in the travelling image chronicles. The Buddha image, because it was created through the agency of both lay and monastic devotees, was an ideal intermediary by which the monks could involve the lay community in their dispute.

The understanding of the Buddha image as an instrument to materialize social values and advance social objectives is also evidenced by another set of historic texts, the hundreds of inscriptions on the bases of Buddha images recorded by Hans Penth in central Chiang Mai. In chapter 6, Penth's data was studied in detail as a whole. In the inscriptions, the creation of an image was recognized as a collaborative effort bringing together and making visible social or karmic networks. The Buddha image was also a material object that invited ongoing change; consecration marked only the beginning of the image's life. The Buddha image constantly exchanges agency with its devotees, who bring to it their wishes, which it may magically fulfil, and who add the material marks of their own agency by donating umbrellas to it, adding an inscription to its base, or affixing a piece of gold leaf to its cheek.

The significance of the image's materiality to devotees was highlighted in chapters 6 and 7. Even as devotees revered the images as sacred representatives of the Buddha, they appreciated the costliness of the specific materials from which the images were made. In Lanna *tamnan* and inscriptions, the features of images that tended to be noted were the material and size. These aspects reflect the economic value of the donation and thus the possible amount of spiritual merit generated by that donation. Buddha images could still be subject to forces of "commoditization," even after they were "singularized" upon their consecration.

In contrast to material and size, the visual appearance, including the iconography, of images was infrequently described in the texts. This was probably *not* due to the fact that the visual appearance or style was unimportant to devotees; instead, it seems more likely that the formal features were not stated because they were assumed to be conforming to standard forms. With the shapes standardized by iconography, the material and size were the features by which the economic and merit values of Buddha images could be judged and compared. The limited range of iconography in Lanna eased the copying of images and supported their proliferation. Thus, iconography facilitated the commoditization of images. Even the most famous Buddha images were described by their material, weight, and size, and depicted as being visually nondistinctive and easily copied. The images' suitability as models was not necessarily related to their forms. Instead, the stories about images highlighted their conceptual significance to devotees as the product of interactions among powerful agencies throughout their lives. To copy a model was not only to replicate visual features but to extend an important social and karmic network. This helps to explain why some images were more highly venerated than others and seen to be more worthy of copying. This adds to the understanding of how models were selected for copying, a topic that has received surprisingly little attention from art historians despite the assumption of constant copying that underlies the entire study of Buddhist art in Thailand.

Chapters 4 and 5 highlighted how Buddha images were distinctive in northern Thai devotion by comparing them with stories of the Buddha's bodily relics in Lanna, as well as with stories from other related Buddhist cultures, particularly those of the Lankans and the Burmese/Mon. As the texts showed, people in the past did not necessarily see Buddha images as deriving their power only from relics enshrined within them—contrary to some claims about images by contemporary scholars. In fact, stories about relics always describe the sight of their performance of miracles and even describe them as appearing in human bodily form, thus providing visual frames for relics and emphasizing that the visual imagery of the relic was key to evidencing its authenticity. This suggests that visuality was important to devotion and therefore puts into question a scholarly assumption that relics more directly channel the Buddha than do images.

Moreover, Lanna stories indicate that Tai people in the past distinguished the material and conceptual characteristics of the two kinds of objects. The structure of the Lanna stories of relics suggests how Buddhism was integrated into local places. In these accounts, the towns of Lanna were not depicted as the passive or lucky recipients of Buddha relics but as the crucial conduits for the ongoing transmission of Buddha agency. This view presents Buddha relics not so much as objects emanating from ancient Buddhist India to benefit distant lands than as objects whose power could only be fully realized by their establishment in specific spots in Lanna. This theme of connection between relics and local place is also present in some Burmese/Mon stories but is less prominent in stories from Lanka, which tended to emphasize the differentiation of local social hierarchies in the handling of relics. The similarities and differences among the Burmese/Mon, Lankan, and Lanna traditions in theme, motif, and structure evidence early Tai Buddhist literature as sharing in cross-regional "intertextuality." At the same time, the distinctive characteristics of *tamnan* show that Lanna's monastic authors were not simply mimicking the earlier Lankan *vaṃsas*.

This Lanna theme of the importance of place was also found in stories about Buddha images. As chapter 4 highlighted, some statues are relic-like and exist to be in place; unlike the travelling images, the postconsecration lives of these images was not depicted. The chronicles culminated with the statues being created at a particular place, often fulfilling a prediction of the Buddha. Though both images and bodily relics could be accounted as in place, relics did not journey in the travelling image mode.

These different types of stories about Buddha images, those travelling and those in place, illustrate ways in which monastic authors sought to manage the complexity of agency relations expressed by an image by providing different examples in which the agencies of the Buddha, lay devotees, and monks were combined in proper ways. This theme was also conveyed by Burmese stories of Buddha images being deployed to serve human schemes. Managing how the Buddha was depicted, in his image and other representations, has been a key task of the monkhood. Maintenance of iconographic conventions was integral to this management of the image of the Buddha, but it was not the only means. Monks at various times emphasized and suppressed the various agencies that could be expressed by an image, as in the example of the destruction of images consecrated by unworthy monks and in the suppression of the agency of the craftsman in the making of an image.

As the focus of this study has been on interactions between Buddha images and their devotees, it may seem odd to some readers that there has been no discussion of personal or individual worship of the images. The chronicles provide almost no detail of such devotions beyond reporting that worshippers were happy and filled with faith, often shouting and waving flags at the sight of the images. The affective and phenomenological nature of worship is not evidenced in these stories. The descriptions of devotion are conventional, intended by their authors to encourage faith and donation though without detailing the individual affective experiences of the worshippers.

This study has relied on texts composed or copied almost entirely by monks. Admittedly, it only provides a small sample of evidence for a society in which oral traditions were much older and more widespread. Many stories likely circulated in oral versions before and at the same time as their written versions were being composed and copied. There are countless other stories of interactions between images and their devotees that have never been recorded. The texts I have discussed here suggest the range of meanings of Buddha images and point to the swirl of assertion, denial, and cooperation among social agencies through them; this complexity suggests how for art objects, even ones of apparently standardized form such as Buddha images, meanings can never quite be fixed. Perhaps this changeability, even mysteriousness, is the defining characteristic of the true object of art.

Notes

Chapter 1: Introduction

1. HRH Princess Maha Chakri Sirindhorn, "Foreword," in M. C. Subhadradis Diskul, *History of the Temple of the Emerald Buddha* (Bangkok: Bureau of the Royal Household, n.d.).

2. John S. Strong, *Relics of the Buddha* (Princeton, NJ: Princeton University Press, 2004), 19–20.

3. Maurice Walshe, trans., *The Long Discourses of the Buddha: A Translation of the Dīgha Nikāya* (Boston: Wisdom, 1995), 270. Prince Damrong Rajanubhab pointed to the Mahāparinibbāna Sutta as evidence to justify the veneration of *dhammacetiya*. Prince Damrong Rajanubhab, *Tamnan Phra Phuttha Chedi* [A history of Buddhist monuments], 2nd ed. (Bangkok: Krom Sinlapakon, 2490 [1947]), 7–8.

4. An English translation of chapters 8 and 9 of *Tamnan Phra Phuttha Chedi nai Sayam* was published as *A History of Buddhist Monuments in Siam*, trans. Sulak Sivaraksa (Bangkok: Siam Society, 1962).

5. Damrong, *Tamnan Phra Phuttha Chedi,* 45–49, 89–93.

6. Damrong, *Tamnan Phra Phuttha Chedi,* 49, cites Foucher regarding the form of flame radiances on Buddha images. Foucher presented his theory that Buddha representations in art were initially "aniconic" in Alfred Foucher, "Les débuts de l'art bouddhique," *Journal Asiatique* 10, no. 17 (1911): 55–79, and in subsequent publications. Foucher's "aniconic" theory was challenged eight decades later by Susan Huntington, whose view was in turn contested by Vidya Dehejia. See Susan L. Huntington, "Early Buddhist Art and the Theory of Aniconism," *Art Journal* 49, no. 4 (1990): 401–408; and Vidya Dehejia, "Aniconism and the Multivalence of Emblems," *Ars Orientalis* 21 (1991): 45–66. See also Susan L. Huntington, "Aniconism and the Multivalence of Emblems: Another Look," *Ars Orientalis* 22 (1992): 111–156; and Vidya Dehejia, "Rejoinder to Susan Huntington," *Ars Orientalis* 22 (1992): 157.

In addition to Foucher's work, Damrong's approach to Buddhist art history also integrated publications by other early European scholars and personal discussions Damrong had with these scholars, particularly George Cœdès, the French pioneer of southeast Asian history and archaeology who was appointed first by Damrong as head of the National Library of Siam from 1918 to 1926 and then as secretary general of the country's Royal Institute of Literature, Archaeology, and Fine Arts from 1927 to 1929. Regarding Damrong's works on Thai history and archaeology in the scholarly context of their time of composition, see A. B. Griswold, "Thoughts on a Centenary," *Journal of the Siam Society* 52, no. 1 (1964): 21–56.

7. The travel account in verse, *Thiao Mueang Phra Ruang* [Journey to the kingdom of Phra Ruang] (1908), by Prince Vajiravudh, the future King Rama VI, includes an attempt to date the monuments of Sukhothai and is considered in Thailand to be the first book on Thai archaeology. In Europe, Alfred Salmony's *Sculpture in Siam* (London: E. Benn, 1925) had limited influence, probably due to criticism of its factual errors.

8. The study of the dating, style, and iconography is so predominant in the field of Thai art history that it is common for survey books and introductory manuals to discuss only the style and iconography of Buddha images with no discussion, beyond present-day assumptions about definitions of iconography, about what the images in the books may have meant for the people who made and used them. See, for example, M. C. Subhadradis Diskul, *Sinlapa nai Prathet Thai* [Art in Thailand] (Bangkok: Thammasat University, 2506 [1963]). This classic reference book of Thai art history has been reprinted more than twenty times in Thailand. See also No Na Paknam, *Phuttha Pratimakam nai Prathet Thai* [Buddha images in Thailand] (Bangkok: Samnak Phim Mueang Boran, 2533 [1990]); and Santi Leksukhum, *Sinlapa Phak Nuea Haripunchai-Lanna* [Art of the north: Hariphunchai-Lanna] (Bangkok: Mueang Boran, 2538 [1995]).

9. Dhida Saraya, "The Development of the Northern Thai States from the Twelfth to the Fifteenth Centuries," PhD diss., University of Sydney, 1982, 103–105.

10. Stanley J. Tambiah, "Famous Buddha Images and the Legitimation of Kings," *Res* 4 (1982): 5–19. See also Stanley Jeyaraja Tambiah, *The Buddhist Saints of the Forest and the Cult of Amulets* (Cambridge: Cambridge University Press, 1984), 230–241.

11. Robert Lingat, "Le culte du Bouddha d'Émeraude," *Journal of the Siam Society* 27, no. 1 (1934): 33.

12. Tambiah, "Famous Buddha Images."

13. Sarassawadee Ongsakul, *History of Lan Na,* trans. Chitraporn Tanratanakul (Chiang Mai: Silkworm Books, 2005), 1–6.

14. Udom Rungrueangsi counted 206, while François Lagirarde estimated 230. Udom Rungrueangsi, "Tamnan," in *Saranukrom Watanatham Thai Phak Nuea* [Encyclopedia of northern Thai culture] (Bangkok: Mulaniti Saranukrom Watanatham Thai, 2542 [1999]), 5:2412–2416. François Lagirarde, "Temps et lieux d'histoires bouddhiques: À propos de quelques 'chroniques' inédites du Lan Na," *Bulletin de l'École française d'Extrême-Orient* 94 (2007): 61.

15. Sarassawadee, *History of Lan Na,* 8. A fascinating recent study of the history of Lanna's Buddhist writing cultures, particularly in Pali, is Daniel Veidlinger, *Spreading the Dhamma: Writing, Orality, and Textual Transmission in Buddhist Northern Thailand* (Honolulu: University of Hawai'i Press, 2006).

16. Hans Penth, *A Brief History of Lān Nā* (Chiang Mai: Silkworm Books, 1994), 13.

17. Justin McDaniel, "Two Buddhist Librarians: The Proximate Mechanisms of Northern Thai Buddhist History," in *Buddhist Manuscript Cultures,* ed. Stephen C. Berkwitz, Juliane Schober and Claudia Brown (London: Routledge, 2009), 137.

18. Lagirarde, "Temps et lieux d'histoires bouddhiques," 60.

19. Hans Penth, "Buddhist Literature of Lān Nā on the History of Lān Nā's Buddhism," *Journal of the Pali Text Society* 23 (1997): 46.

20. Peter Skilling, "Geographies of Intertextuality: Buddhist Literature in Pre-modern Siam," *Aséanie* 19 (2007): 105.

21. Ibid., 107.

22. Kate Crosby, "What Does Not Get Translated in Buddhist Studies and the Impact on Teaching," in *Translation and Religion: Holy Untranslatable?,* ed. Lynne Long (Clevedon, England: Multilingual Matters, 2005), 52.

23. McDaniel, "Two Buddhist Librarians," 125.

24. George Cœdès, "Documents sur l'histoire politique et religieuse du Laos occidental," *Bulletin de l'Ecole française d'Extrême-Orient* 25 (1926): 1–202. Other pioneering researchers who have studied *tamnan* in this mode include Prasert na Nagara and Sommai Premchit. See, for example, Prasert na Nagara, "Kho Sangket Bang Prakan Kiao Kap Wannakam Phutthasasana nai Lanna" [Some observations on Buddhist literature in Lanna] (25–33); Prasert na Nagara, "Bot Namsanoe Tamnan Mūlasāsanā Chiang Mai lae Chiang Tung" [Introduction to the Mūlasāsanā chronicles of Chiang Mai and Chiang Tung] (34–41), and Sommai Premchit, "Wannakam Tamnan Nithan Duek Damban" [Ancient chronicles and legends] (89–96), all in *Wannakam Phutthasasana Nai Lanna* [Buddhist literature in Lanna], ed. Phanphen Khrüathai (Chiang Mai: Suriwong Book Centre, 2540 [1997]). Several other chapters in the book, such as those by Sadupon Changkachit, "Chamathewiwong: Wannakam thi Thuk Luem" [The *Cāmadevīvaṃsa*: a forgotten literary work] (235–251); Prakong Nimmanhaeminda, "Wannakam Phutthasasana Yukkueng Phutthakan khong Lanna" [Buddhist literature in Lanna at the midpoint of the Buddhist era" (97–114); and Udom Rungrueangsi, "Wannakam Chadok thi Mi Laksana Pen 'Lanna'" [*Jātakas* with 'Lanna' characteristics] (51–60) are examples of the mode of research in which *tamnan* are read as sources for extracting historic facts.

25. An important exception among art historians is Phiset Chiechanphong, whose insightful writings on Lanna statues will be discussed at various points in the book. See Phiset Chiechanphong, *Ha Phra Ha Chao* [Looking for the sacred] (Bangkok: Matichon, 2545 [2002]); and Phiset Chiechanphong, *Phra Phuttha*

Sihing 'Jing' Thuk Ong Mai Mi 'Plom' Tae Mai Dai Ma Chak Langka [The Sihing Buddha image: "authentic," but not from Lanka] (Bangkok: Matichon, 2546 [2003]).

26. Udom Rungrueangsi, *Wannakam Lanna* [Lanna literature], 5th ed. (Bangkok: Samnak Ngan Kongthun Sanap Sanun Kanwichai, 2546 [2003]), 304.

27. Anan Ganjanapan, "Early Lan Na Thai Historiography: An Analysis of the Fifteenth and Sixteenth Century Chronicles," MA thesis, Cornell University, 1976, 41. See also Donald K. Swearer, "Myth, Legend and History in the Northern Thai Chronicles," *Journal of the Siam Society* 62 (1974): 70.

28. Donald K. Swearer, "Signs of the Buddha in Northern Thai Chronicles," in *Embodying the Dharma: Buddhist Relic Veneration in Asia,* ed. David Germano and Kevin Trainor (Albany: State University of New York Press, 2004), 157.

29. See, for example, Donald K. Swearer, "Part I. Interpretation," in *The Legend of Queen Cāma: Bodhiraṃsi's Cāmadevīvaṃsa, a Translation and Commentary,* by Donald K. Swearer and Sommai Premchit (Albany: State University of New York Press, 1998), 3–36. Swearer's various works on Lanna will be considered at several points in this book.

30. Jonathan S. Walters, "Buddhist History: The Sri Lankan Pāli Vaṃsas and Their Commentary," in *Querying the Medieval,* by Ronald Inden, Jonathan Walters, and Daud Ali (New York: Oxford University Press, 2000), 100, 148.

31. Dhida, "The Development of the Northern Thai States," 64.

32. David K. Wyatt, "Southeast Asia 'Inside Out,' 1300–1800: A Perspective from the Interior," *Modern Asian Studies* 31, no. 3 (1997): 689–709. See also Sarassawadee Ongsakul's understanding of *tamnan* in Sarassawadee, *History of Lan Na,* 1–2.

33. Lagirarde, "Temps et lieux d'histoires bouddhiques," 88.

34. Peter Skilling, "Worship and Devotional Life: Buddhist Devotional Life in Southeast Asia," in *Encyclopedia of Religion,* 2nd ed., ed. Lindsay Jones (Detroit: Macmillan Reference, 2005), 14: 9828.

35. Robert H. Sharf, "Introduction: Prolegomenon to the Study of Japanese Buddhist Icons," in *Living Images: Japanese Buddhist Icons in Context,* ed. Robert H. Sharf and Elizabeth Horton Sharf (Stanford, CA: Stanford University Press, 2001), 14.

36. Alfred Gell, *Art and Agency* (Oxford: Clarendon, 1998), 6–10.

37. Ibid., 16.

38. Ibid., 22; emphasis in the original.

39. Ibid., 6.

40. Robert Layton, "Art and Agency: A Reassessment," *Journal of the Royal Anthropological Institute* 9 (2003): 447–464. See also Robin Osborne and Jeremy Tanner, eds., *Art's Agency and Art History* (Malden, MA: Blackwell, 2007), which contains essays considering the applicability and implications of Gell's

theory in interpreting a variety of art objects from around the world. The book's "Introduction: *Art and Agency* and Art History" (1–27) by Tanner and Osborne provides a useful overview and analysis of Gell's theory. See the essays by Jessica Rawson, "The Agency of, and the Agency for, the Wanli Emperor" (95–113); Peter Stewart, "Gell's Idols and Roman Cult" (155–178); and Irene J. Winter, "Agency Marked, Agency Ascribed: The Affective Object in Ancient Mesopotamia" (42–69) for examples of writings that advocate the relevance of symbolic approaches to particular examples of art. Another volume of essays that take inspiration from Gell's work to analyze the agency of art in a variety of contexts is Christopher Pinney and Nicholas Thomas, eds., *Beyond Aesthetics: Art and the Technologies of Enchantment* (Oxford: Berg, 2001).

41. Justin Thomas McDaniel, "The Agency between Images: The Relationships among Ghosts, Corpses, Monks, and Deities at a Buddhist Monastery in Thailand," *Material Religion* 7, no. 2 (2011): 242–267.

42. Richard H. Davis, *Lives of the Indian Images* (Princeton, NJ: Princeton University Press, 1997).

43. Sarah J. Horton, *Living Buddhist Statues in Early Medieval and Modern Japan* (New York: Palgrave Macmillan, 2007).

44. Igor Kopytoff, "The Cultural Biography of Things: Commoditization as Process," in *The Social Life of Things: Commodities in Cultural Perspective,* ed. Arjun Appadurai (Cambridge: Cambridge University Press, 1986), 64–91.

45. Eric Reinders, "Recycling Icons and Bodies in Chinese Anti-Buddhist Persecutions," *Res* 48 (2005): 61–68.

46. Schopen's work has demonstrated that contrary to a popularly held view of monks as ascetics removed from commercial affairs, monks in north India in the early medieval period (first or second to fifth or sixth centuries) deployed complex financial and legal arrangements and strategies in the conduct of their relationships with each other and with persons and institutions outside the monastery. Monks' management of reliquary shrines and Buddha images involved access and control, legal entitlement to property, advertisement, and maintenance. Many of Schopen's papers have been conveniently published in three volumes of collected papers. Regarding Buddhist images, see, for example, Gregory Schopen, *Bones, Stones, and Buddhist Monks: Collected Papers on the Archaeology, Epigraphy, and Texts of Monastic Buddhism in India* (Honolulu: University of Hawai'i Press, 1997), chaps. 7 and 11. See also Gregory Schopen, *Buddhist Monks and Business Matters: Still More Papers on Monastic Buddhism in India* (Honolulu: University of Hawai'i Press, 2004), chaps. 2 and 10; and Gregory Schopen, *Figments and Fragments of Mahāyāna Buddhism in India* (Honolulu: University of Hawai'i Press, 2005), chaps. 3 and 4.

47. École française d'Extrême-Orient, "Lanna Manuscripts: A Northern Thai Collection of Manuscripts and Other Texts," accessed August 4, 2015, http://www.efeo.fr/lanna_manuscripts/.

Chapter 2: Buddha Images and Devotees

1. The term "golden age" has been frequently used to describe this period; see, for example, Sarassawadee, *History of Lan Na;* Penth, *A Brief History of Lān Nā*; and Veidlinger, *Spreading the Dhamma.* Justin McDaniel has rightly questioned whether the actual prosperity of the golden age has been overemphasized, at least to the extent that the designation is based on a purported flourishing of literature. Justin McDaniel, "Two Bullets in a Balustrade: How the Burmese Have Been Removed from Northern Thai Buddhist History," *Journal of Burma Studies* 11 (2007): 85–126. Nonetheless, in referring to this period as a golden age, art historians have pointed to the development of styles of Buddhist art and architecture, of which numerous fine examples continue to be influential as sites of worship and artistic models.

2. Four versions of the Sihing chronicle are considered in this chapter: SBCN, SBNJ, SBSM, and SBWN.

3. Phra Thamwimolamali, trans., *Nangsue Tamnan Phra Phuttha Rup 'Phra Saekkham'* [Chronicle of the Saekkham Buddha image] (Phayao, Thailand: n.p., 2544 [2001]); Renu Wichasin, ed. and trans., *Phuen Mueang Saenwi Chabab Ho Kham Mueang Yai* [Chronicle of Saenwi, edition of the royal palace of Mueang Yai] (Chiang Mai: Silkworm Books, 2550 [2007]), 4–6, 332–349 (I thank Jotika Khur-Yearn for bringing this source to my attention); David K. Wyatt, trans., *The Crystal Sands: The Chronicles of Nagara Śrī Dharrmarāja* (Ithaca, NY: Cornell University Southeast Asia Program, 1975), 27–29, 86; Phiset, *Phra Phuttha Sihing 'Jing' Thuk Ong Mai Mi,* 33–37; and Tun Aung Chain, *Chronicle of Ayutthaya: A Translation of the Yodaya Yazawin* (Yangon, Myanmar: Myanmar Historical Commission, 2005), 55–68.

4. Phiset, *Ha Phra Ha Chao,* 5; Penth, "Buddhist Literature of Lān Nā," 71.

5. Four versions of the Emerald Buddha chronicle are considered in this chapter: EBCN, EBNJ, EBSM, and EBWN.

6. Oskar von Hinüber, *A Handbook of Pāli Literature* (Berlin: De Gruyter, 1996), 83.

7. Hiram W. Woodward Jr., "The Emerald and Sihing Buddhas: Interpretations of Their Significance," in *Living a Life in Accord with Dhamma: Papers in Honor of Professor Jean Boisselier on His Eightieth Birthday,* ed. Natasha Eilenberg, M. C. Subhadradis Diskul, and Robert L. Brown (Bangkok: Silpakorn University, 1997), 503; Phiset Chiechanphong, "Introduction," in *Phra Kaeo Morakot Tamnan Phra Kaeo Morakot / The Emerald Buddha: Mythological Accounts and Historical Interpretation,* ed. Suchit Wongthet (Bangkok: Matichon, 2546 [2003]), 16–17.

8. For a detailed history of the Emerald Buddha since the eighteenth century, and particularly of its temple in Bangkok, see Melody Nina Rod-ari, "Visualizing Merit: An Art Historical Study of the Emerald Buddha and Wat Phra Kaew," PhD diss., University of California–Los Angeles, 2010.

9. One version of the Sikhi chronicle is considered in this chapter: SKNJ.

10. In a footnote to their English translation of the *Chiang Mai Chronicle,* David K. Wyatt and Aroonrut Wichienkeeo observe that a Buddha image bearing the name Cao Sikkhi and carved from black stone is now enshrined in Lampang. I have not been able to ascertain whether this image is claimed to be the image referred to in the *JKM*. David K. Wyatt and Aroonrut Wichienkeeo, trans., *The Chiang Mai Chronicle,* 2nd ed. (Chiang Mai: Silkworm Books, 1998), 69n77.

11. Three versions of the Sandalwood Buddha chronicle are considered in this chapter: SWNJ, SWSC, and SWWN.

12. Samuel S. Beal, trans., *Si-Yu-Ki: Buddhist Records of the Western World, Translated from the Chinese of Hiuen Tsiang (A.D. 629)* (London: Kegan Paul, Trench, Trübner, 1906), 1:xliv–xlv. The Chinese monk Xuanzang, who visited ancient India two centuries after Faxian, relates that during his visit to Kauśâmbî, he saw the original sandalwood image, which he attributed to King Udāyana instead of King Prasênajit (Pasenadi). Xuanzang claims he saw in Śrāvastī a sandalwood Buddha image that was made by Prasênajit, who had been inspired by Udāyana. Beal, *Si-Yu-Ki,* 1:235–236 and 2:4. The story of the Sandalwood Buddha is also found in other texts from Lanka and Lanna, and will be discussed in more detail in chapter 4.

13. Horton, *Living Buddhist Statues,* 28. See also Donald F. McCallum, "The Replication of Miraculous Icons: The Zenkoji Amida and the Seiryoji Shaka," in *Images, Miracles, and Authority in Asian Religious Traditions,* ed. Richard H. Davis (Boulder, CO: Westview, 1998), 207–226.

14. Wiluck Sripasang, *Phra Chao Mai Lanna / Lanna Wooden Buddha Images* (Chiang Mai: Sisanphanmai, 2554 [2011]), 70.

15. One version of the Setangkhamani chronicle is considered in this chapter: CBCN.

16. E. W. Hutchinson dated the production of the Setangkhamani image to 1874 based on an inscription on the statue's base. See E. W. Hutchinson, "Sacred Images in Chiengmai," *Journal of the Siam Society* 28, no. 2 (1936): 115. The inscription actually refers, however, to the donation of a base and an umbrella for the statue in 1874 and not to the creation of the image; this inscription will be discussed in more detail in chapter six. The date of composition of the *tamnan* is unknown.

17. The summary herein is based on SBSM.

18. SBSM, 33–36.

19. The people's disregard of the *nāga*'s warning is interesting in view of other accounts in which deities transform themselves into Buddha images on behalf of humans. These include accounts of the encounter between Upagupta and Māra described in texts such as the *Divyādana* and the *Kalpanāmaṇḍitika,* and the meeting of Phussadeva and Māra in the *Sīhaḷavatthuppakaraṇa*. See John Strong, "Buddha Bhakti and the Absence of the Blessed One," in *Premier Colloque Étienne Lamotte,* ed. Jacques Ryckmans (Louvain-la-Neuve, Belgium: Université

Catholique de Louvain, Institut Orientaliste, 1993), 134–135, 138. The trope of a *nāga* transforming his appearance into an image of the Buddha, as in the Sihing story, is also found in the *Mahāvaṃsa,* the chronicle of Lanka written in the late fifth or early sixth century, but there is no mention of a warning against worship or copying the image. See Wilhelm Geiger, trans., *The Mahāvaṃsa or the Great Chronicle of Ceylon* (Colombo: Ceylon Government Information Department, 1960), 33–34.

20. SBSM, 35.

21. Ibid., 37–40.

22. Ibid., 40–44.

23. Ibid., 44–45.

24. Ibid., 45–51.

25. Ibid., 51–54.

26. Luethai is an epithet of two Sukhothai kings, Mahādhammarāja I (Luethai, r. 1346–1347 to 1368–1374) and Mahādhammarāja III (Sai Luethai, r. 1398–1419); it was, however, Mahādhammarāja IV (r. 1419–1438) who was the king who moved to Phitsanulok, around 1430. David K. Wyatt, *Thailand: A Short History,* 2nd ed. (New Haven, CT: Yale University Press, 2003), 58, 309.

27. SBSM, 54–57.

28. Ibid., 57–59.

29. Ibid., 59–60.

30. Ibid., 61–62.

31. Ibid., 62–67.

32. Ibid., 68–71.

33. Ibid., 72–74.

34. Ibid., 75.

35. See, for example, Horton, *Living Buddhist Statues;* Koichi Shinohara, "Changing Roles for Miraculous Images in Medieval Chinese Buddhism: A Study of the Miracle Image Section in Daoxuan's 'Collected Records' " (141–188), and Koichi Shinohara, "Dynastic Politics and Miraculous Images: The Example of Zhuli of the Changlesi Temple in Yangzhou" (189–206), both in Davis, ed., *Images, Miracles, and Authority.*

36. NJSG, 49.

37. SBSM, 58; SBCN, 37; SBNJ, 124; SBWN, 11A–11B.

38. EBSM, 42–43; EBCN, 26–27; EBNJ, 144; EBWN, 16A.

39. SBCN, 20–21, SBSM, 43; SBWN, 10A.

40. SKNJ, 156.

41. Hans Penth has estimated that the section of the *JKM* on events in India and Lanka before the year 1203 takes up 52 percent of the length of the *JKM;* the section on events in Haripuñjaya from ca. 660 to 1296 takes up 7 percent, and the section on events in Chiang Rai and Chiang Mai ca. 1260 to 1527 (that is, Lanna under the Mangrai dynasty), takes up 41 percent. Hans Penth, *Jinakālamālī Index* (Oxford and Chiang Mai: Pali Text Society and Silkworm Books, 1994), vi.

42. EBSM, 22.
43. Ibid., 35.
44. CBCN, 6–9.
45. SBSM, 46. See also SBCN, 22.
46. SBCN, 14–15; SBSM, 38.
47. SBSM, 44–45.
48. SBCN, 27–28; SBSM, 50–52.
49. T. W. Rhys Davids, trans., *The Sacred Books of the East,* vol. 36, *The Questions of King Milinda, Part* 2 (Delhi: Low Price, 2006), 174–175.
50. Phiset, *Phra Phuttha Sihing 'Jing' Thuk Ong Mai Mi,* 24–25.
51. Beal, *Si-Yu-Ki,* 1:134.
52. SBSM, 61.
53. Veidlinger, *Spreading the Dhamma,* 57–58.
54. Kate Crosby, "The Origin of Pāli as a Language Name in Medieval Theravāda Literature," *Journal of the Centre for Buddhist Studies, Sri Lanka* 2 (2004): 95–96.
55. See NJSG, 88–94. Stories of other famous relics enshrined in Lanka, including the southern branch of the Bodhi tree, the right eyetooth and the frontal (forehead) bone, are also included in the *JKM*'s account of the spread of Buddhism from India to Lanka.
56. Bimala Churn Law, *On the Chronicles of Ceylon* (Calcutta: Royal Asiatic Society of Bengal, 1947), 22–23.
57. Bimala Charan Law, trans., *The Dāṭhāvaṁsa: A History of the Tooth-relic of the Buddha* (Lahore, India: Moti Lal Baharsi Das, 1925).
58. Kevin Trainor, *Relics, Ritual, and Representation in Buddhism: Rematerializing the Sri Lanka Theravada Tradition* (Cambridge: Cambridge University Press, 1997). Trainor's illuminating study will be discussed in further detail in chapter 5.
59. Prasert na Nagara and A. B. Griswold, *Epigraphical and Historical Studies* (Bangkok: Historical Society under the Royal Patronage of H.R.H. Princess Maha Chakri Sirindhorn, 1992), 452–453, 453n40.
60. Kate Crosby, "Kamma, Social Collapse or Geophysics? Interpretations of Suffering among Sri Lankan Buddhists in the Immediate Aftermath of the 2004 Asian Tsunami," *Contemporary Buddhism* 9, no. 1 (2008): 65.
61. This summary and quotation is drawn from the translation of the inscription "The Epigraphy of Mahādhammarāja I of Sukhodaya," in Prasert and Griswold, *Epigraphical and Historical Studies,* 450–457.
62. EBSM, 25. See also EBCN, 14.
63. Phiset, "Introduction," 17–18.
64. A. B. Griswold, "The Holy Land Transported," in *Paranavitana Felicitation Volume,* ed. N. A. Jayawickrama (Colombo, Ceylon: Gunasena, 1965), 182.
65. Prasert, "Kho Sangket Bang Prakan Kiao Kap Wannakam Phutthasasana Nai Lanna," 30. Phiset Chiechanphong offered a hypothesis regarding the

chronicle's prediction that at the two thousandth anniversary of the *sāsana* the Sihing would return to Lanka, suggesting that King Sam Fang Kaen of Lanna favored the Suan Dok order over Bodhiraṃsi's monastic order, assumed to be the Pa Daeng, and Bodhiraṃsi felt that the weaker support for the Pa Daeng reflected the decline of the *sāsana,* which would be indicated by the Sihing's departure from Lanna; Phiset, *Ha Phra Ha Chao,* 11–12. In the chronicle, however, Sam Fang Kaen is described as virtuous, glorious, and honored by his people. The chronicle does not describe the announcement of the prophecy of the Sihing's return to Lanka with any sense of doom or dismay: when they heard the prophecy, *arahants,* the king, the people, and gods were "very delighted and happy." SBCN, 15; SBSM, 39.

66. For example, the accounts of the Chinese travellers Faxian (dated 400) and Xuanzang (629) mention various items—including images of Bodhisattvas, a *stūpa* enshrining the Buddha's bodily relics, the Buddha's alms bowl, and an *arahant*'s robe—which were considered to stand for the *sāsana.* See Beal, *Si-Yu-Ki,* 1:134 and 2:116 (Bodhisattva statues); 1:103 (*stūpa*); 1:lxxviii–ix (bowl), and 1:53 (robe).

67. Beal, *Si-Yu-Ki,* 1:lxxviii–ix; Françoise Wang-Toutain, "Le bol du Buddha. Propagation du bouddhisme et légitimité," *Bulletin de l'École française d'Extrême-Orient* 81 (1994): 59–82. Faxian's account of the bowl ends with a description of the decline of human society during the time when there is no *sāsana.* Faxian was on Lanka at the time he received this account, but he says he heard it from a monk from India.

68. Beal, *Si-Yu-Ki,* 2:116.

69. For Xuanzang's account, see Beal, *Si-Yu-Ki,* 1:235–236.

70. See SWSC, 71; and SWWN, 2A. Regarding the Lankan story, see Richard F. Gombrich, "Kosala-Bimba-Vaṇṇanā," in *Buddhism in Ceylon and Studies on Religious Syncretism in Buddhist Countries,* ed. Heinz Bechert (Göttingen, West Germany: Vandenhoek und Ruprecht, 1978), 298. In Cambodia, François Bizot observed that the Buddha image consecration ceremony begins with the new statue conveyed in a procession reenacting Prince Siddhattha's departure from his palace. This apparently draws a correspondence between the Buddha and his image. The same type of procession is also held for a monastic initiate going to his ordination. François Bizot, "La consécration des statues et le culte des morts," in *Recherches nouvelles sur le Cambodge,* ed. François Bizot (Paris: École française d'Extrême-Orient, 1994), 109.

71. SBCN, 44–45; SBSM, 67.

72. SKNJ, 158.

73. SWSC, 87–88; SWWN, 7B–8A.

74. David K. Wyatt, "Relics, Oaths and Politics in Thirteenth-Century Siam," *Journal of Southeast Asian Studies* 32, no.1 (2001): 63.

75. Tambiah, "Famous Buddha Images," 18. Tambiah saw the Sihing chronicle as evidence for his hypothesis that political organization in early Southeast

Asia was "galactic"—that is, that regional political leadership was based on personal charisma and that the support for any one leader was displaced whenever a leader of greater charisma appeared on the scene. Here is not the place to delve into the many scholarly discussions that have already taken place about the "galactic" theory, but it is noteworthy that Tambiah focuses on the social exchange between statues and kings, pointing to how the control of travelling images was considered evidence of the personal charisma of kings.

76. Sarassawadee, *History of Lan Na,* 17.

77. Dhida, "The Development of the Northern Thai States," 103–105, 142.

78. Depicting Lanna as a special place for the *sāsana* could also have been meant to discourage commoners from running away to escape corvée labor duties. In this period, because of a labor shortage, commoners were valued by the ruling class; invading a town to take captives was a typical motivation behind the battles between Lanna and Ayutthaya. As well, some traditional teachings may have been intended to get commoners to resign themselves to their birth status. Sarassawadee, *History of Lan Na,* 88–90.

79. Dhida, "The Development of Northern Thai States," 144.

80. Lingat, "Le culte du Bouddha d'Émeraude," 34–36. Lingat has also suggested that the green stone of the Emerald Buddha may have come from the Khmer Empire of Angkor, based on his interpretation of an Angkorian inscription dated 1011. However, this hypothesis is disputable. See Woodward, "The Emerald and Sihing Buddhas," 506–507.

81. Phra Bat Somdet Phra Chom Klao Chao Yu Hua, "Tamnan Phra Kaeo Morakot samrap Alak An nai Phra Ubosot Wat Phra Sri Ratanasadaram Wan Suat Mon Yen Phra Rachaphithi Sri Sacchapanakan" [Chronicle of the Emerald Buddha for recitation by the royal secretary in the hall of Wat Sri Ratanasadaram on the day of the royal oath-taking ceremony], in Suchit, ed., *Phra Kaeo Morakot Tamnan Phra Kaeo Morakot,* 197–199.

82. Frank E. Reynolds, "The Holy Emerald Jewel: Some Aspects of Buddhist Symbolism and Political Legitimation in Thailand and Laos," in *Religion and Legitimation of Power in Thailand, Laos, and Burma,* ed. Bardwell L. Smith (Chambersburg, PA: Anima, 1978), 178–182. Reynolds has further suggested that the emerald itself provides a special link between the Emerald Buddha and kings, as the divine jewel from which the image is carved, the Amaragaṭa, is "of the same essence as the gem jewel of the great Cakkavatti [universal] king" (183). The *tamnan* of the Emerald Buddha states, however, that the deities guarding Vipulla Mountain pointedly refused Indra's request for the universal king's Maṇījoti jewel; they insisted it was reserved for the use of a *cakkavatti* and told Indra he could take instead the Amaragaṭa (EBCN, 15; EBNJ, 141; EBSM, 27–28; EBWN, 14B). Thus, contrary to Reynolds' reading, the author of the *tamnan* took pains to differentiate the jewel belonging to a universal monarch from the jewel appropriate to meet Nāgasena's wish to make a Buddha image.

83. SWSC, 84–85; SWWN, 6B.

84. EBCN, 21.

85. The reciting of sacred texts to generate magical power is prescribed in the Pali Buddhist canon. Kate Crosby, *Theravada Buddhism: Continuity, Diversity, and Identity* (Chichester, England: Wiley-Blackwell, 2014), 125–126. During the reign of King Tilok the tradition may have begun of inscribing this restatement of the Four Noble Truths in abbreviated form on the bases of Sihing-style Buddha images. At some point the *gāthā* inspired the tradition of preparing Sihing *yanta* (Thai: *yan;* Sanskrit: *yantra*), magical diagrams on cloth (Thai: *Pha Yan Phra Sihing*), which people made and worshipped for protection against dangers. Thus M. L. Surasawasdi Sooksawasdi has suggested that the Sihing image may have had tantric associations. M. L. Surasawasdi Sooksawasdi, "Laksana Phra Phuttha Rup Baep Pala nai Khwaen Benggol thi Prakot nai Sinlapa Thai: Karani Sueksa chak Phra Phuttha Sihing" [Characteristics of Pala-style Buddha images of Bengal in Thai art: a study of the Sihing Buddha image], *Muang Boran Journal* 36, no. 3 (2010): 89–96. Regarding the Sihing *gāthā,* see also Hans Penth, "An Inscribed Buddha Image in Wat Ket Sī," in *Bauddhavidyāsudhākaraḥ: Studies in Honour of Heinz Bechert on the Occasion of His 65th Birthday,* ed. Petra Kieffer-Pülz and Jens-Uwe Hartmann (Swisttal-Odendorff, Germany: Indica et Tibetica Verlag, 1997), 495–503.

86. Phiset Chiechanphong, "Pratu Phi lae Nathi khong Phra Kaeo Morakot" [The spirit door and the duties of the Emerald Buddha], in Suchit, ed., *Phra Kaeo Morakot: Tamnan Phra Kaeo Morakot,* 343–354.

87. Sarassawadee, *History of Lan Na,* 106.

88. Justin T. McDaniel, "Transformative History: *Nihon Ryōiki* and *Jinakālamālīpakaraṇam,*" *Journal of the International Association of Buddhist Studies* 25, nos. 1–2 (2002): 163.

89. Veidlinger, *Spreading the Dhamma,* 105–106. Veidlinger also notes that there are strong indications that a high proportion of the monastic patrons of manuscripts belonged to the Wat Pa Daeng order, which was formed by monks from mainland Southeast Asia who visited Lanka in the early fifteenth century (128).

90. Dhida, "The Development of the Northern Thai States," 169–175.

91. SBSM, 68–69. See also SBCN, 49–50.

92. SWSC, 80; SWWN, 5A.

93. EBSM, 33–34.

94. Schopen, *Buddhist Monks and Business Matters,* 80.

95. Justin Thomas McDaniel, *Gathering Leaves and Lifting Words: Histories of Buddhist Monastic Education in Laos and Thailand* (Seattle: University of Washington Press, 2008), 74, 84.

96. Schopen, *Figments and Fragments of Mahāyāna Buddhism in India*, 137.

97. McDaniel, *Gathering Leaves and Lifting Words,* 89.

98. Hutchinson, "Sacred Images in Chiengmai," 136–137.

99. SWSC, 2:54–67. See also other versions of this chronicle in Hutchinson, "Sacred Images in Chiengmai," 124–142; and Donald K. Swearer, *Becoming the*

Buddha: The Ritual of Image Consecration in Thailand (Princeton, NJ: Princeton University Press, 2004), 205–210.

Chapter 3: Buddha Images and the Monkhood

1. See Schopen, *Buddhist Monks and Business Matters,* esp. chapters 2, 3, and 10.

2. The texts of the Flower Garden order are originally in Yuan language with some Pali. PNWS was found at Wat Mueang Mang in Haiya, Amphoe Mueang, Chiang Mai Province, and was copied in year 2472 BE (1929). PNYK was found at Wat Ban Ueam in Ban Ueam, Lampang Province, and bears a copying year equivalent to 1920).

The texts of the Redwood Grove order are originally in the Yuan language with some Pali except for the Chiang Tung Pa Daeng chronicle (SMPD), which is originally in Khoen instead of Yuan. PNPD was found at Wat Buppharam, Ban Ueam, Lampang Province, and bears a copying year of 1274 CS (1912). SMPD was found at Wat P̱āḍaeng in Chiang Tung, and it does not bear a date; the translator gives the title as the *P̱āḍaeng Chronicle,* but it covers many of the same events as in the texts labelled as *Mūlasāsanā* of Wat Pa Daeng. The main difference is that SMPD tends to have greater detail about some local Chiang Tung occurrences. Sao Sāimöng Mangrāi, the translator of SMPD, has described some differences between SMPD and SSPD in *The P̱āḍaeng Chronicle and the Jengtung State Chronicle Translated,* 45–47.

SSPD, according to its translators Sommai Premchit and Donald K. Swearer, is based on "a text of volume IX of the Transliteration Series, Department of Sociology and Anthropology, Chiang Mai University. However, the translation is not a literal one. On occasion we have tried to resolve some of the confusions in the text by consulting two other manuscripts" (74n2). They believe that SSPD was composed in Chiang Tung (73n1); the last date cited in the text is 2064 BE (1521), although the chronicle relates events following that date.

3. See Penth, "Buddhist Literature of Lān Nā," 66; Sarassawadee, *History of Lan Na,* 2–3; Swearer, "Myth, Legend and History in the Northern Thai Chronicles," 69; and A. B. Griswold, "Foreword," in Mangrāi, *The P̱āḍaeng Chronicle and the Jengtung State Chronicle Translated*, xiii.

4. Prasert, "Kho Sangket Bang Prakan Kiao Kap Wannakam Phutthasasana Nai Lanna," 30.

5. Victor Lieberman, "Introduction," in Mangrāi, *The P̱āḍaeng Chronicle and the Jengtung State Chronicle Translated*, ix.

6. In PNYK, he is called Dhammagambhīra. It is possible that this name does not refer to the same person as Ñāṇagambhīra. In SMPD, 106, 112, Ñāṇagambhīra is contrasted to a monk called Dhammagambhīra, who is said to have fought with his preceptor, run off to Lanka, returned to Chiang Mai to criticize his former order, and then disrobed and married a nobleman's daughter. Nevertheless, it is clear that SMPD, in referring to Ñāṇagambhīra, and PNYK, in referring to Dhammagambhīra,

both indicate the founder of the Redwood Grove order. Prasert has suggested that they are one and the same individual and that the monk's name probably changed at the time of his reordination in Lanka. Prasert, "Bot Namsanoe Tamnan Mūlasāsanā Chiang Mai lae Chiang Tung," 39.

7. François Bizot, *Le Bouddhisme des Thaïs* (Bangkok: Éditions des Cahiers de France, 1993), 37–50.

8. See, for example, Donald K. Swearer and Sommai Premchit, "The Relationship between the Religious and Political Orders in Northern Thailand (14th–16th Centuries)," in Smith, ed., *Religion and Legitimation of Power in Thailand, Laos, and Burma,* 20–33; and Prasert, "Bot Namsanoe Tamnan Mūlasāsanā Chiang Mai lae Chiang Tung."

9. Strong, *Relics of the Buddha,* 148. Strong also quotes another example of the subordination of the monkhood in the performance of patronage: Juliane Schober, writing of the construction of relic *stūpas* in contemporary Myanmar, noted that such sites of patronage "create a field of merit and source of political legitimation separate and distinct from . . . the saṃgha, [one that] diminish[es] the saṃgha's position as a religious institution and source of merit and charisma." Juliane Schober, "Buddhist Just Rule and Burmese National Culture: State Patronage of the Chinese Tooth Relic in Myanma," *History of Religions* 36, no. 3 (1997): 242, quoted in Strong, *Relics of the Buddha,* 148.

10. SSPD, 91. See also PNPD, 176–177.

11. SMPD, 113–116.

12. SMPD, 121. See also PNPD, 193; and SSPD, 101.

13. SMPD, 128–129.

14. SMPD, 124.

15. SMPD, 137–139.

16. PNWS, 43–44; PNYK, 112–113.

17. PNWS, 50; PNYK, 115–116.

18. Choy Fah Kong, *Saccakiriyā: The Belief in the Power of True Speech* (Singapore: Choy Fah Kong, 2012), 37–39.

19. Ibid., 29–30.

20. Inscriptions left by donors on the bases of Lanna Buddha statues will be discussed in detail in chapter 6.

21. In the last two decades a number of scholars have critically evaluated the influence of Max Weber on the academic study of Buddhism. See, for example, John Holt, "Protestant Buddhism?," *Religious Studies Review* 17, no. 4 (1991): 307–312; Steven Collins, *Nirvana and Other Buddhist Felicities: Utopias of the Pali Imaginaire* (Cambridge: Cambridge University Press, 1998); Pattana Kitiarsa, "Beyond the Weberian Trails: An Essay on the Anthropology of Southeast Asian Buddhism, *Religion Compass* 3, no. 2 (2009): 200–204; and Phibul Choompolpaisal, "Reassessing Modern Thai Political Buddhism: A Critical Study of Sociological Literature from Weber to Keyes," PhD diss., University of London, 2011.

22. Tambiah, *The Buddhist Saints of the Forest,* 248.

23. Ibid., 254.

24. See PNPD, 158, 169; SMPD, 102, 109; and SSPD, 80.

25. See Swearer, *Becoming the Buddha.*

26. Regarding the correspondence in Cambodia between the procession of a new Buddha statue and that of a monastic initiate, see chapter 2.

27. As Daniel Veidlinger has pointed out, this episode is also interesting as it suggests the importance that the Pa Daeng monks, to whom the inscription of many fifteenth century manuscripts are attributed, placed on written forms. Veidlinger, *Spreading the Dhamma,* 69.

28. PNPD, 203; SMPD, 136–137; SSPD, 107. According to Tun Aung Chain, a version of this story of the pious lady who rescued Buddha statues thrown away by a heretic king is found on an inscription erected by Banya Htaw and Dhammazedi in 1470. Tun Aung Chain, trans., *A Chronicle of the Mon* (Yangon, Myanmar: SEAMEO Regional Centre for History and Tradition, 2010), 31n107. A Mon chronicle probably composed in the mid- to late eighteenth century and translated by Robert Halliday, the *Slapat rājāwaṅ datow smiṅ roṅ,* also contains a version of this story of a devoted woman who retrieved Buddha statues disposed by a heretic king. This Mon version says the lady survived the king's punishment because she "sent out her loving kindness [to her punishers] and repeated the Three Refuges." Further, her vow of devotion to the Three Gems caused the Buddha images to miraculously fly into the air. The Mon version of the story describes precisely the virtuous thoughts that enable the lady to be saved; the less-detailed Pa Daeng versions only mention devotion to the Buddha and his image, emphasizing their exchange of agencies with the lady. See Robert Halliday, *The Mons of Burma and Thailand,* vol. 2, *Selected Articles,* ed. Christian Bauer (Bangkok: White Lotus, 2000), 93–95, 116. Whether the story originated in the Shan or Mon areas or elsewhere is unknown, as far as I am aware. At the least, the inclusion of the story in the Chiang Tung *Mūlasāsanā* indicates that it had some particular resonance for local interests.

29. PNPD, SSPD.

30. Writing of his observations of Sri Lankan Buddhist communities, Richard F. Gombrich stated that while Theravādin doctrine clearly states the Buddha is no longer present, "in moments of great crisis some individuals do pray to him for help, but that is the spontaneous outburst of emotion and in their calmer moments they know that it can do no good except as a psychological relief to themselves." Richard F. Gombrich, *Theravāda Buddhism: A Social History from Ancient Benares to Modern Colombo* (London: Routledge, 2005), 120. Differences between doctrinal statements and actual practices in the expression of devotion to the Buddha and his representations have been much discussed by present-day scholars of Buddhism. For a lucid discussion of the issues, see Kate Crosby, "Devotion to the Buddha in Theravada and Its Role in Meditation," in *The Intimate Other: Love Divine in Indic Religions,* ed. Anna S. King and John

Brockington (New Delhi: Orient Longman, 2005), 244–277. See also Crosby, *Theravada Buddhism,* 48–53.

31. PNWS, 58–59, 61. See also PNYK, 120, 122.

32. Reinders, "Recycling Icons and Bodies," 65.

33. Sarassawadee, *History of Lan Na,* 32.

34. Swearer and Sommai, *The Legend of Queen Cāma,* 59.

35. Ibid., 105–106.

36. Wyatt and Aroonrut, *The Chiang Mai Chronicle,* 36–37.

37. Pe Maung Tin and G. H. Luce, trans., *The Glass Palace Chronicle of the Kings of Burma* (London: Oxford University Press, 1923), 26–28. Tun Shwe Khine has suggested that the large image in the story is the Mahāmuni; a Śrī Kṣetran king, Supannanagara Seinda, invaded Arakan in the year 81 and attempted to bring it home to Śrī Kṣetra but was unable to do so. Tun Shwe Khine, *A Guide to Mrauk-U: An Ancient City of Rakhine, Myanmar* (Sittway, Myanmar: Sittway Degree College, 1992), 102. There are no references in these accounts to the Mahāmuni being destroyed by the Śrī Kṣetran king, however.

38. Pe Maung Tin and Luce, *The Glass Palace Chronicle,* 147–148. See also Bimala Churn Law, trans., *The History of the Buddha's Religion (Sāsanavaṃsa)* (London: Luzac, 1952), 76–78.

Chapter 4: Buddha Images and Place

1. Swearer, "Signs of the Buddha in Northern Thai Chronicles," 157. As far as I am aware, the expression *"buddhadesa"* does not appear in any northern Thai monastic chronicles but seems to be a useful term created by Swearer and developed in his many rich writings on northern Thai Buddhism. See also Donald K. Swearer, *Wat Haripuñjaya: A Study of the Royal Temple of the Buddha's Relic, Lamphun, Thailand* (Missoula, MT: Scholars Press for the American Academy of Religion, 1976), 47; Donald K. Swearer, "Presencing the Buddha in Northern Thailand: Perspectives from Ritual and Narrative," in *Buddhist Legacies in Mainland Southeast Asia: Mentalities, Interpretations and Practices,* ed. François Lagirarde and Paritta Chalermpow Koanantakool (Paris and Bangkok: École française d'Extrême-Orient and Princess Maha Chakri Sirindhorn Anthropology Centre, 2006), 281. See also see Swearer and Sommai, *The Legend of Queen Cāma,* 6.

2. *Tamnan Phra Non Khon Muang* [Chronicle of the Buddha Image Lying on a Mango-Tree Log], Siam Society, Bangkok, EFEO 001 002. Inscription date 2505 BE (1962). Yuan language with some Pali. Hereafter, page numbers will be cited parenthetically in the text; the page numbers given for this and all other manuscripts in the École française d'Extrême-Orient (EFEO) Lanna Collection will follow the EFEO's system and not the numbering of the original manuscript.

3. Udom Rungrueangsi, "Phra Non Khon Muang," in *Saranukrom Watanatham Thai Phak Nuea* [Encyclopedia of northern Thai culture] (Bangkok: Mulaniti Saranukrom Watanatham Thai, 2542 [1999]), 8:4328–4329.

4. Wyatt and Aroonrut, *The Chiang Mai Chronicle,* 187–192. Wyatt believed this version of the chronicle was written in 1827, based on dates of the most recent events it relates (xxxi).

5. Buppha Khunyotying, "Phra Non Khon Muang, Wat," in *Saranukrom Watanatham Thai Phak Nuea,* 9:4487.

6. *Tamnan Wat Phra Non Khon Muang* [Chronicle of the Monastery of the Buddha Image Lying on a Mango-Tree Log] (Chiang Mai: Wat Phra Non Khon Muang, 2501 BE [1958]), 12.

7. Walshe, *The Long Discourses of the Buddha,* 266.

8. Ibid., 289–290.

9. Donald K. Swearer, Sommai Premchit, and Phaithoon Dokbuakaew, *Sacred Mountains of Northern Thailand and Their Legends* (Chiang Mai: Silkworm Books, 2004), 38, 44. This manuscript is in the microfilm archive at the Social Research Institute, Chiang Mai University. Swearer and colleagues note that in the text there is a reference to King Kawila that indicates the text may have been composed in the early nineteenth century.

10. *Tamnan Phra Chao Ton Luang* [Chronicle of the Grand Lord], Wat Phra Luang Sung Men, Sung Men, Phrae, EFEO 003 007. Inscription date unknown. Yuan language with some Pali. Hereafter, page numbers will be cited parenthetically in the text.

11. Buppha Khunyotying, "Phra Chao Ton Luang," in *Saranukrom Watanatham Thai Phak Nuea,* 8:4305.

12. The inscription is No. Lamphun/29. Buppha, "Phra Chao Ton Luang," 4308.

13. *Tamnan Wat Phra Kaeo Don Tao Wiang Din* [Chronicle of Wat Phra Kaeo Don Tao Wiang Din], Siam Society, Bangkok, EFEO 003 019. Inscription date 1288 CS (1926). Yuan language with some Pali. Hereafter, page numbers will be cited parenthetically in the text. See also Buppha Khunyotying, "Phra Kaeo Don Tao, Wat," in *Saranukrom Watanatham Thai Phak Nuea,* 8:4271–4273.

14. Buppha Khunyotying, "Suchadaram, Wat," in *Saranukrom Watanatham Thai Phak Nuea,* 13:6971.

15. There is a statue of Phra Kaeo presently at Wat Phra Kaeo Don Tao. Apparently, though, this was given by Wat Suthasanathep Woraram in Bangkok in 1958. Buppha, "Phra Kaeo Don Tao, Wat," 4275–4276. For an investigation into the possible history of the original Wat Phra Kaeo Don Tao image, see Sak Rattanachai, "Rueang Chuankhit thi At Cha Pen Pai Dai Kiao Kap Khao Nguen Phra Kaeo Khu Ballang Phutthachak Chieng Saen thi Lampang / Hypotheses concerning Images of the Buddha Palladia of Chiang Saen," *Muang Boran Journal* 5, no. 4 (1979): 69–84.

16. Barbara Watson Andaya has noted that "positive images of motherhood are fostered by images projected in village 'texts'—sermons, folk operas, courting songs, agricultural rituals and myths." Barbara Watson Andaya, "Localising the Universal: Motherhood and the Appeal of Early Theravāda Buddhism," *Journal*

of Southeast Asian Studies 33, no. 1 (2002): 7. Monica Lindberg Falk has noted that, in Thailand, "[t]he symbol of woman as mother is prevalent and contributes to associating women with the secular realm." Monica Lindberg Falk, *Making Fields of Merit: Buddhist Female Ascetics and Gendered Orders in Thailand* (Seattle: University of Washington Press, 2007), 7. Charles F. Keyes has observed that "mother" is the dominant image of woman, but there is also a pop-culture image of woman as "lover" or "adulterer." Charles F. Keyes, "Mother or Mistress but Never a Monk: Buddhist Notions of Female Gender in Rural Thailand," *American Ethnologist* 11, no. 2 (1984), 227, 230.

17. Keyes, "Mother or Mistress but Never a Monk," 229.

18. Kate Crosby, "Gendered Symbols in Theravada Buddhism: Missed Positives in the Representation of the Female," *Hsuan Chuang Journal of Buddhist Studies* 9 (2008), 42. Bernard Faure has observed that Sujātā's providing of milk rice to the Buddha represented another symbolic milk debt that enabled the Buddha to achieve enlightenment, itself a kind of rebirth. Bernard Faure, *The Power of Denial: Buddhism, Purity, and Gender* (Princeton, NJ: Princeton University Press, 2003), 163.

19. According to the northern Thai chronicle, the *Jinakālamālīpakaraṇaṁ*, when many lifetimes ago the future Buddha Gotama first committed to the path to Buddhahood, the reason was that he wanted to care for his mother. NJSG, 2–3, cited in Andaya, "Localising the Universal," 17.

20. The *Nidāna-kathā* of the Jātaka collection declares that the womb of a Bodhisatta's mother is "like the relic-chamber of a shrine, and no other being can lie in it or occupy it, the mother of the Bodhisatta dies seven days after the Bodhisatta's birth and is reborn in the City of Tusita." N. A. Jayawickrama, *The Story of Gotama Buddha: The Nidāna-kathā of the Jātakaṭṭhakathā* (Oxford: Pali Text Society, 1990), 69. The fact that Māyā's lifespan was expected to be ten months and seven days was one of the considerations that led the future Buddha, while in heaven planning his final rebirth, to select her as his mother. The other factors were the time, country, district, the family and the mother's virtues (66).

21. Alan Sponberg, "Attitudes toward Women and the Feminine in Early Buddhism," in *Buddhism, Sexuality, and Gender*, ed. José Ignacio Cabezón (Albany: State University of New York Press, 1992), 13.

22. Ashley Thompson, "Introductory Remarks between the Lines: Writing Histories of Middle Cambodia," in *Other Pasts: Women, Gender and History in Early Modern Southeast Asia*, ed. Barbara Watson Andaya (Honolulu: Center for Southeast Asian Studies, University of Hawai'i at Manoa, 2000), 68.

23. When the Buddha returned to visit his hometown of Kapilavatthu, his father objected to his begging from door to door because he is of the Khattiya lineage. The Buddha replied, "Your Majesty, this royal lineage is your descent, but mine is this lineage of Buddhas, from Dipaṅkara, Koṇḍañña and others right down to Kassapa." Jayawickrama, *The Story of Gotama Buddha*, 121.

24. Strong, *Relics of the Buddha,* 7; emphasis in the original.

25. Ibid., 143.

26. Swearer, "Signs of the Buddha in Northern Thai Chronicles," 157.

27. Juliane Schober, "Venerating the Buddha's Remains in Burma: From Solitary Practice to the Cultural Hegemony of Communities," *Journal of Burma Studies* 6 (2001): 111–139.

28. Mircea Eliade, *The Sacred and the Profane,* trans. William R. Trask (Orlando, FL: Harcourt, 1987), 11.

29. Edward S. Casey, *Remembering: A Phenomenological Study* (Bloomington: Indiana University Press, 2000), 202.

30. Strong, *Relics of the Buddha,* 41.

31. Ibid., 33, 43.

32. Elizabeth H. Moore, *Early Landscapes of Myanmar* (Bangkok: River Books, 2007), 25.

33. Ibid., 243.

34. H. L. Shorto, "The 'Dewatau Sotāpan': A Mon Prototype of the 37 'Nats,'" *Bulletin of the School of Oriental and African Studies, University of London* 30, no. 1 (1967): 140.

35. The *Mahāvaṃsa* recounts the Buddha's subduing and conversion of the *yakṣas* on Lanka and his subduing and conversion of the *nāgas* at Nāgadīpa in the northwest part of Lanka Island. See Geiger, *The Mahāvaṃsa,* 3–4, 6–7.

36. Walshe, *The Long Discourses of the Buddha,* 237.

37. Ibid., 245–246. Walshe states that the Bahuputta Shrine was an old banyan tree at which people made prayers for sons (269n398). T. W. and C. A. F. Rhys-Davids suggested that all of these shrines were for "pre-Buddhistic worship" and may have been trees and mounds. T. W. and C. A. F. Rhys-Davids, trans., *Dialogues of the Buddha* (London: Oxford University Press, 1910), 2:110n2.

38. Walshe, *The Long Discourses of the Buddha,* 263–264.

39. Jayawickrama, *The Story of Gotama Buddha,* 92–93.

40. Ibid., 94.

41. Ibid., 97.

42. Ibid., 103.

43. I. B. Horner, trans., *The Minor Anthologies of the Pali Canon,* vol. 3, *Chronicles of Buddhas (Buddhavaṁsa) and Basket of Conduct (Cariyāpiṭaka)* (London: Pali Text Society, 1975), xxxix.

44. Beal, *Si-Yu-Ki,* 2:114.

45. Strong, *Relics of the Buddha,* 55.

46. Gombrich, "Kosala-Bimba-Vaṇṇanā," 281–286.

47. Wilhelm Geiger, *Culture of Ceylon in Mediaeval Times,* ed. Heinz Bechert (Wiesbaden, West Germany: Harrassowitz, 1960), 101–102.

48. Jonathan Walters, "Buddhist History," 102–108.

49. Juliane Schober, "In the Presence of the Buddha: Ritual Veneration of the Burmese Mahāmuni Image," in *Sacred Biography in the Buddhist Traditions*

of South and Southeast Asia, ed. Juliane Schober (Honolulu: University of Hawai'i Press, 1997), 263.

50. Emanuel Forchhammer, *Report on the Antiquities of Arakan* (Rangoon, Burma: Superintendent, Government Printing, 1892), 2–5. The name of the second text is given by Forchhammer as Sappadānapakaraṇa or Sarvasṭhānaprakaraṇa. No dates or names of authors or scribes are given for these manuscripts by Forchhammer.

51. Other manuscripts contain varying accounts of how the statue was made. According to one text, the work of creating the statue was first assigned to a thousand Arakanese sculptors, but they were unsuccessful, so the king called to the gods for help. Jacques P. Leider, "Relics, Statues, and Predictions: Interpreting an Apocryphal Sermon of Lord Buddha in Arakan," *Asian Ethnology* 68, no. 2 (2009): 357n31.

52. Forchhammer, *Report on the Antiquities of Arakan,* 5–6.

53. San Shwe Bu, "The Story of Mahamuni," *Journal of the Burma Research Society* 6 (1916): 226.

54. Forchhammer, *Report on the Antiquities of Arakan,* 5–7.

55. San Shwe Bu, "The Story of Mahamuni," 227. According to another account, the image was lost in the mid-seventeenth century and later discovered, though missing its right leg and most of its back. Tun Shwe Khine, *A Guide to Mrauk-U,* 103. Another story says that the statue became damaged when raiders tried to melt it, while yet another claims that the image was thrown into a creek and sunk in the sea, only to miraculously emerge in the twelfth century. Leider, "Relics, Statues, and Predictions," 342–343.

56. Schober, "In the Presence of the Buddha," 266.

57. Pyi Phyo Kyaw and Kate Crosby, "The Buddha and His Brothers: Expressions of Power, Place and Community by the Network of Mahāmuni Images of Arakan, Bangladesh and Burma," in *Art of Merit: Studies in Buddhist Art and Its Conservation,* ed. David Park, Kuenga Wangmo, and Sharon Cather (London: Archetype, 2012), 266–268, 272).

58. Beal, *Si-Yu-Ki,* 2:4.

59. Swearer, *Becoming the Buddha,* 15. An English translation of the story, from a Pali text titled *Zinme Paññāsa* (*Chiang Mai Fifty*) found in Burma, is given in Padmanabh S. Jaini, trans., *Apochryphal Birth-Stories (Paññasa-Jātaka)* (London: Pali Text Society, 1986), 2:103–121. See also Padmanabh S. Jaini, "On the Buddha Image," in *Studies in Pali and Buddhism,* ed. A. K. Narain and L. Zwilling (Delhi: B. R., 1979), 183–188.

60. Leider, "Relics, Statues, and Predictions," 337–338, 348.

61. Tun Aung Chain, "The Mingun Bell Inscription: The King as Dhammarāja," in *Selected Writings of Tun Aung Chain* (Yangon: Myanmar Historical Commission Golden Jubilee Publication Committee, 2004), 187–192.

62. Ibid., 195–196.

63. Schober, "In the Presence of the Buddha," 266.

64. Phiset Chiechanphong has noted the motif in Thai Buddhist literature in which virtuous persons obtain blessings by repairing broken Buddha images, and he has suggested that the author of the Sihing Buddha chronicle may have wanted to include this motif to highlight the repair of Buddha images as a suitable act of patronage. Phiset, *Ha Phra Ha Chao,* 39–46.

Chapter 5: Buddha Images and Relics

1. Walshe, *The Long Discourses of the Buddha,* 262–264.

2. Steven Collins, "Nirvāṇa, Time, and Narrative," *History of Religions* 31, no. 3 (1992): 237, quoted in Strong, *Relics of the Buddha,* 20.

3. EBSM, 30–31. See also EBCN, 16–17; EBWN, 14B–15A; and NJSG, 142.

4. Robert H. Sharf, "On the Allure of Buddhist Relics," *Representations* 66 (1999): 75–99.

5. Ashley Thompson, "In the Absence of the Buddha: 'Aniconism' and the Contentions of Buddhist Art History," in *A Companion to Asian Art and Architecture,* ed. Rebecca M. Brown and Deborah S. Hutton (Chichester, England: Wiley-Blackwell, 2011), 416.

6. Strong, *Relics of the Buddha,* 223–224.

7. Thompson, "In the Absence of the Buddha," 403–404.

8. SBSM, 46. See also SBCN, 22.

9. *Tamnan Wat Suan Dok* [Chronicle of the Flower Garden Monastery], Wat Pa Sak Noi, Sankhamphaeng, Chiang Mai, EFEO 002 003. Inscription date 1309 CS (1947). Yuan language with some Pali. Hereafter, page numbers will be cited parenthetically in the text; the page numbers given for this and all other manuscripts in the École française d'Extrême-Orient (EFEO) Lanna Collection will follow EFEO's system and not the numbering of the original manuscript. Another version of this chronicle is the *Tamnan Suan Dokmai* [Chronicle of the Flower Garden Monastery], Wat Pa Sak Noi, Sankhamphaeng, Chiang Mai, EFEO 002 004. Inscription date 1296 CS (1934). See also NJSG, 117–120, 126–127; and the translation of *Tamnan Phra That Suthep* [Chronicle of the relic of Suthep] in Donald K. Swearer et al., *Sacred Mountains of Northern Thailand,* 69–83.

10. NJSG, 117–120, 126.

11. Ibid., 126.

12. *Tamnan Wat Suan Dok,* 2A, and *Tamnan Suan Dokmai,* 2A.

13. According to Sarassawadee Ongsakul, the enshrining of the Great Relic of Haripuñjaya took place around 1157. Sarassawadee, *History of Lan Na,* 38. The story of the enshrinement of the Great Relic can be found in a number of manuscripts and published sources. Aside from the EFEO chronicles discussed here, the story is also recounted in the *JKM* (see NJSG, 106–109) and in different versions of the *Mūlasāsanā* (for example, PNYK, 94–95, and SSPD, 77). The story of the Great Relic of Haripuñjaya is also part of the chronicle of Queen Cāmadevī, the

Cāmadevīvaṃsa, dated by scholars to the early fifteenth century. See Cœdès, "Documents sur l'histoire politique et religieuse du Laos occidental," 12–15, 141–171; Camille Notton, trans., *Annales du Siam,* vol. 2, *Chronique de La:p'un* (Paris: Charles-Lavauzelle, 1930), and Swearer and Sommai, *The Legend of Queen Cāma.*

14. *Tamnan Phra That Chao Lamphun lae Tamnan Wat Ton Kaeo* [Chronicle of the relic of Lamphun and Chronicle of Wat Ton Kaeo], Siam Society, Bangkok, EFEO 001 005, 21B–25B. Inscription date 1275 CS (1913). Yuan language with some Pali. Hereafter, page numbers will be cited parenthetically in the text.

15. Swearer and Sommai, *The Legend of Queen Cāma,* 3–36.

16. Ibid., 7.

17. *Tamnan Phra Kesa That* [Chronicle of the hair relics], Wat Pa Sak Noi, Sankhamphaeng, Chiang Mai, EFEO 002 005. Inscription date 2501 BE (1958). Yuan language with some Pali. Hereafter, page numbers will be cited parenthetically in the text.

18. For analyses of various accounts about Trapuṣa and Bhallika, see Pe Maung Tin, "The Shwe Dagon Pagoda," *Journal of the Burma Research Society* 24, no. 1 (1934): 1–91; and Strong, *Relics of the Buddha,* 73–82.

19. Stephen C. Berkwitz, *Buddhist History in the Vernacular* (Leiden, Netherlands: Brill, 2004), 36.

20. According to N. A. Jayawickrama, the accounts of the right eyetooth relic and the forehead (frontal) bone found in the *JKM* are mainly drawn from the *Lalāṭadhātuvaṁsa,* with additional information from the *Mahāvaṁsa,* and the source for the account of the arrival of the Tooth Relic is the *Dāṭhāvaṁsa.* N. A. Jayawickrama, "Translator's Introduction," in NJSG, xxi.

21. Strong, *Relics of the Buddha,* 43.

22. Geiger, *The Mahāvaṃsa,* 99–109.

23. Trainor, *Relics, Ritual, and Representation in Buddhism,* 134.

24. Ibid., 151.

25. Strong, *Relics of the Buddha,* 166–167.

26. NJSG, 66–68.

27. Geiger, *The Mahāvaṃsa,* 116–121.

28. Strong, *Relics of the Buddha,* 165–167.

29. Lagirarde, "Temps et lieux d'histoires bouddhiques," 67.

30. Charles F. Keyes, "Buddhist Pilgrimage Centers and the Twelve-Year Cycle: Northern Thai Moral Orders in Space and Time," *History of Religions* 15, no. 1 (1975): 87.

31. Pe Maung Tin, "The Shwe Dagon Pagoda," 48, 54.

32. Ibid., 56–57.

33. Ibid., 57. Pe Maung Tin references the Burmese edition of the *Manorathapūranī* (Rangoon: Kawi Myet Hman Press, 1908), 1:71, and the Pali Text Society edition (London: Pali Text Society, 1924), 1:91.

34. Tun Aung Chain, "Prophecy and Planets: Forms of Legitimation of the Royal City in Myanmar," in *Selected Writings,* 124–128.

35. François Tainturier, "The Foundation of Mandalay by King Mindon," PhD diss., University of London, 2010, 45–46. See also Tun Aung Chain, "Prophecy and Planets,"126.

36. Tainturier, "The Foundation of Mandalay by King Mindon," 63–64.

37. Tun Aung Chain, "Prophecy and Planets," 128–131.

38. Tainturier, "The Foundation of Mandalay by King Mindon," 233–273.

39. Ibid., 39–42. The gathering of earth from special sites is also referred to in the Burmese chronicle *Sāsanavaṃsa* (1861), in which it is noted that in the year 1860, a delegation of monastic and lay devotees from Lanka arrived in Mandalay bringing gifts, including "a casket of silver and gold, a shrine of silver and gold with a relic, a Buddha image made of ivory, leaves of the great Bo-tree, bark of the great Bo-tree, *earth from the resting place of the great Bo-tree,* leaves of the southern branch of the Bo-tree in Sīhala [Lanka], and the *earth from the place of waking* [i.e., the seat of enlightenment] *in the second week.*" Law, *The History of the Buddha's Religion,* 161; emphasis added.

40. Tainturier, "The Foundation of Mandalay by King Mindon," 59.

41. Juliane Schober, "Mapping the Sacred in Theravada Buddhist Southeast Asia," in *Sacred Places and Modern Landscapes,* ed. Ronald A. Lukens-Bull (Tempe: Monograph Series Press, Arizona State University Program for Southeast Asian Studies, 2003), 16.

42. Tainturier, "The Foundation of Mandalay by King Mindon," 41.

43. See the central Thai translation of this chronicle in Aroonrut Wichienkeeo and David K. Wyatt, trans., *Tamnan Phuen Mueang Chiang Mai* [Chiang Mai Chronicle] (Chiang Mai: Silkworm Books, 2543 [2000]), 40–46; and the English translation of the same in Wyatt and Aroonrut, *The Chiang Mai Chronicle,* 41–47. Regarding the dating of the manuscript, see the introduction in both books: 30–33 in the Thai version and xxxv–xxxix in the English.

44. *Tamnan Phra Phuttha Rup Chao Nang Din* [Chronicle of the Buddha Image Seated on the Earth], Wat San Pa Kha, Ton Pao, Sankhamphaeng, Chiang Mai, EFEO 025 001. Inscription date unknown, 1B.

45. Geiger, *The Mahāvaṃsa,* 191–192; N. A. Jayawickrama, trans., *Chronicle of the Thūpa and the Thūpavaṃsa* (London: Luzac, 1971), 100–101.

46. Jayawickrama, *Chronicle of the Thūpa and the Thūpavaṃsa,* 100.

47. T. W. Rhys Davids and William Stede, eds., "Marumba," in *The Pali Text Society's Pali-English Dictionary* (Chipstead, England: Pali Text Society, 1999), 524.

48. T. Richard Blurton, *Hindu Art* (London: British Museum Press, 1992), 40, 155.

49. David Dean Shulman, *Tamil Temple Myths: Sacrifice and Divine Marriage in the South Indian Śaiva Tradition* (Princeton, NJ: Princeton University Press, 1980), 17–18.

50. Ibid., 48.

51. Ibid., 55–56.

52. Pe Maung Tin and Luce, *The Glass Palace Chronicle,* 87–88.

53. Ibid., 87.

54. See Arthur P. Phayre, *History of Burma* (London: Trübner, 1883), 8n1, cited in Gordon H. Luce, *Old Burma—Early Pagan* (New York: Artibus Asiae and the Institute of Fine Arts, New York University, 1969), 1:89.

55. Pe Maung Tin and Luce, *The Glass Palace Chronicle,* 82.

56. Ibid., 113–115.

57. Luce, *Old Burma—Early Pagan,* 1:83.

58. Pe Maung Tin and Luce, *The Glass Palace Chronicle,* 120. Five hundred years later, the Shinbyu and Shinhla images were apparently still being venerated, according to records of the reign of King Min-ye-kyaw-din (1673–1698). Min-ye-kyaw-din had two famous Buddha images, one from Pahkangyi and the other from Thiha-daw, transported to Ava to be venerated by lay and monastic devotees for a week. The images were made from sacred wood and said to date from the time of Alaungsithu. Than Htut, "State, Saṁgha and Laity during the Nyaungyan Period," in *Myanmar Two Millenia, vol. 3, Proceedings of the Myanmar Two Millennia Conference, 15–17 December 1999* (Yangon, Myanmar: Universities Historical Research Centre, 2000), 84.

59. Pe Maung Tin and Luce, *The Glass Palace Chronicle,* 90.

60. Ibid., 81–82, 87, and 122.

61. Skilling, "Geographies of Intertextuality," 98–101.

62. McDaniel, "Two Buddhist Librarians," 137.

63. Trainor, *Relics, Ritual, and Representation in Buddhism,* 143.

64. Thant Myint-U, *The Making of Modern Burma* (Cambridge: Cambridge University Press, 2001), 20.

65. Ibid., 79–81.

66. John Clifford Holt, *Spirits of the Place: Buddhism and Lao Religious Culture* (Chiang Mai: Silkworm Books, 2011), 20–28, 65.

67. Sarassawadee, *History of Lan Na,* 111–123.

68. See SWSC, 77–83, 87. See also *Tamnan Phra Chao Ton Luang Phayao* [Chronicle of the Grand Lord of Phayao], Siam Society, Bangkok, EFEO 001 009. Inscription date 2505 BE, 1324 CS (1962), 11A–11B. See also *Tamnan Phra Chan Phra Sing Phra Kaeo,* 4B, 5A, 6A, 7B.

69. Hans Penth, "Editor's Introduction," in Committee to Research the History of Phra Thāt Dòi Tung, *History of Phra Thāt Dòi Tung* (Bangkok and Chiang Rai: Mae Fah Luang Foundation and Social Research Institute, Chiang Mai University, 1993), 63–66.

70. Davis, *Lives of the Indian Images,* 138.

Chapter 6: Buddha Images as Objects of Donation

1. See, for example, Hiram W. Woodward Jr., *The Sacred Sculpture of Thailand* (Bangkok: River Books, 1997), 20; and Aroonrut Wichienkeeo, "Buddha Images in Lan Na (Northern Thailand): A Study from Palm-Leaf Texts and Inscriptions," in *Buddhist Legacies in Mainland Southeast Asia: Mentalities, Inter-*

pretations and Practices, ed. François Lagirarde and Paritta Chalermpow Koanantakool (Paris and Bangkok: École française d'Extrême-Orient and Princess Maha Chakri Sirindhorn Anthropology Centre, 2006), 35–37. In his catalogue, Penth himself provided only a brief analysis of the data as a whole. Hans Penth, *Khamcharuek thi Than Phra Phuttha Rup nai Nakhon Chiang Mai* [Inscriptions on the bases of Buddha images in Chiang Mai] (Bangkok: Khana Kamakan Chat Phim Ekasan Thang Prawatisat, Samnak Nayok Ratamontri, 2519 [1976]), 6–8.

2. Penth, *Khamcharuek thi Than Phra Phuttha Rup,* 54.

3. Ibid., 7.

4. J. C. Eade, *The Calendrical Systems of Mainland South-East Asia* (Leiden, Netherlands: Brill, 1995), 17.

5. Crosby, *Theravada Buddhism,* 48–49.

6. J. C. Eade, *The Thai Historical Record: A Computer Analysis* (Tokyo: Centre for East Asian Cultural Studies for UNESCO, 1996), 100.

7. For explanation of the different calendars used in inscriptions, see Eade, *The Calendrical Systems of Mainland South-East Asia.*

8. Eade, *The Thai Historical Record,* ix.

9. Penth, *Khamcharuek thi Than Phra Phuttha Rup,* 8.

10. Carol Stratton, *Buddhist Sculpture of Northern Thailand* (Chiang Mai: Silkworm Books, 2004); chaps. 6–9 cover the fourteenth to mid-sixteenth centuries, and chap. 10 covers the sixteenth to twentieth centuries.

11. Among the few studies to date on Lanna wooden Buddha images are Naengnoi Punjabhan, Aroonrut Wichienkeeo, and Somchai Na Nakhonphanom, *The Charm of Lanna Wood Carving,* trans. Lawrence Maund (Bangkok: Rerngrom, 2537 [1994]); and Wiluck, *Phra Chao Mai Lanna.*

12. Donald M. Stadtner, *Sacred Sites of Burma* (Bangkok: River Books, 2011), 12–13.

13. Aroonrut Wichienkeeo assembled a list of wishes of donors of Buddha images from a review of inscriptions, chronicles, and interviews. Aroonrut Wichienkeeo, "Buddha Images in Lan Na (Northern Thailand), 33–52.

14. Penth, *Khamcharuek thi Than Phra Phuttha Rup,* No. 1 (1465), No. 3 (1473–74), No. 5 (1482), No. 6 (1482), No. 19 (1520), No. 282, and No. 285. For the last two, which do not bear a date, Penth suggested that they may have been made around 1490–1520. Penth, "An Inscribed Buddha Image in Wat Ket Sī," 498n11.

15. Penth, *Khamcharuek thi Than Phra Phuttha Rup,* Nos. 2, 20, 22, 24, 34, 50, 76, 114, 209, 236, 249, 254, and 277.

16. Ibid., Nos. 25, 27, 34, 53, 74, 78, 91, 98, 114, 117, 120, 137, 141, 142, 166, 168, 173, 178, 198, 209, 221, 236, 239, 250, 252, and 255.

17. Peter Skilling, "For Merit and Nirvana: The Production of Art in the Bangkok Period," *Arts Asiatiques* 62 (2007): 90.

18. Penth, *Khamcharuek thi Than Phra Phuttha Rup,* Nos. 81, 105, 110, 119, 144, 198, 232, 252, 254, and 287.

19. Crosby, *Theravada Buddhism,* 129–130.

20. Susan L. Huntington, *Leaves from the Bodhi Tree: The Art of Pāla India (8th–12th Centuries) and Its International Legacy* (Dayton, OH: Dayton Art Institute in association with the University of Washington Press, 1990), 207.

21. J. E. van Lohuizen-de Leeuw, "The Stone Buddha of Chiengmai and Its Inscription," *Artibus Asiae* 24, nos. 3–4 (1961): 324–329.

22. Hutchinson, "Sacred Images in Chiengmai," 136–137.

23. Hans Penth, Phanphen Khrüathai, and Silao Ketphrom, *Corpus of Lān Nā Inscriptions,* vol. 2, *King Kāwila Inscriptions, A.D. 1791–1814* (Chiang Mai: Archive of Lan Na Inscriptions, Social Research Institute, Chiang Mai University, 1998), 25–34. Penth transcribes and translates this inscription to modern central Thai in *Khamcharuek thi Than Phra Phuttha Rup* (see Image No. 254), but I have chosen to consult his more recent transcription and translation to Thai from this later publication. As with the other inscriptions in this chapter, the translation to English is mine.

24. Sarassawadee, *History of Lan Na,* 134–136.

25. Penth, *Khamcharuek thi Than Phra Phuttha Rup,* 133n119.

26. Ibid.; the name list appears on pages 35–52. There are 464 entries; however, I excluded twelve that are duplicates or blank.

27. Sarassawadee, *History of Lan Na,* 136 and 202.

28. Veidlinger, *Spreading the Dhamma,* 105.

29. Penth, *Khamcharuek thi Than Phra Phuttha Rup,* Nos. 1, 12, 17, 19, 20, 27, 137, 143, 178, 221, 231, 236, and 246.

30. Ibid., Nos. 5, 16, 18, 22, 24, 25, 28, 34, 50, 53, 78, 91, 98, 105, 114, 117, 120, 141, 142, 166, 168, 171, 198, 209, 233, 237, 239, 243, 252, 254, 255, and 277.

31. Jonathan S. Walters, "Communal Karma and Karmic Community in Theravāda Buddhist History," in *Constituting Communities: Theravāda Buddhism and the Religious Cultures of South and Southeast Asia,* ed. John Clifford Holt, Jacob N. Kinnard, and Jonathan S. Walters (Albany: State University of New York Press, 2003), 9–39.

32. Penth, *Khamcharuek thi Than Phra Phuttha Rup,* 8–22.

33. After the battles with Burma in the late eighteenth century, materials such as silver and bronze may have been very expensive. Aroonrut Wichienkeeo, *Boranwatthu—Boransathan nai Wat Lanna* [Ancient artifacts and sites in Lanna monasteries] (Chiang Mai: Sathaban Phasa Sinlapa lae Wathanatham, Mahawithayalai Rachaphat Chiang Mai, 2549 [2006]), 89.

34. Wiluck, *Phra Chao Mai Lanna,* 62–77.

35. SWSC, 81.

36. Penth, *Khamcharuek thi Than Phra Phuttha Rup,* 61.

37. Wyatt and Aroonrut, *The Chiang Mai Chronicle,* 181–182.

38. Ibid., 182n66.

39. Penth, *Khamcharuek thi Than Phra Phuttha Rup,* 113n110.

40. Ibid., 155n134.

41. *Tamnan Phraya Thammikarat* [Chronicle of the King of the Dhamma], Wat Pa Sak Noi, Sankhamphaeng, Chiang Mai, EFEO 002 007. Inscription date 1316 CS (1954 CE), 4B, 8A.

42. This palm leaf manuscript is preserved on microfilm in the collection of the Social Research Institute, Chiang Mai University. It has been translated into English by Donald K. Swearer and Sommai Premchit and published in Swearer, *Becoming the Buddha,* 60–63. According to Swearer, the manuscript was copied in 1841 but the original date of composition is not known.

43. Swearer, *Becoming the Buddha,* 61–62.

44. These postures are: reclining (Pali: *sayāsana,* Thai: *saiyat*), fifteen images (5 percent); standing (Thai: "*prathap yuen* (1)" in Penth's categorization), seventeen images (6 percent); walking ("*prathap yuen* (2) and (3)"), nine images (3 percent); forbidding the relatives (*ham yat*), ten images (3 percent); holding bowl (*um bat*), five images (2 percent); forbidding the Sandalwood Image (*ham phra kaenchan*), three images (1 percent); contemplating (*ramphueng*), two images (1 percent); subduing the Nālāgiri elephant (*prap chang nalakhiri*), two images (1 percent), and staring (*thawai net*), one image (less than 1 percent). These numbers include five sculptures that consist of pairs of statues in different postures on the same base; I counted each of these ten statues on its own. Not included are the nine non-Buddha images.

45. Woodward, *The Sacred Sculpture of Thailand,* 115.

46. Elizabeth H. Moore, personal communication with the author, 2011.

47. SBCN, 8; SBSM, 35. The posture and iconography are omitted in SBNJ, the shortened version of the Sihing story in the *JKM.*

48. Penth transliterates "Sahing" in the inscription as "Sihing," like the name of the famous Buddha image. However, Phiset Chiechanphong has proposed that "Sahing" derives from a Mon phrase, *sahing sahoei,* meaning "that which pleases." Thus Buddha Image No. 2 in Phiset's view is that "which when seen brings happiness," like the Buddha himself. He suggests that over time the name shifted to Sihing, perhaps because of the association of the image with the Lankan (Sihala) sect that spread in Chiang Mai in the fifteenth century. Phiset, *Ha Phra Ha Chao,* 23.

49. Penth, *Khamcharuek thi Than Phra Phuttha Rup;* the material is specified in Nos. 22, 34, 50, 53, 98, 114, 142, 143, 168, 221, 236, 239, 252, 254, and 255; in addition, Nos. 2, 9, 17, 19, 24, 209, 231, and 246 do not state the material but refer to the image being "cast."

50. Penth, *Khamcharuek thi Than Phra Phuttha Rup,* Nos. 2, 4, 9, 12, 13, 16, 17, 19, 20, 22, 23, 209, and 255.

51. NJSG, 110, 115 (two examples), 120 (two examples), 124, 126 (two examples), 142, 145–146, 148–149, 150, 155–156, 161, 173, 175 (two examples), and 178.

52. Penth, *Khamcharuek thi Than Phra Phuttha Rup,* 179n146, 179n147.

53. NJSG, 150.

54. Sakchai Saisingha, *Phra Phuttha Rup Samkhan lae Phuttha Sin nai Dindaen Thai* [Important Buddha images and Buddhist art in Thai lands] (Bangkok: Muang Boran, 2554 [2011]), 394.

55. Beal, *Si-Yu-Ki,* 1:218.

56. Than Tun, *History of Buddhism in Burma, A.D. 1000–1300* (Rangoon: Burma Research Society, 1978), 64, 67, 68.

57. See Pe Maung Tin and Luce, *The Glass Palace Chronicle,* 113, for a donation by King Alaungsithu, and 148 for another by King Narapatisithu. The latter donation is also described in Law, *The History of the Buddha's Religion,* 77–78. The latter also notes a donation by a king of Toungoo of a bronze Buddha image made in his own weight (88).

58. Penth, *Khamcharuek thi Than Phra Phuttha Rup,* 139.

59. Ibid., 95.

60. Skilling, "Worship and Devotional Life," 9829.

61. Skilling, "For Merit and Nirvana," 77.

Chapter 7: Buddha Images as Objects of Transferrable Power

1. See, for example, Luang Boribal Buribhand, *Rueang Phra Phuttha Sihing kap Wichan* [A study of the Sihing Buddha image] (Bangkok: Krom Sinlapakon, 2477 [1934]); and A. B. Griswold, *Dated Buddha Images of Northern Siam, Artibus Asiae* Supplementum 16 (Ascona, Switzerland: Artibus Asiae, 1957), 42–45. A perceptive analysis of the *Chronicle of the Emerald Buddha Image* is found in Sakchai Saisingha, *Phra Phuttha Rup Samkhan lae Phuttha Sin nai Dindaen Thai,* 142–144.

2. The Mahābodhi Temple has inspired multiple copies across Buddhist Asia, with several in China as well as replicas in Chiang Mai and Bago (Pegu). Scholars have suggested various reasons for the creation of each of these copies. See A. B. Griswold, "The Holy Land Transported," 173–222; Donald M. Stadtner, "A Fifteenth-Century Royal Monument in Burma and the Seven Stations in Buddhist Art," *Art Bulletin* 73, no. 1 (1991): 39–52; Atsuko Naono, "The Buddhist Kings of Chiengmai and Pegu, the Purification of the *Saṅgha,* and the Mahābodhi Replicas in the Late Fifteenth Century," MA thesis, University of Michigan, 1996; and Isabelle Charleux, "Copies de Bodhgayā en Asie orientale: les stupas de type Wuta à Pékin et Kökeqota (Mongolie-Intérieure)," *Arts Asiatiques* 61 (2006): 120–142.

3. Griswold, *Dated Buddha Images of Northern Siam,* 17.

4. Ibid., 18, 52–54.

5. Ibid., 42–43.

6. Ibid., 42.

7. For more on Griswold's view of copying of Buddha images, see also A. B. Griswold, "Imported Images and the Nature of Copying in the Art of Siam," in *Essays Offered to G. H. Luce by His Colleagues and Friends in Honour of His*

Seventy-Fifth Birthday, ed. Ba Shin, Jean Boisselier, and A. B. Griswold, *Artibus Asiae* Supplementum 23, vol. 2 (Ascona, Switzerland: Artibus Asiae, 1966), 37–73.

8. Luang Boribal Buribhand, *Chumnum Boranakadi* [A collection on archaeology] (Bangkok: Kasem Bannakich Book Store, 2503 [1960]), 140.

9. See Jean Boisselier, *The Heritage of Thai Sculpture,* trans. James Emmons (Bangkok: Asia Books, 1975), 27, 38, 40.

10. Tambiah, "Famous Buddha Images," 16.

11. Ibid., 18.

12. Ibid., 5–6.

13. Tambiah, *The Buddhist Saints of the Forest,* 240–241. See also Tambiah, "Famous Buddha Images," 17–18.

14. Woodward has suggested that the views of Griswold and Tambiah on copying provide only a "partial" explanation for the highly venerated status of the Sihing and other Buddha images. He posits that the significance of Buddha images may instead derive from their ability to represent abstract ideas, such as systems of proportional ideals or conceptions of the symbolic value of different body parts, which might be reflected in texts or *yantras* (magical diagrams). He does not elaborate further, providing no evidence for how such concepts had a relation to the Sihing or to any other particular Buddha image. Woodward, "The Emerald and Sihing Buddhas," 507–508.

15. Piriya has been developing and revising a system of periodization of art in Thailand through works published over the course of more than three decades. While his earlier analyses divided the chronology of art into periods named after ethnic categories, since the late 1990s he has been advocating a periodization using names of religious groups. The rationale behind his method of chronology is given in detailed form most recently in Piriya Krairiksh, *Aryatham Thai Phuenthan thang Prawatisat Sinlapa* [Art historical foundations of Thai civilization], vol. 1 (Bangkok: Amarin, 2544 [2001]), esp. chaps. 1 and 2.

16. Piriya Krairiksh, *The Roots of Thai Art,* trans. Narisa Chakrabongse (Bangkok: River Books, 2012), 14–16.

17. Piriya, *Aryatham Thai,* 3.

18. Piriya, *The Roots of Thai Art,* 12.

19. The full detail of Piriya's periodization is not provided here as it is beyond the scope of the argument in this chapter. See Piriya, *The Roots of Thai Art,* 19.

20. Nandana Chutiwongs, "To Dr. Piriya Krairiksh Prap Plien Yuk Samai khong Phuttha Sin nai Prathet Thai" [Response to Dr. Piriya Krairiksh's "Changing the eras of Buddhist art in Thailand"], *Sinlapa Wathanatham* 22, no. 1 (2543 [2000]): 50–55.

21. Nicolas Revire, review of Piriya Krairiksh, *The Roots of Thai Art,* trans. Narisa Chakrabongse, *Journal of the Siam Society* 101 (2013): 236.

22. Piriya, *The Roots of Thai Art,* 18. The Pali Text Society's *Pali-English Dictionary* defines *paṭimā* as "counterpart, image, figure." Rhys Davids and

Stede, "*Paṭimā*," in *The Pali Text Society's Pali-English Dictionary,* 397. In my view, defining it as "replication," as Piriya does, suggests a closer resemblance between original and copy than is implied by the society's definition.

23. See, for example, the images in Michael Sullivan, "The P'ra Sila of Chiengmai and Its Replicas," *Artibus Asiae* Supplementum 23 (Ascona, Switzerland: Artibus Asiae, 1966), 175–178.

24. Piriya, *The Roots of Thai Art,* 378.

25. Piriya, *Aryatham Thai,* 43.

26. M. L. Pattaratorn Chirapravati, "From Text to Image: Copying as Buddhist Practice in Late Fourteenth Century Sukhothai," in *Buddhist Manuscript Cultures,* ed. Stephen C. Berkwitz, Juliane Schober, and Claudia Brown (London: Routledge, 2009), 176.

27. Ibid., 176–178.

28. Ibid., 178.

29. Ibid., 178–179.

30. Ibid., 180–181.

31. Walshe, *The Long Discourses of the Buddha,* 441–442.

32. SBCN, 7–8; SBSM, 3; SBWN, 8B.

33. Swearer, *Becoming the Buddha,* 68.

34. Ibid., 54–55. According to Swearer, 262n33, "robber [king]" may refer to *Jātaka* 1.264 or 2.104.

35. Woodward, *The Sacred Sculpture of Thailand,* 23.

36. Ibid.

37. Swearer, *Becoming the Buddha,* 46–48.

38. Ibid., 79.

39. Ibid., 5.

40. CBCN, 8–9; EBSM, 30–32; SBCN, 15; SWSC, 2:56; *Tamnan Phayao,* 9A; *Tamnan Phra Non Khon Muang,* 9B; *Tamnan Phra Kaeo Don Tao Wiang Din,* 6B.

41. SBCN, 13–14; SBSM, 37–38.

42. SBCN, 37; SBSM, 56–58.

43. SBCN, 38, 43; SBSM, 59–60, 65.

44. EBCN, 33.

45. SWSC, 73–75. See also SWWN, 2B–3A.

46. EBSM, 28. EBWN, 14B, also states the Emerald Buddha's height, but with a different figure: one *sok,* four *niu* (49–53 centimeters). One *sok* is about 43–45 centimeters; one *niu* is 1.5–2 centimeters. The conversion of the units of measure is based on Penth, *Jinakālamālī Index,* 318–320.

47. SWSC, 71; see also SWWN, 2A–2B. One *ongkhuli* (Pali/Sanskrit: *aṅgula*] is equal to one *niu,* or 1.5–2 centimeters. One *wa* (Sanskrit: *vyāma*) is about 1.75 meters. One *khuep* is about 20 centimeters. For a Buddha image, one unit of weight is about 1 gram. Penth, *Jinakālamālī Index,* 318–320.

48. *Tamnan Phra Chao Ton Luang,* 7B.

49. See *Tamnan Nong Eiang Phayao* [Chronicle of the Eiang Pond of Phayao], Wat Pa Sak Noi, Sankhamphaeng, Chiang Mai, EFEO 002 018. Inscription date 1313 CS (1951), 10A–10B; and *Tamnan Phayao,* 8A.

50. *Tamnan Phra Chao Ton Luang,* 5B.

51. See *Tamnan Nong Eiang Phayao,* 7A–7B; and *Tamnan Phayao,* 8A–8B.

52. *Tamnan Phra Chao Ton Luang,* 4A.

53. *Tamnan Phra Phuttha Rup Chao Nang Din,* 1B–2A.

54. Robert L. Brown, "Expected Miracles: The Unsurprisingly Miraculous Nature of Buddhist Images and Relics," in Davis, ed., *Images, Miracles, and Authority,* 24. Notably, Brown interprets this focus by Xuanzang on size and materials as detaching the images from the agency of their donors: "Because the images are rarely linked to any human agency, they appear as if self-immanent. With their wondrous size and priceless material, they appear not so much as artistic or archaeological fact, but rather as part of a miraculous epistemology, a way of knowing the miraculous" (26). Brown's source for Xuanzang's account, Samuel Beal's *Si-Yu-Ki,* contains, by my count, sixty-one references to Buddha images, and another eighteen to images of bodhisattvas and other beings that are part of Buddhist tradition. Of these seventy-nine mentions of Buddhist statues, thirty-one refer to the miracle-working powers of the image; as Brown notes, the miraculous nature of images was a subject of interest to Xuanzang. There are thirty-five references to material of the image, thirty to size, twenty-three to posture, and fourteen to the image's adornments. There are also fourteen mentions of the image's sponsor and eight references to the skill or work of the craftsman. Throughout his account Xuanzang also refers to kings who as patrons of Buddhism sponsored monasteries and monuments. He apparently appreciated the human input to the making of images. After all, what is miraculous is that a human-crafted object of familiar materials can emit light or speak. Although Brown pointedly notes that Xuanzang's attention to Buddha images' powers was part of his "miraculous epistemology," it seems too strong to assert, as Brown does, that the Chinese monk saw them as "rarely linked to any human agency" (26).

55. Geiger, *Culture of Ceylon in Mediaeval Times,* 101. The *Mahāvaṃsa* is dated by scholars to the late fifth or early sixth centuries and its extensions, together known as the *Culavaṃsa,* were written from the thirteenth century to the early nineteenth century.

56. SWSC, 2:55; Hutchinson, "Sacred Images in Chiengmai," 131. Sanguan's text uses the Thai word *pang* to refer to the posture of the image, while Hutchison's manuscript does not.

57. Horton, *Living Buddhist Statues,* 162.

58. Shinohara, "Changing Roles for Miraculous Images," 148.

59. NJSG, 145–146.

60. Griswold, *Dated Buddha Images of Northern Siam,* 56.

61. NJSG, 150.

62. Ibid., 160–161.

63. Kopytoff, "The Cultural Biography of Things," 64–91.

64. Reinders, "Recycling Icons and Bodies," 66.

65. Ibid., 67.

66. SWSC, 78–80, 87. See also SWWN, 4B, 7B.

67. *Tamnan Phayao,* 11A–11B.

68. Walter Benjamin, *Illuminations,* ed. Hannah Arendt and trans. Harry Zohn (London: Fontana, 1973), 218.

69. David Freedberg, *The Power of Images: Studies in the History and Theory of Response* (Chicago: University of Chicago Press, 1989), 113.

Bibliography

Archival Sources

Manuscripts from the Collection of the École française d'Extrême-Orient at the Princess Maha Chakri Sirindhorn Anthropology Centre, Bangkok

Tamnan Cho Hae [Chronicle of Mount Cho Hae], Wat Phra Luang Sung Men, Sung Men, Phrae, EFEO 003 003. Inscription date 1234 CS (1872).

Tamnan Nong Eiang Phayao [Chronicle of the Eiang Pond of Phayao], Wat Pa Sak Noi, Sankhamphaeng, Chiang Mai, EFEO 002 018. Inscription date 1313 CS (1951).

Tamnan Phra Chan Phra Sing Phra Kaeo [Chronicle of the Sandalwood Buddha Image, the Sihing Buddha Image, and the Emerald Buddha Image], Wat Nantharam, Amphoe Mueang, Chiang Mai, EFEO 006 003. Inscription date unknown.

Tamnan Phra Chao Ton Luang [Chronicle of the Grand Lord], Wat Phra Luang Sung Men, Sung Men, Phrae, EFEO 003 007. Inscription date unknown.

Tamnan Phra Chao Ton Luang Phayao [Chronicle of the Grand Lord of Phayao], Siam Society, Bangkok, EFEO 001 009. Inscription date 2505 BE, 1324 CS (1962).

Tamnan Phra Kesa That [Chronicle of the hair relics], Wat Pa Sak Noi, Sankhamphaeng, Chiang Mai, EFEO 002 005. Inscription date 2501 BE (1958).

Tamnan Phra Non Khon Muang [Chronicle of the Buddha Image Lying on a Mango-Tree Log], Siam Society, Bangkok, EFEO 001 002. Inscription date 2505 BE (1962).

Tamnan Phra Phuttha Rup Chao Nang Din [Chronicle of the Buddha Image Seated on the Earth], Wat San Pa Kha, Ton Pao, Sankhamphaeng, Chiang Mai, EFEO 025 001. Inscription date unknown.

Tamnan Phra That Chao Lamphun lae Tamnan Wat Ton Kaeo [Chronicle of the relic of Lamphun and Chronicle of Wat Ton Kaeo], Siam Society, Bangkok, EFEO 001 005. Inscription date 1275 CS (1913).

Tamnan Phraya Thammikarat [Chronicle of the King of the Dhamma], Wat Pa Sak Noi, Sankhamphaeng, Chiang Mai, EFEO 002 007. Inscription date 1316 CS (1954).

Tamnan Suan Dokmai [Chronicle of the Flower Garden Monastery], Wat Pa Sak Noi, Sankhamphaeng, Chiang Mai, EFEO 002 004. Inscription date 1296 CS (1934).

Tamnan Wat Phra Kaeo Don Tao Wiang Din [Chronicle of Wat Phra Kaeo Don Tao Wiang Din], Siam Society, Bangkok, EFEO 003 019. Inscription date 1288 CS (1926).

Tamnan Wat Suan Dok [Chronicle of the Flower Garden Monastery], Wat Pa Sak Noi, Sankhamphaeng, Chiang Mai, EFEO 002 003. Inscription date 1309 CS (1947).

Published Sources

(Following Thai convention, Thai names are alphabetized according to given names, rather than surnames, of the authors.)

Anan Ganjanapan. "Early Lan Na Thai Historiography: An Analysis of the Fifteenth and Sixteenth Century Chronicles." MA thesis, Cornell University, 1976.

Andaya, Barbara Watson. "Localising the Universal: Motherhood and the Appeal of Early Theravāda Buddhism." *Journal of Southeast Asian Studies* 33, no. 1 (2002): 1–30.

Aroonrut Wichienkeeo. *Boranwatthu—Boransathan nai Wat Lanna* [Ancient artifacts and sites in Lanna monasteries]. Chiang Mai: Sathaban Phasa Sinlapa lae Wathanatham, Mahawithayalai Rachaphat Chieng Mai, 2549 [2006].

———. "Buddha Images in Lan Na (Northern Thailand): A Study from Palm-Leaf Texts and Inscriptions." In *Buddhist Legacies in Mainland Southeast Asia: Mentalities, Interpretations and Practices,* edited by François Lagirarde and Paritta Chalermpow Koanantakool, 33–52. Paris and Bangkok: École française d'Extrême-Orient and Princess Maha Chakri Sirindhorn Anthropology Centre, 2006.

Aroonrut Wichienkeeo and David K. Wyatt, trans. *Tamnan Phuen Mueang Chiang Mai* [Chiang Mai Chronicle]. Chiang Mai: Silkworm Books, 2543 [2000].

Beal, Samuel S., trans. *Si-Yu-Ki: Buddhist Records of the Western World, Translated from the Chinese of Hiuen Tsiang (A.D. 629)*. 2 vols. London: Kegan Paul, Trench, Trübner, 1906.

Benjamin, Walter. *Illuminations*. Edited by Hannah Arendt. Translated by Harry Zohn. London: Fontana, 1973.

Berkwitz, Stephen C. *Buddhist History in the Vernacular.* Leiden, Netherlands: Brill, 2004.

Bizot, François. *Le Bouddhisme des Thaïs*. Bangkok: Éditions des Cahiers de France, 1993.

———. "La consécration des statues et le culte des morts." In *Recherches Nouvelles sur le Cambodge,* edited by François Bizot, 101–135. Paris: École française d'Extrême-Orient, 1994.

Blurton, T. Richard. *Hindu Art*. London: British Museum Press, 1992.

Boisselier, Jean. *The Heritage of Thai Sculpture*. Translated by James Emmons. Bangkok: Asia Books, 1975.

Boribal Buribhand, Luang. *Chumnum Boranakadi* [A collection on archaeology]. Bangkok: Kasem Bannakich Book Store, 2503 [1960].

———. *Rueang Phra Phuttha Sihing kap Wichan* [A study of the Sihing Buddha image]. Bangkok: Krom Sinlapakon, 2477 [1934].

Brereton, Bonnie Pacala. *Thai Tellings of Phra Malai*. Tempe: Arizona State University Program for Southeast Asian Studies, 1995.

Brown, Robert L. "Expected Miracles: The Unsurprisingly Miraculous Nature of Buddhist Images and Relics." In *Images, Miracles, and Authority in Asian Religious Traditions*, edited by Richard H. Davis, 23–36. Boulder, CO: Westview, 1988.

Buppha Khunyotying. "Phra Chao Ton Luang." In *Saranukrom Watanatham Thai Phak Nuea* [Encyclopedia of northern Thai culture], 8:4305–4309. Bangkok: Mulaniti Saranukrom Watanatham Thai, 2542 [1999].

———. "Phra Kaeo Don Tao, Wat." In *Saranukrom Watanatham Thai Phak Nuea* [Encyclopedia of northern Thai culture], 8:4271–4277. Bangkok: Mulaniti Saranukrom Watanatham Thai, 2542 [1999].

———. "Phra Non Khon Muang, Wat." In *Saranukrom Watanatham Thai Phak Nuea* [Encyclopedia of northern Thai culture], 9:4487–4489. Bangkok: Mulaniti Saranukrom Watanatham Thai, 2542 [1999].

———. "Phra That Cho Hae, Wat." In *Saranukrom Watanatham Thai Phak Nuea* [Encyclopedia of northern Thai culture], 9:4397–4400. Bangkok: Mulaniti Saranukrom Watanatham Thai, 2542 [1999].

———. "Suchadaram, Wat." In *Saranukrom Watanatham Thai Phak Nuea* [Encyclopedia of northern Thai culture], 13:6971. Bangkok: Mulaniti Saranukrom Watanatham Thai, 2542 [1999].

Casey, Edward S. *Remembering: A Phenomenological Study*. Bloomington: Indiana University Press, 2000.

Charleux, Isabelle. "Copies de Bodhgayā en Asie orientale: les stupas de type Wuta à Pékin et Kökeqota (Mongolie-Intérieure)." *Arts Asiatiques* 61 (2006): 120–142.

Chiu, Angela S. "Drawn to an 'Extremely Loathsome' Place: The Buddha and the Power of the Northern Thai Landscape." In *From Mulberry Leaves to Silk Scrolls: New Approaches to the Study of Asian Manuscript Traditions*, edited by Justin Thomas McDaniel and Lynn Ransom, 107–130. Philadelphia: University of Pennsylvania Libraries, 2015.

Chiu, Angela Shih Chih. "The Social and Religious World of Northern Thai Buddha Images: Art, Lineage, Power and Place in Lan Na Monastic Chronicles (*Tamnan*)." PhD diss., University of London, 2012.

Cœdès, George. "Documents sur l'Histoire Politique et Religieuse du Laos Occidental." *Bulletin de l'Ecole française d'Extrême-Orient* 25 (1926): 1–202.

Cowell, E. B. *The Jātaka or Stories of the Buddha's Former Births.* Oxford: Pali Text Society, 1995.

Crosby, Kate. "Devotion to the Buddha in Theravada." In *The Intimate Other: Love Divine in Indic Religions,* edited by Anna S. King and John Brockington, 244–277. New Delhi: Orient Longman, 2005.

———. "Gendered Symbols in Theravada Buddhism: Missed Positives in the Representation of the Female." *Hsuan Chuang Journal of Buddhist Studies* 9 (2008): 31–47.

———. "Kamma, Social Collapse or Geophysics? Interpretations of Suffering Among Sri Lankan Buddhists in the Immediate Aftermath of the 2004 Asian Tsunami." *Contemporary Buddhism* 9, no. 1 (2008): 53–76.

———. "The Origin of Pāli as a Language Name in Medieval Theravāda Literature." *Journal of the Centre for Buddhist Studies, Sri Lanka* 2 (2004): 70–116.

———. *Theravada Buddhism: Continuity, Diversity, and Identity.* Chichester, England: Wiley-Blackwell, 2014.

———. "What Does Not Get Translated in Buddhist Studies and the impact on Teaching." In *Translation and Religion: Holy Untranslatable?,* edited by Lynne Long, 41–53. Clevedon, England: Multilingual Matters, 2005.

Damrong Rajanubhab, Prince. *Tamnan Phra Phuttha Chedi* [A history of Buddhist monuments]. 2nd ed. Bangkok: Krom Sinlapakon, 2490 [1947].

Davis, Richard H. *Lives of the Indian Images.* Princeton, NJ: Princeton University Press, 1997.

Dhida Saraya. "The Development of the Northern Thai States from the Twelfth to the Fifteenth Centuries." PhD diss., University of Sydney, 1982.

Eade, J. C. *The Calendrical Systems of Mainland South-East Asia.* Leiden, Netherlands: Brill, 1995.

———. *The Thai Historical Record: A Computer Analysis.* Tokyo: Centre for East Asian Cultural Studies for UNESCO, 1996.

École française d'Extrême-Orient. "Lanna Manuscripts: A Northern Thai Collection of Manuscripts and Other Texts." http://www.efeo.fr/lanna_manuscripts/.

Eliade, Mircea. *The Sacred and the Profane.* Translated by William R. Trask. Orlando, FL: Harcourt, 1987.

Falk, Monica Lindberg. *Making Fields of Merit: Buddhist Female Ascetics and Gendered Orders in Thailand.* Seattle: University of Washington Press, 2007.

Faure, Bernard. *The Power of Denial: Buddhism, Purity, and Gender.* Princeton, NJ: Princeton University Press, 2003.

Forchhammer, Emanuel. *Report on the Antiquities of Arakan.* Rangoon, Burma: Superintendent, Government Printing, 1892.

Freedberg, David. *The Power of Images: Studies in the History and Theory of Response.* Chicago: University of Chicago Press, 1989.

Geiger, Wilhelm. *Culture of Ceylon in Mediaeval Times.* Edited by Heinz Bechert. Wiesbaden, West Germany: Harrassowitz, 1960.

———, trans. *The Mahāvaṃsa or the Great Chronicle of Ceylon.* Colombo: Ceylon Government Information Department, 1960.

Gell, Alfred. *Art and Agency.* Oxford: Clarendon, 1998.

Gombrich, Richard F. "Kosala-Bimba-Vaṇṇanā." In *Buddhism in Ceylon and Studies on Religious Syncretism in Buddhist Countries,* edited by Heinz Bechert, 281–303. Göttingen, West Germany: Vandenhoek und Ruprecht, 1978.

———. *Theravāda Buddhism: A Social History from Ancient Benares to Modern Colombo.* London: Routledge, 2005.

Griswold, A. B. *Dated Buddha Images of Northern Siam. Artibus Asiae* Supplementum 16. Ascona, Switzerland: Artibus Asiae, 1957.

———. "Foreword." In Sao Sāimöng Mangrāi, *The P̱āḍaeng Chronicle and the Jengtung State Chronicle Translated,* xiii–xv. Ann Arbor: University of Michigan Centers for South and Southeast Asian Studies, 2002.

———. "The Holy Land Transported." In *Paranavitana Felicitation Volume,* edited by N. A. Jayawickrama, 173–222. Colombo, Ceylon: Gunasena, 1965.

———. "Imported Images and the Nature of Copying in the Art of Siam." In *Essays Offered to G. H. Luce by His Colleagues and Friends in Honour of His Seventy-Fifth Birthday,* edited by Ba Shin, Jean Boisselier, and A. B. Griswold. *Artibus Asiae* Supplementum 23, vol. 2 (Ascona, Switzerland: Artibus Asiae, 1966), 37–73.

Griswold, A. B., and Prasert na Nagara. *Epigraphical and Historical Studies.* Bangkok: Historical Society under the Royal Patronage of H.R.H. Princess Maha Chakri Sirindhorn, 1992.

Halliday, Robert. *The Mons of Burma and Thailand.* Vol. 2, *Selected Articles.* Edited by Christian Bauer. Bangkok: White Lotus, 2000.

Hinüber, Oskar von. *A Handbook of Pāli Literature.* Berlin: Walter de Gruyter, 1996.

Holt, John Clifford. *Spirits of the Place: Buddhism and Lao Religious Culture.* Chiang Mai: Silkworm Books, 2011.

Horner, I. B., trans. *The Minor Anthologies of the Pali Canon.* Vol. 3, *Chronicles of Buddhas (Buddhavaṁsa) and Basket of Conduct (Cariyāpiṭaka).* London: Pali Text Society, 1975.

Horton, Sarah J. *Living Buddhist Statues in Early Medieval and Modern Japan.* New York: Palgrave Macmillan, 2007.

Huntington, Susan L. *Leaves from the Bodhi Tree: The Art of Pāla India (8th–12th Centuries) and Its International Legacy.* Dayton, OH: Dayton Art Institute in association with the University of Washington Press, 1990.

Hutchinson, E. W. "Sacred Images in Chiengmai." *Journal of the Siam Society* 28, no. 2 (1936): 114–142.

Jayawickrama, N. A., trans. *Chronicle of the Thūpa and the Thūpavaṃsa.* London: Luzac, 1971.

———, trans. *The Sheaf of Garlands of the Epochs of the Conqueror, Being a Translation of the Jinakālamālīpakaraṇaṁ of Ratanapañña Thera of Thailand.* London: Pali Text Society, 1978.

———, trans. *The Story of Gotama Buddha: The Nidāna-kathā of the Jātakaṭṭhakathā.* Oxford: Pali Text Society, 1990.

Keyes, Charles F. "Buddhist Pilgrimage Centers and the Twelve-Year Cycle: Northern Thai Moral Orders in Space and Time." *History of Religions* 15, no. 1 (1975): 71–89.

———. "Mother or Mistress but Never a Monk: Buddhist Notions of Female Gender in Rural Thailand." *American Ethnologist* 11, no. 2 (1984): 223–241.

Khaimuk Uthayaoli. "Phra Chao Nang Din." In *Saranukrom Watanatham Thai Phak Nuea* [Encyclopedia of northern Thai culture], 8:4311–4312. Bangkok: Mulaniti Saranukrom Watanatham Thai, 2542 [1999].

Kong, Choy Fah. *Saccakiriyā: The Belief in the Power of True Speech.* Singapore: Choy Fah Kong, 2012.

Kopytoff, Igor. "The Cultural Biography of Things: Commoditization as Process." In *The Social Life of Things: Commodities in Cultural Perspective,* edited by Arjun Appadurai, 64–91. Cambridge: Cambridge University Press, 1986.

Lagirarde, François. "Temps et lieux d'histoires bouddhiques: À propos de quelques 'chroniques' inédites du Lan Na." *Bulletin de l'École française d'Extrême-Orient* 94 (2007): 59–94.

Law, Bimala Churn, trans. *The Dāṭhāvaṁsa: A History of the Tooth-Relic of the Buddha.* Lahore, India: Moti Lal Baharsi Das, 1925.

———, trans. *The History of the Buddha's Religion (Sāsanavaṃsa).* London: Luzac, 1952.

———. *On the Chronicles of Ceylon.* Calcutta: Royal Asiatic Society of Bengal, 1947.

Layton, Robert. "Art and Agency: A Reassessment." *Journal of the Royal Anthropological Institute* 9 (2003): 447–464.

Leider, Jacques P. "Relics, Statues, and Predictions: Interpreting an Apocryphal Sermon of Lord Buddha in Arakan." *Asian Ethnology* 68, no. 2 (2009): 333–364.

Lieberman, Victor. "Introduction." In Sao Sāimöng Mangrāi, *The P̱āḍaeng Chronicle and the Jengtung State Chronicle Translated,* ix–x. Ann Arbor: University of Michigan Centers for South and Southeast Asian Studies, 2002.

Lingat, Robert. "Le culte du Bouddha d'Émeraude." *Journal of the Siam Society* 27, no. 1 (1934): 9–38.

Luce, Gordon H. *Old Burma—Early Pagan.* Vol. 1. New York: Artibus Asiae and the Institute of Fine Arts, New York University, 1969.

Maha Chakri Sirindhorn, HRH Princess. "Foreword." In M.C. Subhadradis Diskul, *History of the Temple of the Emerald Buddha,* n.p. Bangkok: Bureau of the Royal Household, n.d.

Mangrāi, Sao Sāimöng. *The Pādaeng Chronicle and the Jengtung State Chronicle Translated*. Ann Arbor: University of Michigan Centers for South and Southeast Asian Studies, 2002.

McDaniel, Justin T. "The Agency between Images: The Relationships among Ghosts, Corpses, Monks, and Deities at a Buddhist Monastery in Thailand." *Material Religion* 7, no. 2 (2011): 242–267.

———. *Gathering Leaves and Lifting Words: Histories of Buddhist Monastic Education in Laos and Thailand*. Seattle: University of Washington Press, 2008.

———. "Transformative History: *Nihon Ryōiki* and *Jinakālamālīpakaraṇam*." *Journal of the International Association of Buddhist Studies* 25, nos. 1–2 (2002): 151–207.

———."Two Buddhist Librarians: The Proximate Mechanisms of Northern Thai Buddhist History." In *Buddhist Manuscript Cultures*, edited by Stephen C. Berkwitz, Juliane Schober, and Claudia Brown, 124–139. London: Routledge, 2009.

Moore, Elizabeth H. *Early Landscapes of Myanmar*. Bangkok: River Books, 2007.

Moore, Elizabeth, Hansjörg Mayer, and U Win Pe. *Shwedagon: Golden Pagoda of Myanmar*. London: Thames and Hudson, 1999.

Nandana Chutiwongs. "To Dr. Piriya Krairiksh Prap Plien Yuk Samai khong Phuttha Sin nai Prathet Thai" [Response to Dr. Piriya Krairiksh's "Changing the eras of Buddhist art in Thailand"], *Sinlapa Wathanatham* 22, no. 1 (2543 [2000]): 50–55.

Naono, Atsuko. "The Buddhist Kings of Chiengmai and Pegu, the Purification of the *Saṅgha*, and the Mahābodhi Replicas in the Late Fifteenth Century." MA thesis, University of Michigan, 1996.

Notton, Camille, trans. *Annales du Siam*. Vol. 2, *Chronique de La:p'un*. Paris: Charles-Lavauzelle, 1930.

———, trans. *The Chronicle of the Emerald Buddha*. 2nd ed. Bangkok: Bangkok Times Press, 1933.

———, trans. *P'ra Buddha Sihiṅga*. Bangkok: Bangkok Times Press, 1933.

———, trans. *P'ră Setaṃgamaṇī*. Bangkok: Bangkok Times Press, 1936.

Osborne, Robin, and Jeremy Tanner, eds. *Art's Agency and Art History*. Malden, MA: Blackwell, 2007.

Pattaratorn Chirapravati, M. L. "From Text to Image: Copying as Buddhist Practice in Late Fourteenth Century Sukhothai." In *Buddhist Manuscript Cultures*, edited by Stephen C. Berkwitz, Juliane Schober, and Claudia Brown, 172–188. London: Routledge, 2009.

Pe Maung Tin. "The Shwe Dagon Pagoda." *Journal of the Burma Research Society* 24, no. 1 (1934): 1–91.

Pe Maung Tin and G. H. Luce, trans. *The Glass Palace Chronicle of the Kings of Burma*. London: Oxford University Press, 1923.

Penth, Hans. *A Brief History of Lān Nā*. Chiang Mai: Silkworm Books, 1994.

———. "Buddhist Literature of Lān Nā on the History of Lān Nā's Buddhism." *Journal of the Pali Text Society* 23 (1997): 43–81.

———. "Editor's Introduction." In Committee to Research the History of Phra Thāt Dòi Tung, *History of Phra Thāt Dòi Tung,* 53–104. Bangkok and Chiang Rai: Mae Fah Luang Foundation and Social Research Institute, Chiang Mai University, 1993.

———. "An Inscribed Buddha Image in Wat Ket Sī." In *Bauddhavidyāsudhākaraḥ: Studies in Honour of Heinz Bechert on the Occasion of His 65th Birthday,* edited by Petra Kieffer-Pülz and Jens-Uwe Hartmann, 495–503. Swisttal-Odendorff, Germany: Indica et Tibetica Verlag, 1997.

———. *Jinakālamālī Index.* Oxford and Chiang Mai: Pali Text Society and Silkworm Books, 1994.

———. *Khamcharuek thi Than Phra Phuttha Rup nai Nakhon Chiang Mai* [Inscriptions on the bases of Buddha images in Chiang Mai]. Bangkok: Khana Kamakan Chat Phim Ekasan Thang Prawatisat, Samnak Nayok Ratamontri, 2519 [1976].

Penth, Hans, Phanphen Khrüathai, and Silao Ketphrom. *Corpus of Lān Nā Inscriptions.* Vol. 2, *King Kāwila Inscriptions, A.D. 1791–1814.* Chiang Mai: Archive of Lan Na Inscriptions, Social Research Institute, Chiang Mai University, 1998.

Phiset Chiechanphong. *Ha Phra Ha Chao* [Looking for the sacred]. Bangkok: Matichon, 2545 [2002].

———. "Introduction." In *Phra Kaeo Morakot Tamnan Phra Kaeo Morakot / The Emerald Buddha: Mythological Accounts and Historical Interpretation,* edited by Suchit Wongthet, 9–27. Bangkok: Matichon, 2546 [2003].

———. *Phra Phuttha Sihing 'Jing' Thuk Ong Mai Mi 'Plom' Tae Mai Dai Ma Chak Langka* [The Sihing Buddha image: "authentic," but not from Lanka], Bangkok: Matichon, 2546 [2003].

———. "Pratu Phi lae Nathi khong Phra Kaeo Morakot" [The spirit door and the duties of the Emerald Buddha]. In *Phra Kaeo Morakot Tamnan Phra Kaeo Morakot* [The Emerald Buddha: mythological accounts and historical interpretation], edited by Suchit Wongthet, 343–354. Bangkok: Matichon, 2546 [2003].

Phra Bat Somdet Phra Chom Klao Chao Yu Hua. "Tamnan Phra Kaeo Morakot samrap Alak An nai Phra Ubosot Wat Phra Sri Ratanasadaram Wan Suat Mon Yen Phra Rachaphithi Sri Sacchapanakan" [The Chronicle of the Emerald Buddha for recitation by the royal secretary in the hall of Wat Phra Sri Ratanasadaram on the day of the royal oath-taking ceremony]. In *Phra Kaeo Morakot Tamnan Phra Kaeo Morakot / The Emerald Buddha: Mythological Accounts and Historical Interpretation,* edited by Suchit Wongthet, 196–209. Bangkok: Matichon, 2546 [2003].

Piriya Krairiksh. *Aryatham Thai Phuenthan thang Prawatisat Sinlapa* [Art historical foundations of Thai civilization]. Vol. 1. Bangkok: Amarin, 2544 [2001].

———. *Rakngao haeng Sinlapa nai Prathet Thai*. Bangkok: River Books, 2553 [2010]. Translated by Narisa Chakrabongse as *The Roots of Thai Art* (Bangkok: River Books, 2012).

Prasert na Nagara. "Kho Sangket Bang Prakan Kiao Kap Wannakam Phutthasasana nai Lanna" [Some observations on Buddhist literature in Lanna]. In *Wannakam Phutthasasana nai Lanna* [Buddhist literature in Lanna], edited by Phanphen Khrüathai, 25–33. Chiang Mai: Suriwong Book Centre, 2540 [1997].

———. "Tamnan Mulasasana Chiang Mai lae Chiang Tung" [Mūlasāsanā chronicles of Chiang Mai and Chiang Tung]. In *Wannakam Phutthasasana nai Lanna* [Buddhist literature in Lanna], edited by Phanphen Khrüathai, 34–41. Chiang Mai: Suriwong Book Centre, 2540 [1997].

Prasert na Nagara and Puangkham Tuikhiao, trans. *Tamnan Mulasasana Chiang Mai lae Chiang Tung* [Mūlasāsanā chronicles of Chiang Mai and Chiang Tung]. Bangkok: Samakhom Prawatisat, 2537 [1994].

Prima Mallikamas, Narisa Chakrabongse, and Paisarn Piammattawat, eds. *Oxford–River Books English-Thai Dictionary*. Oxford and Bangkok: Oxford University Press and River Books, 2010.

Pyi Phyo Kyaw and Kate Crosby. "The Buddha and His Brothers: Expressions of Power, Place and Community by the Network of Mahāmuni Images of Arakan, Bangladesh and Burma." In *Art of Merit: Studies in Buddhist Art and Its Conservation*, edited by David Park, Kuenga Wangmo, and Sharon Cather, 263–274. London: Archetype, 2012.

Reinders, Eric. "Recycling Icons and Bodies in Chinese Anti-Buddhist Persecutions." *Res* 48 (2005): 61–68.

Renu Wichasin, ed. and trans. *Phuen Mueang Saenwi Chabab Ho Kham Mueang Yai* [Chronicle of Saenwi, edition of the Royal Palace of Mueang Yai]. Chiang Mai: Silkworm Books, 2550 [2007].

Revire, Nicolas. Review of Piriya Krairiksh, *The Roots of Thai Art*, translated by Narisa Chakrabongse. *Journal of the Siam Society* 101 (2013): 233–242.

Reynolds, Frank E. "The Holy Emerald Jewel: Some Aspects of Buddhist Symbolism and Political Legitimation in Thailand and Laos." In *Religion and Legitimation of Power in Thailand, Laos, and Burma*, edited by Bardwell L. Smith, 175–193. Chambersburg, PA: Anima, 1978.

Rhys Davids, T. W., trans. *The Sacred Books of the East*. Vol. 36, *The Questions of King Milinda, Part* 2. Edited by Max Müller. Delhi: Low Price, 2006.

Rhys-Davids, T. W., and C. A. F. [Rhys-Davids], trans., *Dialogues of the Buddha*, vol. 2. London: Oxford University Press, 1910.

Rhys Davids, T. W., and William Stede, eds. *The Pali Text Society's Pali-English Dictionary*. Oxford: Pali Text Society, 1999.

Rod-ari, Melody Nina. "Visualizing Merit: An Art Historical Study of the Emerald Buddha and Wat Phra Kaew." PhD diss., University of California–Los Angeles, 2010.

Saeng Manawithun, trans. *Nithan Phra Phuttha Sihing* [Story of the Sihing Buddha]. Bangkok: Krom Sinlapakon, 2506 [1963].

———, trans. *Ratanaphimphawong* [Chronicle of the Emerald Buddha]. Bangkok: Krom Sinlapakon, 2510 [1967].

Sakchai Saisingha. *Phra Phuttha Rup Samkhan lae Phuttha Sin nai Dindaen Thai* [Important Buddha images and Buddhist art in Thai lands]. Bangkok: Muang Boran, 2554 [2011].

Salmony, Alfred. *Sculpture in Siam*. London: E. Benn, 1925.

Sa-nguan Chotisukharat. *Prachum Tamnan Lanna Thai* [A collection of Lanna chronicles]. Vol. 2. Bangkok: Odeon Store, 2515 [1972].

San Shwe Bu. "The Story of Mahamuni." *Journal of the Burma Research Society* 6 (1916): 225–229.

Santi Leksukhum. *Sinlapa Phak Nuea: Hariphunchai—Lanna* [Art of the north: Hariphunchai—Lanna]. Bangkok: Muang Boran, 2538 [1995].

Sarassawadee Ongsakul. *History of Lan Na*. Translated by Chitraporn Tanratanakul. Chiang Mai: Silkworm Books, 2005.

Schober, Juliane. "In the Presence of the Buddha: Ritual Veneration of the Burmese Mahāmuni Image." In *Sacred Biography in the Buddhist Traditions of South and Southeast Asia,* edited by Juliane Schober, 259–288. Honolulu: University of Hawai'i Press, 1997.

———. "Mapping the Sacred in Theravada Buddhist Southeast Asia." In *Sacred Places and Modern Landscapes,* edited by Ronald A. Lukens-Bull, 1–27. Tempe: Monograph Series Press, Arizona State University Program for Southeast Asian Studies, 2003.

———. "Venerating the Buddha's Remains in Burma: From Solitary Practice to the Cultural Hegemony of Communities." *Journal of Burma Studies* 6 (2001): 111–139.

Schopen, Gregory. *Bones, Stones, and Buddhist Monks: Collected Papers on the Archaeology, Epigraphy, and Texts of Monastic Buddhism in India*. Honolulu: University of Hawai'i Press, 1997.

———. *Buddhist Monks and Business Matters: Still More Papers on Monastic Buddhism in India*. Honolulu: University of Hawai'i Press, 2004.

———. *Figments and Fragments of Mahāyāna Buddhism in India*. Honolulu: University of Hawai'i Press, 2005.

Sharf, Robert H. "Introduction: Prolegomenon to the Study of Japanese Buddhist Icons." In *Living Images: Japanese Buddhist Icons in Context,* edited by Robert H. Sharf and Elizabeth Horton Sharf, 1–18. Stanford, CA: Stanford University Press, 2001.

———. "On the Allure of Buddhist Relics." *Representations* 66 (1999): 75–99.

Shinohara, Koichi. "Changing Roles for Miraculous Images in Medieval Chinese Buddhism: A Study of the Miracle Image Section in Daoxuan's 'Collected Records.'" In *Images, Miracles, and Authority in Asian Religious Traditions,* edited by Richard H. Davis, 141–188. Boulder, CO: Westview, 1998.

Shorto, H. L. "The 'Dewatau Sotāpan': A Mon Prototype of the 37 'Nats.'" *Bulletin of the School of Oriental and African Studies, University of London* 30, no. 1 (1967): 127–141.

Shulman, David Dean. *Tamil Temple Myths: Sacrifice and Divine Marriage in the South Indian Śaiva Tradition.* Princeton, NJ: Princeton University Press, 1980.

Skilling, Peter. "For Merit and Nirvana: The Production of Art in the Bangkok Period." *Arts Asiatiques* 62 (2007): 76–94.

———. "Geographies of Intertextuality: Buddhist Literature in Pre-modern Siam." *Aséanie* 19 (2007): 91–112.

———. "Worship and Devotional Life: Buddhist Devotional Life in Southeast Asia." In *Encyclopedia of Religion,* 2nd ed., edited by Lindsay Jones, 14:9826–9834. Detroit: Macmillan Reference, 2005.

Sommai Premchit and Donald K. Swearer. "A Translation of Tamnān Mūlasāsanā Wat Pā Daeng: The Chronicle of the Founding of Buddhism of the Wat Pā Daeng Tradition." *Journal of the Siam Society* 65, no. 2 (1977): 73–110.

Sponberg, Alan. "Attitudes toward Women and the Feminine in Early Buddhism." In *Buddhism, Sexuality, and Gender,* edited by José Ignacio Cabezón, 3–36. Albany: State University of New York Press, 1992.

Stadtner, Donald M. "A Fifteenth-Century Royal Monument in Burma and the Seven Stations in Buddhist Art," *Art Bulletin* 73, no. 1 (1991): 39–52.

———. *Sacred Sites of Burma.* Bangkok: River Books, 2011.

Stratton, Carol. *Buddhist Sculpture of Northern Thailand.* Chiang Mai: Silkworm Books, 2004.

Strong, John. "Buddha Bhakti and the Absence of the Blessed One." In *Premier Colloque Étienne Lamotte,* edited by Jacques Ryckmans, 131–140. Louvain-la-Neuve, Belgium: Université Catholique de Louvain, Institut Orientaliste, 1993.

Strong, John S. *Relics of the Buddha.* Princeton, NJ: Princeton University Press, 2004.

Subhadradis Diskul, M. C. *History of the Temple of the Emerald Buddha.* Bangkok: Bureau of the Royal Household, n.d.

———. *Sinlapa nai Prathet Thai* [Art in Thailand]. Bangkok: Thammasat University, 2506 [1963].

Surasawasdi Sooksawasdi, M. L. "Laksana Phra Phuttha Rup Baep Pala nai Khwaen Benggol thi Prakot nai Sinlapa Thai: Karani Sueksa chak Phra Phuttha Sihing" [Characteristics of Pala-style Buddha images of Bengal in Thai art: a study of the Sihing Buddha image], *Muang Boran Journal* 36, no. 3 (2010): 83–100.

Swearer, Donald K. *Becoming the Buddha: The Ritual of Image Consecration in Thailand.* Princeton, NJ: Princeton University Press, 2004.

———. "Consecrating the Buddha." In *Buddhism in Practice,* edited by Donald S. Lopez Jr., 50–58. Princeton, NJ: Princeton University Press, 1995.

———. "Myth, Legend and History in the Northern Thai Chronicles." *Journal of the Siam Society* 62 (1974): 67–88.

———. "Presencing the Buddha in Northern Thailand: Perspectives from Ritual and Narrative." In *Buddhist Legacies in Mainland Southeast Asia: Mentalities, Interpretations and Practices,* edited by François Lagirarde and Paritta Chalermpow Koanantakool, 277–284. Paris and Bangkok: École française d'Extrême-Orient and Princess Maha Chakri Sirindhorn Anthropology Centre, 2006.

———. "Signs of the Buddha in Northern Thai Chronicles." In *Embodying the Dharma: Buddhist Relic Veneration in Asia,* edited by David Germano and Kevin Trainor, 145–162. Albany: State University of New York Press, 2004.

Swearer, Donald K., and Sommai Premchit. *The Legend of Queen Cāma: Bodhiraṃsi's Cāmadevīvaṃsa, a Translation and Commentary.* Albany: State University of New York Press, 1998.

———. "The Relationship between the Religious and Political Orders in Northern Thailand (14th–16th Centuries)." In *Religion and Legitimation of Power in Thailand, Laos, and Burma,* edited by Bardwell L. Smith, 20–33. Chambersburg, PA: Anima, 1978.

Swearer, Donald K., Sommai Premchit, and Phaithoon Dokbuakaew. *Sacred Mountains of Northern Thailand and Their Legends.* Chiang Mai: Silkworm Books, 2004.

Tainturier, François. "The Foundation of Mandalay by King Mindon." PhD diss., University of London, 2010.

Tambiah, Stanley J. "Famous Buddha Images and the Legitimation of Kings." *Res* 4 (1982): 5–19.

Tambiah, Stanley Jeyaraja. *The Buddhist Saints of the Forest and the Cult of Amulets.* Cambridge: Cambridge University Press, 1984.

Tamnan Phra Kaeo Khao (Setangkhamani) kap Phra Sila (Phra Hin On) [Chronicles of the Setangkhamani and Sila Buddha images]. Chiang Mai: Wat Chiengman, 2539 [1996].

Tamnan Wat Phra Non Khon Muang [Chronicle of the Monastery of the Buddha Image Lying on a Mango-Tree Log]. Chiang Mai: Wat Phra Non Khon Muang, 2501 [1958].

Tawee Swangpanyangkoon, trans. *Tamnan Mueang Chieng Tung* [Chiang Tung State Chronicle]. Chiang Mai: Krongkan Tamra Mahawithayalai, 2529 [1986].

Thamwimolamali, Phra, trans. *Nangsue Tamnan Phra Phuttha Rup 'Phra Saekkham'* [Chronicle of the Saekkham Buddha Image]. Phayao: n.p., 2544 [2001].

Than Htut. "State, Saṅgha and Laity during the Nyaungyan Period." In *Myanmar Two Millennia.* Vol. 3, *Proceedings of the Myanmar Two Millennia Conference, 15–17 December 1999,* 73–93. Yangon, Myanmar: Universities Historical Research Centre, 2000.

Than Tun. *History of Buddhism in Burma, A.D. 1000–1300*. Rangoon, Burma: Burma Research Society, 1978.

Thant Myint-U. *The Making of Modern Burma*. Cambridge: Cambridge University Press, 2001.

Thienchai Aksondit. *Phra That Cho Hae* [The Relic of Cho Hae]. Chiang Mai: Silkworm Books, 2546 [2003].

Thompson, Ashley. "In the Absence of the Buddha: 'Aniconism' and the Contentions of Buddhist Art History." In *A Companion to Asian Art and Architecture*, edited by Rebecca M. Brown and Deborah S. Hutton, 398–420. Chichester, England: Wiley-Blackwell, 2011.

———. "Introductory Remarks between the Lines: Writing Histories of Middle Cambodia." In *Other Pasts: Women, Gender and History in Early Modern Southeast Asia*, edited by Barbara Watson Andaya, 47–68. Honolulu: Center for Southeast Asian Studies, University of Hawai'i at Manoa, 2000.

Trainor, Kevin. *Relics, Ritual, and Representation in Buddhism: Rematerializing the Sri Lanka Theravada Tradition*. Cambridge: Cambridge University Press, 1997.

Tun Aung Chain. *Chronicle of Ayutthaya: A Translation of the Yodaya Yazawin*. Yangon: Myanmar Historical Commission, 2005.

———, trans. *A Chronicle of the Mon*. Yangon, Myanmar: SEAMEO Regional Centre for History and Tradition, 2010.

———. *Selected Writings of Tun Aung Chain*. Yangon: Myanmar Historical Commission Golden Jubilee Publication Committee, 2004.

Tun Shwe Khine. *A Guide to Mrauk-U: An Ancient City of Rakhine, Myanmar*. Sittway, Myanmar: Sittway Degree College, 1992.

Udom Rungrueangsi. "Phra Non Khon Muang." In *Saranukrom Watanatham Thai Phak Nuea* [Encyclopedia of northern Thai culture], 8:4328–4329. Bangkok: Mulaniti Saranukrom Watanatham Thai, 2542 [1999].

———. "Tamnan." In *Saranukrom Watanatham Thai Phak Nuea* [Encyclopedia of northern Thai culture], 5:2412–2416. Bangkok: Mulaniti Saranukrom Watanatham Thai, 2542 [1999].

———. *Wannakam Lanna* [Lanna literature]. 5th ed. Bangkok: Samnak Ngan Kongthun Sanap Sanun Kanwichai, 2546 [2003].

Van Lohuizen-de Leeuw, J. E. "The Stone Budddha of Chiengmai and Its Inscription." *Artibus Asiae* 24, nos. 3–4 (1961): 324–329.

Veidlinger, Daniel. *Spreading the Dhamma: Writing, Orality, and Textual Transmission in Buddhist Northern Thailand*. Honolulu: University of Hawai'i Press, 2006.

Walshe, Maurice, trans. *The Long Discourses of the Buddha: A Translation of the Dīgha Nikāya*. Boston: Wisdom, 1995.

Walters, Jonathan S. "Buddhist History: The Sri Lankan Pāli Vaṃsas and Their Commentary." In Ronald Inden, Jonathan Walters, and Daud Ali, *Querying the Medieval*, 99–164. New York: Oxford University Press, 2000.

———. "Communal Karma and Karmic Community in Theravāda Buddhist History." In *Constituting Communities: Theravāda Buddhism and the Religious Cultures of South and Southeast Asia,* edited by John Clifford Holt, Jacob N. Kinnard, and Jonathan S. Walters, 9–39. Albany: State University of New York Press, 2003.

Wang-Toutain, Françoise. "Le bol du Buddha. Propagation du bouddhisme et légitimité." *Bulletin de l'École française d'Extrême-Orient* 81 (1994): 59–82.

Wiluck Sripasang. *Phra Chao Mai Lanna / Lanna Wooden Buddha Images.* Chiang Mai: Sisanphanmai, 2554 [2011].

Woodward, Hiram W., Jr. "The Emerald and Sihing Buddhas: Interpretations of Their Significance." In *Living a Life in Accord with Dhamma: Papers in Honor of Professor Jean Boisselier on His Eightieth Birthday,* edited by Natasha Eilenberg, M. C. Subhadradis Diskul, and Robert L. Brown, 502–513. Bangkok: Silpakorn University, 1997.

———. *The Sacred Sculpture of Thailand.* Bangkok: River Books, 1997.

Wyatt, David K., trans. *The Crystal Sands: The Chronicles of Nagara Śrī Dharrmarāja.* Ithaca, NY: Cornell University Southeast Asia Program, 1975.

———. "Relics, Oaths and Politics in Thirteenth-Century Siam." *Journal of Southeast Asian Studies* 32, no. 1 (2001): 3–66.

———. "Southeast Asia 'Inside Out,' 1300–1800: A Perspective from the Interior." *Modern Asian Studies* 31, no. 3 (1997): 689–709.

———. *Thailand: A Short History.* 2nd ed. New Haven, CT: Yale University Press, 2003.

Wyatt, David K., and Aroonrut Wichienkeeo, trans. *The Chiang Mai Chronicle.* 2nd ed. Chiang Mai: Silkworm Books, 1998.

Index

Page numbers in italic type refer to illustrations.

About the Author

Angela S. Chiu is an independent scholar, formerly research associate in the Department of the History of Art and Archaeology at the School of Oriental and African Studies, University of London.